FOLLOWING JESUS IN THE MODERN WORLD

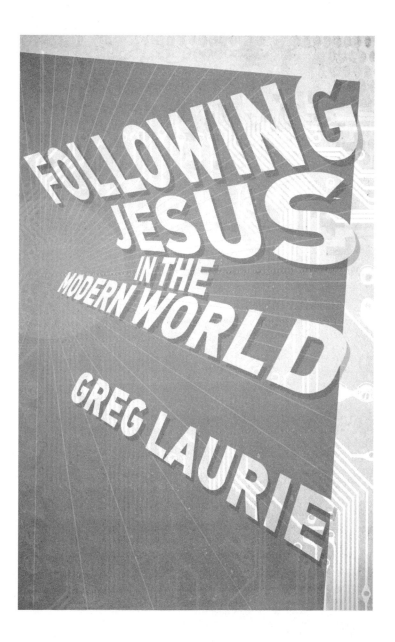

FOLLOWING JESUS IN THE MODERN WORLD

GREG LAURIE

KERYGMA™
PUBLISHING

ALLEN DAVID BOOKS

Following Jesus in the Modern World

Copyright ©2013 by Greg Laurie

All rights reserved.

International Standard Book Number: 978-1-61291-316-2

Published by: Kerygma Publishing

Coordination: FM Management, Ltd.

Contact: mgf@fmmgt.net

Cover design: Jeff Storm

Production: Mark Ferjulian

Printed in the United States of America

1 2 3 4 5 6 7 / 18 17 16 15 14 13

CONTENTS

1

"FOLLOW ME"

"I am a follower of Jesus Christ."

You and I hear someone say that, and we think to ourselves, *Isn't that wonderful?* But what does it really mean?

Sometimes the word *follower* has a negative connotation. It all depends on whom you are following!

Since the development of Twitter, we hear the word *follower* quite a bit. If you send out tweets and people read your tweets, they are called followers. As you may know, there are people who follow every tweet of certain famous individuals or celebrities. It's become something of a status symbol: The more people who follow your tweets, the more famous or influential you are thought to be.

If you are on Facebook, you don't have *followers*; you have *friends*.

Why do I bring this up? Because I think that Jesus Christ has a lot of so-called friends, but I wonder how many real followers He actually has.

CALLED TO FOLLOW

Throughout history, there have been any number of people who have admired Jesus Christ, viewing Him as a great teacher or heroic figure. In a poll taken in 2001, Jesus was "the most widely admired hero" in the United States.

That's all right, as far as it goes.

But the fact is, Jesus never said, "Admire Me."

He said, "Follow Me."

Toward the end of His Sermon on the Mount, Jesus said,

"Not everyone who says to Me, 'Lord, Lord,' shall enter the kingdom of heaven, but he who does the will of My Father in heaven. Many will say to Me in that day, 'Lord, Lord, have we not prophesied in Your name, cast out demons in Your name, and done many wonders in Your name?' And then I will declare to them, 'I never knew you; depart from Me, you who practice lawlessness!'" (Matthew 7:21-23)

In other words, just because you have admiration for Jesus or think positive thoughts about Jesus doesn't mean you are really one of His followers. Jesus concluded His Sermon on the Mount with a little story meant to distinguish between real followers and those who are only admirers:

"Anyone who listens to my teaching and follows it is wise, like a person who builds a house on solid rock. Though the rain comes in torrents and the floodwaters rise and the winds beat against that house, it won't collapse because it is built on bedrock." (Matthew 7:24-25, NLT)

A follower is one who builds his house on the rock; it is the person who hears God's Word *and does it*.

Are you a follower of Jesus Christ? Frankly, it isn't an easy thing to be or do in today's culture. In fact, there are so many pressures *not to* follow Jesus in the twenty-first century.

MATTHEW'S PERSPECTIVE

In the pages that follow, we will dip into the gospel of Matthew, seeking to learn more about the life, ministry, death, and resurrection of Jesus—and what it means to follow Him.

Matthew, also known as Levi, has an interesting story. As far as we can tell from the Gospel accounts, he became a follower of Jesus rather quickly. We don't read of any extended conversations that Christ had with Matthew, as He did with the woman at the well or Nicodemus or the rich young ruler. As far as we know, Matthew never witnessed any great miracles of Christ before deciding to follow Him.

So why did he? What moved him? What caused him to decide in a flash and literally leave everything to walk with Jesus for the rest of his life? As we read in Matthew's own account, the Teacher from Galilee simply walked up to the tax booth where Matthew was sitting and said two words to him: "Follow Me."

And with that—after hearing those two words— Matthew got up from his table, left *everything* behind, followed Jesus from that moment forward, and never once looked back.

How did that happen? What were the dynamics that led to such an instant change in this man's life course?

A LIFE-TRANSFORMING ENCOUNTER

> As Jesus passed on from there, He saw a man named Matthew sitting at the tax office. And He said to him, "Follow Me." So he arose and followed Him.
>
> Now it happened, as Jesus sat at the table in the house, that behold, many tax collectors and sinners came and sat down with Him and His disciples. And when the Pharisees saw it, they said to His disciples, "Why does your Teacher eat with tax collectors and sinners?"
>
> When Jesus heard that, He said to them, "Those who are well have no need of a physician, but those who are sick. But go and learn what this means: 'I desire mercy and not sacrifice.' For I did not come to call the righteous, but sinners, to repentance."
> (Matthew 9:9-13)

Jesus compares Himself to a physician in this passage. I can certainly appreciate His point, but the fact is that I hate going to the doctor or the dentist. When the doctor does a checkup on me, I'm always afraid he'll find something wrong.

It reminds me of the story of the man who went in for a checkup. As it turns out, it took a long time. Finally the doctor set down his instruments and said, "I'm afraid I have some bad news for you."

"Oh no," the man said. "What is it?"

"I am sorry to tell you this," the doctor told him, "but you don't have long to live."

Distraught at hearing such grim news, the patient said, "How long do I have?"

"Ten," the doctor replied.

"Ten? Ten *what*? Ten months? Ten weeks? Ten days?"

The doctor shook his head and said, "Ten . . . nine . . . eight . . . seven . . ."

That was a doctor who needed a little improvement in his bedside manner! Jesus, as the Great Physician, knew exactly how to deal with every individual He encountered because He sees people from the inside out. As we read about the Lord's conversations in the Gospels, we see that He never dealt with any two people in exactly the same way. His method with Nicodemus was far different from the way He interacted with the woman at the well in Samaria. To Peter and Andrew He said, "Follow Me, and I will make you fishers of men" (Matthew 4:19). But He didn't say that to Matthew, did He? Why? Because Peter and Andrew were career fishermen and had spent their lives casting nets and pursuing fish. The fact is, Jesus related to people in His world as individuals, and He does that with us as well. God always comes to us in a way that we can understand.

In his classic book *The Knowledge of the Holy*, author A. W. Tozer wrote, "The self-condemned will find Him generous and kind. To the frightened He is friendly, to the poor in spirit He is forgiving, to the ignorant, considerate; to the weak, gentle; to the stranger, hospitable."[1]

In the case of Matthew, the Great Physician made a house call. Doctors don't do that much these days because they are just too busy. If you're not feeling well, you can't really expect your physician to arrive on your doorstep, black bag in hand. No, you will be told to go to the emergency room at the hospital or some walk-in urgent care clinic. Though doctors in previous generations used to make house calls, it just isn't done much anymore.

But in this case, it was.

Matthew, the tax collector, desperately needed healing, and he was about to receive a house call from the greatest Healer of all. We see Jesus going to where Matthew was, his place of business. And in that day and age, what Matthew was doing wasn't a respected business at all. Far from it! In Matthew 9:9, we read that he was "sitting at the tax office."

Matthew's occupation as a tax collector is just a little difficult for us to understand in today's culture. Being a Jewish tax officer employed by Rome is not the same as being an IRS agent. To be a tax officer for Rome meant that Matthew was a collaborator with the enemy—a turncoat, a Benedict Arnold.

Rome was the occupying power over Israel at that time, and the Jewish people who lived under that iron control didn't like it one bit. It was supremely offensive to Jews that Matthew, a Jew himself, would work for the dark side, the occupying power, and actually collect revenue from his fellow citizens.

But if that weren't bad enough, most of these tax collectors were corrupt; they would collect the money Rome wanted and add some on top for themselves. And there was nothing the people of Israel could do about it. For this reason and more, the tax collectors became wealthy, powerful, and utterly despised.

As a tax collector, Matthew had effectively abandoned his faith and turned his back on his own people. Apparently, he had turned his back on God as well. Think of an ambulance-chasing lawyer mixed with a sleazy used-car salesman who is a telemarketer at night, and you'll get an idea of how people would have viewed a tax collector in that day. These guys were barely above plankton on the food chain.

So there was Matthew. He had turned his back on God and turned his back on his people. And then . . . along comes Jesus. There was something about Jesus that arrested Matthew's attention, a man very well-versed in the Scriptures. How do we know this? We know this because the gospel he ended up writing brims over with almost one hundred references to Old Testament passages. So Matthew knew the Word of God, but for some reason he had turned against what it taught.

But Jesus?

There was something *different* about Him. He wasn't like the rabbis or the self-righteous religious hypocrites of the day. Matthew would have seen the crowds who followed Jesus growing larger by the day. He may have seen Jesus interact with children and young people. How would he see all this? In a sense, he had a box seat.

A tax collector's booth was located in an elevated place, so he could observe all the deals and transactions going down all around him. From that vantage point, he probably saw—and heard—a lot.

As he watched Jesus and heard the people talking about Him, something began to stir in this man's heart. I believe that he secretly longed to be a follower of Jesus. But he probably thought to himself, *Even if I stepped up and volunteered, surely Christ would turn me down. If I were to say, "Hey, Jesus, I want to join Your team," Christ would probably turn and say, "You think I am so desperate that I would take a* tax collector? *Forget about it!"*

Matthew must have felt hopelessly trapped in the life and lifestyle he had created for himself and didn't see any way that he could get out of it or change direction. So when he saw Jesus walk by, everything in him wanted to follow. But he probably thought it was impossible.

AN UNEXPECTED INVITATION

What Matthew didn't take into account is that we have a God who responds to our longings. If we long for God—long to know Him, walk with Him, and be with Him—we will soon find Him knocking on our front door.

So there came a day when the unexpected happened. In fact, for Matthew, it was the greatest thing imaginable. Jesus was walking by, and Matthew was watching Him, with eyes full of longing.

Suddenly Jesus turned toward him and began to walk in his direction, keeping eye contact.

In Matthew 9:9 we read, "As Jesus passed on from there, He saw a man named Matthew sitting at the tax office."

The Greek word used here for *saw* is very suggestive. It means to gaze intently up, to stare, or to fix one's eyes constantly on an object. Jesus was looking directly into Matthew's eyes—directly into Matthew's soul—and He walked right up to him and spoke those two words that changed this man's life forever: "Follow Me!"

It's a little difficult for us to imagine what this experience would have been like for this hated tax collector. It would be like being a major Yankees fan and watching your favorite team go through its warm-ups before a game. Suddenly Mark Teixeira, the Yankees' first baseman, makes eye contact with you in the stands and waves you down to the front row. He says to you, "Hey, come on down from the stands. Come out here with me! Why don't you come and join the team?"

Or maybe you've paid big bucks for a ticket to a U2 concert because you have such a great admiration for this band and Bono, the lead singer. Before the concert begins, Bono singles you out in the crowd and says, "Hey, come on up and play with us tonight! Join the band!"

You are being asked to come into the inner circle — the ultimate club, if you will.

Those are just poor examples of how the Lord's invitation would have hit Matthew on that day. It was stunning! He was being asked to be a follower of Jesus Christ.

Have you and I even begun to realize what a privilege it is that we have been called by God to follow His Son? That's exactly what has happened. In 1 Corinthians 1:9, the apostle Paul said, "God, who has called you into fellowship with his Son Jesus Christ our Lord, is faithful" (NIV).

Chew on that for a moment: You have been called into fellowship — friendship, relationship — with the Son of God by God the Father Himself.

One day God looked at you and said, "Follow Me!" He called you, chose you, and selected you to walk with Christ and to be in Christ. Why in the world did He call someone like me? I don't know, but I will be eternally grateful that He did!

This is good news for all of us who were always last to be chosen for the team. I wasn't a very good athlete in high school, so when the teams were being put together — for baseball, kickball, whatever — I was always one of the last ones chosen.

"Oh, I guess I will take Laurie. Ugh. Laurie, you are first base."

The truth is, I always ended up way, way out in the outfield, standing there with my little mitt, hoping something would come my way.

Maybe that's your story, too. Maybe you were the last one chosen. You weren't a great student or a star athlete or a good singer or one of the popular crowd. You were the last one chosen. You weren't the top of anything. But then Jesus called you.

That is what He did for Matthew. The Bible tells us in 1 Peter 2:9, "But you are a chosen generation, a royal priesthood, a holy nation, His own special people, that you may proclaim the praises of Him who called you out of darkness into His marvelous light."

"FOLLOW ME": WHAT DOES IT MEAN?

What does it mean in the twenty-first century to be a follower of Christ?

The phrase *follow Me* is a fascinating expression in the Greek. It comes from the word that means "to walk the same road." To follow Jesus, then, means you walk the same road as He walks. And because that word is in the imperative mode, it is not just an invitation; it is a command. In addition, the verb is in the present tense, commanding the beginning of an action and continuing habitually in it.

So what does that add up to when we put it all together?

Jesus was saying, "I command you to follow Me each and every day."

This isn't just a Sunday pursuit; it is every day at all times. So many begin the journey of the Christian life but never finish it. Toward the end of his earthly life, Paul said his objective was to finish his race with joy. That's the idea. Don't just start well, but *finish* well.

Jesus wants to be a part of everything that you do. He's not just a Sunday Jesus, but an everyday Jesus. He wants to go with you to church and to school and to work. He wants to be at your side when you're at the movies or on the Internet. Jesus wants to go with you wherever you go. That is why we are told in Romans 13:14, "But put on the Lord Jesus Christ, and make no provision for the flesh, to fulfill its lusts." That phrase *put on* conveys the idea of the clothes you put on in the morning. You pick out your clothes, and then you wear your clothes.

Your clothing goes with you into the day, and you expect your clothes to move wherever and whenever and however you do. In the same way, Jesus wants to be a part of everything that you and I say and do. The J. B. Phillips translation of that same verse reads like this: "Let us be Christ's men from head to foot, and give no chances to the flesh to have its fling."

Jesus is saying, "I command you to follow Me each and every day. I want you to finish what you have started."

But here is something interesting. In the original language, the word *with* would be included in the *follow Me* command. In other words, it could be translated, "Follow *with* Me."

There's a whole world of meaning in that one word *with*.

Jesus is saying, "Yes, I want your obedience, but I also want your friendship and companionship." In essence, He was saying to Matthew, "I am your Lord and Master, and I command you to follow Me. But do you know what else I am, Matthew? I am your Friend. I want you to walk with Me . . . and I want to walk with you for the rest of your life."

That is what Jesus says to you, too.

We know Him as Master and Lord, and we bow before Him. The Lord says, "Yes, that is all true, but I want to be your Friend too. I want to walk with you through life. I want to be there as we go through it together."

So it was that Matthew, understanding the great privilege being offered to him, just went for it. Matthew 9:9 says that "he arose and followed Him."

Don't you love that?

There were no deliberations, no speeches, no "Just a minute, Lord, while I close things up." The tax collector said, in essence, "Right, Lord. Let's go. I'm out of here!"

Luke's version of the account gives an additional detail. Luke writes that Matthew "left everything and followed him" (Luke 5:28, NIV).

He left everything . . . and he had a lot to leave.

Again, in Luke's gospel we read that Matthew "held a great banquet for Jesus at his house, and a large crowd of tax collectors and others were eating with them" (Luke 5:29, NIV).

To give a great banquet that serves a large crowd implies that you have a really big house. But Matthew walked away from it all. He probably gave up more than any other disciple to follow Jesus. Yes, Peter, Andrew, and John gave up their fishing business and their nets, but Matthew gave up a powerful position and a lucrative career. Of all the disciples, he made the greatest sacrifice of material possessions and power, and yet in his modesty, he made no mention of it.

I think this serves as a reminder not to mention "what we gave up" when we share our story of following Christ. After all, what is the pittance of what we gave up compared to the wonderful and awesome privileges that

God has given to us? Seen in that light, we've given up nothing at all.

Looking back at his own past, the apostle Paul expressed it in these graphic terms:

> I once thought these things were valuable, but now I consider them worthless because of what Christ has done. Yes, everything else is worthless when compared with the infinite value of knowing Christ Jesus my Lord. For his sake I have discarded everything else, counting it all as garbage, so that I could gain Christ and become one with him. (Philippians 3:7-9, NLT)

Garbage. Trash. Rubbish. Rotten stuff, right out of a landfill. That's what you gave up to follow Jesus.

I don't know about you, but I want to get rid of the garbage in my house as quickly as I can. It's no great sacrifice for me to haul out the garbage at night and stuff it into the can. I don't mind parting with it at all. Of course not. Garbage is something you want to go away. Our family was gone last week, and we hadn't managed to get the garbage containers out to the curb. So we came home to full trash cans that had been baking in the sun. It wasn't smelling really good, I can assure you, and all the flies in the neighborhood were having a big party around it. I was so glad when the trash man came to haul it away.

That is how Paul referred to his past life and all his supposed accomplishments. He was saying, "Compared to walking with Jesus, it's a pile of rotting garbage."

That is how the old life is, and I'm not just talking about old sins and old habits. I mean everything. Even the old trophies and newspaper clippings we used to be so proud of and hold in such high value. Whatever it may be, it is nothing and less than nothing compared to being a son or daughter of God and living with Him through all eternity in heaven.

Matthew forsook all and followed Jesus. He lost a career, but he gained a destiny. He lost material possessions, but he gained a spiritual fortune. He lost temporary security, but he gained eternal life. He lost emptiness and loneliness, but he found fulfillment and companionship. He gave up all the world had to offer, and he found Jesus.

So what else do you do at a time like that but throw a party?

MATTHEW THROWS A BANQUET

> Now it happened, as Jesus sat at the table in the house, that behold, many tax collectors and sinners came and sat down with Him and His disciples. (Matthew 9:10)

After making up his mind to follow Jesus, Matthew had a sudden impulse to bring all his friends and associates together for one last party. He thought to himself, *I want everybody to meet Jesus.*

Do you remember how it felt when you first came to faith in Christ? You wanted to tell everyone. You may not have had a lot of sophistication or tact at that point, and you might have even been a little abrupt with people. (I know that I was.) But more than anything else, you just wanted to reach your friends for Christ. You wanted to introduce them to your new Savior and Friend, Jesus.

The sad thing is that as we mature in our faith, we do that less and less. Sometimes it seems to me that those who know the most do the least, and those who know the least do the most. I know people who have been Christians for decades but who literally can't remember the last time they initiated a conversation about Jesus Christ. But then there are people who are brand-new in the faith — sometimes less than a week old — who are out bringing people to church with them and leading people to the Lord.

That's what Matthew did. He invited all his rowdy friends over, and Jesus was the guest of honor. We can conclude from the accounts in Matthew and Luke that in addition to all the tax collectors, most of the notorious sinners from town showed up at Matthew's farewell banquet: prostitutes, thieves, con artists — you name it, they were there. And there was Jesus in the midst of them, having a great time. Isn't that classic?

Matthew responded immediately to the Lord's call, left everything, and followed Jesus. Sadly, however, there were others whom Jesus called who decided against following Christ . . . missing the very most important opportunity of their whole lives.

TWO WOULD-BE FOLLOWERS

In Matthew the tax collector, we have a true follower of Jesus. But in Matthew 8, we have the story of two would-be followers who also heard the call but ended up missing the boat, possibly forever.

> Then a certain scribe came and said to Him, "Teacher, I will follow You wherever You go."
>
> And Jesus said to him, "Foxes have holes and birds of the air have nests, but the Son of Man has nowhere to lay His head."

> Then another of His disciples said to Him, "Lord,
> let me first go and bury my father."
>
> But Jesus said to him, "Follow Me, and let the
> dead bury their own dead." (verses 19-22)

This first man, a scribe, seems to have been caught up in the emotion of the moment. A scribe was one of the religious elites of the day—a highly educated man who had dedicated his life to the transcription of the Scriptures.

In a human sense, he would have been a great addition to the Lord's team. To have a scribe in your following would have been a very big deal. Having a fisherman or a tax collector wouldn't have impressed anyone. But a scribe? That would have been a significant acquisition for Jesus' little band of disciples.

One day this guy apparently had been listening to Jesus and found himself caught up by the Lord's words. So he declared, "Teacher, I will follow You wherever You go."

You might have expected Jesus to reply, "Are you kidding Me? *A scribe?* Come on in! Welcome to the team! Everyone else move over to make room for this guy."

Jesus, however, responded in an interesting way: "Foxes have holes and birds of the air have nests, but the Son of Man has nowhere to lay His head."

In other words, "Hey, buddy, I don't know if you even understand what you are saying. We don't sleep in the Jerusalem Hilton every night, and I'm not headed for an earthly throne—not yet. In fact, within mere months from now, I will be rejected by the people and by the authorities, and I will die on a Roman cross for the sins of the world. Are you sure you're up for that? Is that what you want to do?"

And the scribe must have replied (backing away), "Umm, not so much. Catch You later."

In the impulse of the moment, people will sometimes say, "I want to be a Christian. I want to follow Jesus." But it really isn't a decision at all. It's just a rash, impulsive statement, with no real commitment behind it. A person who really wants to follow Jesus must first count the cost of what they're about to do.

People often will follow impulses and then regret it later. That's why banks offer free credit cards to people. People will sign up without really thinking much about it or reading the fine print, and then they get themselves into financial trouble. They will find out (too late) that if they are one hour late on their payment, their interest rate will jump from 9 percent to 49 percent.

Or maybe you're at the grocery store, and as you're waiting to check out, you find yourself grabbing some of those handy little items and snacks placed so strategically near the register.

They call those "impulse items," and they put them there because they understand our human tendency to make quick purchases without really thinking about it.

It's the same with impulse commitments to Jesus Christ. Jesus reminds us that we are to count the cost before we commit to following Him—and despite what you may have heard, He never promises us an easy road.

The second would-be follower was hung up with relationship issues. In verses 21-23, we read, "Then another of His disciples said to Him, 'Lord, let me first go and bury my father.' But Jesus said to him, 'Follow Me, and let the dead bury their own dead.' Now when He got into a boat, His disciples followed Him.'"

If you don't understand the culture of the time, the

Lord's reply to this man might come off sounding a little heartless. This man seems to be saying, "Lord, my dad just died, and I need to make some funeral arrangements. I could use a little extra time."

But that is not at all what was happening here. The man was actually using an expression, a common idiom of the day, when he said, "Let me first go and bury my father." What he meant by those words was, "Let me wait until my father gets older and eventually dies. Then, when it's more convenient, I will follow You. I can't do it now, but I will do it later."

In the same way, there are people today who will say, "Yes, I'd like to follow Christ, but I'm concerned about how it might affect people around me. How would it impact my family? What would my wife say if I went home today and announced, 'I've decided to be a follower of Christ'? What would my parents say? How would my friends react? What would happen with my coworkers? I need some space here. I have to think this thing through."

Yes, there might very well be friction in the home or on the job if you take a stand for Christ. And it's true that some friends might want nothing more to do with you. Jesus Himself declared, "Do you think I have come to give peace to the earth? No! Rather, strife and division! From now on families will be split apart, three in favor of me, and two against—or perhaps the other way around" (Luke 12:51-52, TLB).

We think sometimes that the highest values in life are peace and harmony. You know, "Let's just all coexist in peace and love and tolerance."

But those aren't the highest values, and unity and tolerance aren't always good things. *Truth is more important than unity.* The fact is that people can be unified around a lie.

Let's say that you go home one night and say, "I've become a Christian today."

That announcement may very well trigger some tension, anger, and even a few arguments. There may be people under your roof who won't like that turn of events at all. That conflict, however, could be a good thing because your family members may be under the conviction of the Holy Spirit, and a battle may be raging for their souls.

It's generally true that the most difficult people to reach with the gospel are members of your own family. You would think they might be the easiest, but no, they can be the hardest. Jesus said, "A prophet is not without honor except in his own country and in his own house" (Matthew 13:57). Even Jesus' own siblings did not believe in Him until His death and resurrection.

That amazes me. Who was a better, kinder, more loving, more consistent example than Jesus Christ? He never messed up, not even once. He never had to say to one of His brothers, "Hey, man, I'm sorry. I shouldn't have said that." He never did anything wrong. *Ever.* And He was never prideful, arrogant, sarcastic, or impatient with His parents, brothers, or sisters. Still, they refused to believe.

Can you imagine being one of His siblings? Can you imagine hearing Mary say, "Why can't you be more like your brother Jesus? Why don't you treat me like Jesus does?" Most likely, that was tough to handle sometimes.

How did they feel toward Him? They thought He was off His rocker. They thought He was delusional until they realized that He had been raised from the dead and that everything He had been saying was true. My point is that if Jesus Christ, God incarnate, had a challenge in His own family, we certainly will have it in ours.

My advice? Just live the life.

Yes, it's good to preach sermons, but there comes a point when there's been enough preaching and it's time to just start walking it out. Live it day in and day out, in good circumstances and bad. Let your actions speak. You've already told them what you believe, explained to them what Jesus said, and showed them how to believe in Him. Now the important thing is to demonstrate how Christ can change a life by the way that you live.

The point is, don't let potential conflict with your mate or family members or friends keep you away from God. Here is your choice in life: You can have harmony with God and conflict with people, or you can have harmony with people and find yourself in conflict with the living God who loves you. If you want to get along with everyone, you will eventually alienate God, because that means you are making compromises. But if you want to get along with God, do what He wants, and stay in step with Him, it's going to offend some people.

It isn't because you're obnoxious or mean or narrow-minded or whatever other label someone wants to pin on you. It's just that there are certain people who don't want anything to do with God and don't like what God says. And if you happen to be doing what God says, they won't like you, either.

What do you do about it? Again, you live the life. Go on loving those people and praying for them, but don't let them keep you from following the Lord.

Jesus said, "Let the dead bury the dead. You come and follow Me."

ARE WE REALLY FOLLOWERS OF CHRIST?

What is a follower of Christ? Who is a follower of Christ?

1. A follower of Jesus follows Him each and every day.

It is not just starting out in the Christian life with a grand flourish and a brass band; it is running the race for the rest of your life. It's staying in that race and aiming for the finish line, not allowing yourself to become distracted or wander off the track. Jesus commanded that we follow Him, but He also has invited us to follow Him, enjoying His nearness and friendship and an ongoing conversation with Him through every waking hour.

2. A follower of Jesus can't say goodbye to the old life fast enough.

Remember the example of Matthew, who bolted up from that tax table and left everything to follow Christ. We need to gladly shed every old sin, old vice, or old habit that slows us down from keeping in step with Jesus.

And let me add this: Whatever you give up to follow Jesus will be replaced by something far better. Sometimes I will hear people say, "I gave up a friendship to follow Jesus." Or "I broke off a relationship with my boyfriend," or "I gave up my career."

Yes, and God will make it up to you, in this life and in the life to come . . . but especially in the life to come.

3. A follower of Jesus cares about unbelievers and wants to reach them.

Again, I love the example of Matthew. Using his influence and his wealth and his network of friends, he threw a huge party and brought in Jesus Christ as the guest speaker!

Reaching his friends and colleagues was the first thing he wanted to do after he became a follower of Jesus.

4. A follower of Jesus loves Him more than anyone or anything else.

Jesus is number one in this person's life, even if it means the painful severing of other relationships. What's more, a true follower of Jesus is always on guard against those temptations, habits, attitudes, activities, or associations that would grieve the Lord or steal away their love for Him. As it says in the Song of Solomon, "Catch all the foxes, those little foxes, before they ruin the vineyard of love, for the grapevines are blossoming!" (2:15, NLT).

Follow Me! Jesus said that, Matthew did it, and he never regretted it.

This very day, he is still following Jesus along the paths of heaven.

2

FOLLOWING JESUS THROUGH THE STORMS OF LIFE

People have a lot more warning about approaching storms than they used to. Now when a huge storm approaches an area, residents usually get a heads-up from the TV, radio, or Internet. If that storm system builds itself up to monumental proportions, with hurricane strength, they might even give it a name. There are certain hurricanes that are famous—or infamous—now, like Hurricanes Carla, Camille, Isabel, Andrew, Katrina, and Sandy.

Some hurricanes, of course, don't receive the same level of notoriety. Was it because they weren't as powerful, or because they had mild-sounding names? There was actually a Hurricane Fabian at one point and a Hurricane Larry. Really? Could anybody get intimidated by a Hurricane Larry? Or how about a Hurricane Teddy? Doesn't that just strike fear into your heart? Probably not. The bottom line, however, is that we give names to certain powerful storms because of their significance and potential for great damage and destruction.

There are storms in life, too.

Sometimes these storms will be expected, and we watch them build and brew with great concern in our hearts. But at other times, storms seem to slam into our world out of nowhere, with no warning at all.

Maybe it's a heart attack . . . or a rebellious child . . . or a pink slip at work . . . or a crumbling marriage. It might even be the death of someone you love very much. These sorts of storms can alter the very landscape of our lives.

Here is what you need to know about life storms in general: *You're going to have them.*

There are really two kinds of people in the world: those who are experiencing a crisis, and those who are about to experience a crisis. You're either in a storm or you're headed into another. That is not pessimism; that is *life*.

According to the Bible, the rain will fall on both the righteous and the unrighteous. Jesus Himself said, "In this godless world you will continue to experience difficulties. But take heart! I've conquered the world" (John 16:33, MSG).

The simple fact is that we can't control whether storms will come into our lives; all we can control is how we *respond* to them. For the next few pages, let's consider a literal storm that came into the lives of Jesus' disciples.

A STORM THAT LOOKED LIKE DEATH

Now when He got into a boat, His disciples followed Him. And suddenly a great tempest arose on the sea, so that the boat was covered with the waves. But He was asleep. Then His disciples came to Him and awoke Him, saying, "Lord, save us! We are perishing!"

But He said to them, "Why are you fearful, O you of little faith?" Then He arose and rebuked the winds and the sea, and there was a great calm. So the men marveled, saying, "Who can this be, that even the winds and the sea obey Him?" (Matthew 8:23-27)

In the last chapter, we looked at the two words Jesus spoke to Matthew, the tax collector: *Follow Me.*

In the original language, those words implied both the beginning and the ending of something. In other words, Jesus was effectively saying to Matthew, "I want you to follow Me each and every day." So Matthew followed Jesus.

In fact, all of the disciples followed Jesus. And where did that lead them? *Directly into a storm.*

Sometimes when storms or hardships come into our lives, we may think, *This is probably happening because I did something wrong.* But that certainly wasn't true in this case. These disciples were in the will of God, men who had committed their very lives to following Jesus. *The storm came even as they were obeying the Lord, not because they had disobeyed Him.*

So what do we learn from this story?

1. Storms will come into our lives.

This was a serious storm, so frightening that these seasoned sailors feared for their lives. In the original language, the word used to describe it is also used to speak of an earthquake. One translation says that "high waves began to break into the boat until it was nearly full of water and about to sink" (Mark 4:37, TLB).

So it was a seismic megastorm that covered the boat with crashing waves.

Have you ever been in a storm at sea? I've been in a few, but never in a boat like Jesus and the disciples were in that day. It was a very simple, primitive boat, and none of them were wearing life jackets.

So what was Jesus doing while this terrifying storm swept over them? Amazingly, He was sound asleep in the lower part of the boat.

Does it ever seem to you as though God is asleep or not paying attention to what's going on in your life? It can be rather disheartening when someone falls asleep just at the moment when we really need them.

Some people can sleep through anything. My wife can do that quite well. Once she goes to sleep, she is *asleep*. That's not the case with me. I wake up when a bird chirps and then can't go back to sleep again.

Have you ever been talking with someone and had them actually fall asleep while you were talking? It happens to me all the time as a preacher. And don't think I don't notice! People can pretend like they have just been praying after their head lurches forward, but I'm not buying it.

People are people, and they will occasionally fall asleep in your presence or take a nap at the very moment when you need them most. But God never does that. Psalm 121:4 says, "Indeed, he who watches over Israel will neither slumber nor sleep" (NIV).

In a technical sense, Jesus the man, weary from a hard day's work, was asleep. But in the broader sense, God never sleeps. He is always on watch, always on duty, always paying attention. Jesus was asleep because He rested confidently in the will of the Father. And that is what the disciples should have done, too. They should have realized that God would see them through that storm and they would be fine. Instead, they were beside themselves with fear.

What should we do when storms come into our lives?

2. We need to cry out to Jesus in the midst of our storms.

They cried out, "Lord, save us!" And by the way, I don't think they whispered those words.

When I say cry out to Jesus, I mean *cry out*—whatever is on your heart. You will never offend God by raising your voice. Tell Him just how you're feeling. He already knows!

God, why?
God, what?
God, where are You?
Lord, I don't get this.
Lord, I don't like this.
Lord, this is really hard.
Jesus, this doesn't make any sense to me.
Lord, HELP!

All of those expressions are perfectly legitimate. In fact, you can read prayers of much greater intensity in the book of Psalms.

Sometimes I think we feel as though we need to sanitize our prayers or pretty them up a little. No, God wants to hear you speak from your heart. He wants honest prayer, even if it's shouted or cried out through tears. Again, read the honesty of David and others in the Psalms as they cried out to God, pouring out their frustration to Him. Even Jesus, hanging on the cross, said, "My God, My God, why have You forsaken Me?"

Talk to God about it. Call out to Him. That is what those disciples did when they were slammed by that storm.

Though the shrieking of the storm did not wake Jesus, the cry of His people did. You can be sure they had tried everything possible to get out of that mess on their own. But after exhausting all of their efforts, they knew Jesus was their only hope. That's the way it is with us sometimes. God will let us get to the very end of our rope, coming to the end of ourselves, so that we might (finally) cry out to Him.

The story is told of a hardened old sea captain who was quite vocal about his atheism. One night during a terrible storm, he was swept overboard. Someone quickly threw him a rope, but as he was thrashing about in the dark ocean, his men heard him yelling and crying out to God for help and for mercy.

After his crew rescued him and got him dried off, one of his men said to him, "Captain, I thought you didn't believe in God."

The salty old captain replied, "Well, even if there isn't a God, there *ought* to be at times like this."

That is how many people respond. C. S. Lewis said that even atheists have moments of doubt. Sometimes, in quiet moments when no one else is around, that individual who seems so confident in his atheism and hatred of Christianity has moments of doubt about his philosophy. When great trials come, he might instinctively turn toward God . . . or at least want to.

Will God hear that person when he cries out to Him? Yes, He will. We might imagine God saying something like, "Forget it! You made your bed, and now you can sleep in it." But that is not the kind of God He is. When Jesus walked this earth, He responded to the cries of those in distress and need.

In Psalm 91:14-15, the Lord says, "I will rescue those who love me. I will protect those who trust in my name. When they call on me, I will answer; I will be with them in trouble. I will rescue and honor them" (NLT).

It was Thomas Watson who said, "When God lays men on their backs, then they look up to heaven."

Not long ago, I got a letter from a woman who came to our crusade in Chicago. It was a crisis that got her attention. This is what she wrote:

Dear Greg,

My husband and I have been going through a lot. He had a stroke a few weeks ago, and we have really been struggling I became upset with God and all of these things that were hitting me at once. So last week, I was told by my mother that I never fit into our family and never would and was not welcome in their home anymore. . . . I was ready to take my own life.

So here was a woman enduring deep hardship, rejected by her own mother and devastated by her husband's stroke, who was ready to commit suicide. How did God reach her? It was through her eight-year-old daughter, who, in her words, "loved the Lord and wanted to go to the crusade." Reluctantly, the little girl's mom relented and took her.

When the invitation was given, her little girl wanted to go forward. The mom didn't really want to go forward, but she went down to the front with her little girl who wanted to commit her life to Christ.

But something happened to her once she began to move toward Christ. When she got to the front, she dropped down on her knees. "I felt His love," she wrote, "and I knew He loved me and had forgiven me."

I love that story. You see, as soon as this distraught woman began to move toward Jesus, Jesus rushed to help her. She needed help, and He responded to her. And that is the way He responds to all of us when we cry out to Him.

3. God has His purposes in the storms of life.

> Then He arose and rebuked the winds and the sea, and there was a great calm. (Matthew 8:26)

Maybe you are in a storm right now, and you have cried out for it to stop . . . but it hasn't. In fact, it has gotten worse. You think, *Why? Why is God allowing this?*

There are no easy answers to that question, but know this: Where there are no trials in life, there will be no triumphs. It has been said, "The hammer shatters glass, but it forges steel." And strangely enough, God often brings surprise benefits to our lives in the midst of our hardships. It is in the difficult places of life, the dark valleys and the steep paths, where we learn and discover truths we couldn't learn anywhere else.

Everyone loves Psalm 23, and many of us have committed it to memory. Its opening verses paint such a beautiful picture:

> The LORD is my shepherd;
> I shall not want.
> He makes me to lie down in green pastures;
> He leads me beside the still waters.
> He restores my soul. (verses 1-3)

The scene is very soothing and pastoral, with sheep grazing on green grass and a cool stream winding through the meadow. It was written by a shepherd named David, who went on to become the first great king of Israel. David knew quite a bit about sheep because he had cared for them for years. He knew they were one of the dumbest animals on the face of the earth and needed the constant care and protection of the shepherd. And that is why he humbled himself and said, "The Lord Himself is *my* Shepherd."

But then David continued on, saying,

> Yea, though I walk through the valley of the shadow
>   of death,
> I will fear no evil;
> For You are with me;
> Your rod and Your staff, they comfort me.
> You prepare a table before me in the presence of
>   my enemies. (verses 4-5)

"Hold on!" we say. "I signed up for green pastures and still waters, not for dark valleys. I don't like valleys. I don't do valleys. And what's this business about the presence of enemies?"

Yes, if you are a child of God, if you are one of His sheep, then you will do the valleys as well as the green pastures. You will endure the storms as well as relax in the gentle breezes. But He will be with you when you leave the pleasant pastures and quiet waters, and He will take care of you in the dark valleys. It is in and through those valleys that we will learn our most important lessons. When you think about it, fruit doesn't grow on mountaintops; it grows in valleys.

The secret to making it through all the highs and lows of life is *knowing that you are not alone and that God will get you through whatever you are facing.*

How could David get through that valley? "Yea, though I walk through the valley of the shadow of death, I will fear no evil; *for You are with me*" (emphasis added).

That is both the promise and the hope. God is with you, and He will be with you in your storm, no matter how severe.

THREE KINDS OF LIFE STORMS

When it comes to the storms we face in life, I have placed them in three categories: correcting storms, protecting storms, and perfecting storms.

1. Correcting Storms

Jonah faced such a storm when he rejected God's command and tried to run from the presence of the Lord on a ship bound for the edge of civilization. As a result, the Lord sent a great storm that rocked the reluctant prophet's world and put his life back on course. That storm was the result of Jonah's disobedience to God and the sacred call on his life.

Many times we bring storms on ourselves. If we deliberately do wrong or hurtful things, we will reap the repercussions of those acts. If you rob a gas station, get caught, and are thrown in jail, there is really no need to pray, *Oh Lord, why did You bring me into this storm?*

If it's a storm of your own making, you will face the consequences of your own actions. Maybe you have neglected or mistreated your spouse, and he or she abandons you. You ask, "Why is this storm coming on me?" The truth is that you brought it on yourself. God is letting you reap what you sow, with the objective being that you will change your actions.

Even in the consequences of your own foolishness or sin, God is at work. He will use the painful consequences of those sinful actions to discipline you and train you. The book of Hebrews counsels us to "endure hardship as discipline; God is treating you as sons" (12:7, NIV). When you go astray and face discipline for your actions, it is a reminder that you are a son or daughter of God.

> My child, don't make light of the LORD's discipline,
>   and don't give up when he corrects you.
> For the LORD disciplines those he loves,
>   and he punishes each one he accepts as his
>   child. (Hebrews 12:5-6, NLT)

We don't discipline other people's children, do we? But we would *like* to sometimes, wouldn't we? You know what I mean. You're in a store and some child is having a total meltdown. The mom is flustered and simply doesn't know what to do or how to control her own child. There are times when you would like to step in, but you can't because that isn't your role. Discipline is your legitimate role with your own children, but not with someone else's.

When God disciplines us for rebelling against Him and going our own way, it's an indication that we really belong to Him and that He loves us.

Back in the twenty-third psalm, David wrote, "Yea, though I walk through the valley of the shadow of death, I will fear no evil; for You are with me; Your rod and Your staff, they comfort me" (verse 4).

I can see getting some comfort from the staff, but . . . *from the rod?*

The staff was a long pole with a crook on the end, and the shepherd used it to pull a wayward sheep back into line.

But a rod was basically just a club.

How does a club comfort a sheep?

It comforts me to realize that God won't let me go too far astray without reminding me that I'm on the wrong path, that He loves me, and that He wants me to return to Him and remain close to Him. His discipline may hurt, but He knows exactly what it will take to get my attention. Sometimes He will use the staff, and sometimes He will use the rod.

Either way, "the Lord disciplines those he loves" (Hebrews 12:6, NIV). He doesn't bring pain into your life because He is against you, but because He is *for* you.

We can all think of times when we've pushed the envelope and walked right up to the edge of some cliff, wondering, *How far can I go?*

That's when the Lord may answer us with His discipline and say, "Not any further than this."

Did you know that sometimes a shepherd actually will take that rod and break a sheep's leg if necessary?

We might say, "Oh, poor little sheep!"

But it's better to have a broken leg than become leg of lamb. If a sheep keeps wandering away from the flock, it will become easy prey for predators in the mood for a little fresh mutton. So the shepherd will have to take drastic measures to keep that wayward sheep from completely destroying itself. He will try to protect that wayward sheep — *and the others that follow it* — from its own foolish actions. That is another crazy thing about sheep. When one goes astray, the others will blindly follow along. Not long ago, I read in a newspaper about one sheep that walked off a cliff, fell to its death, and was followed by a thousand more!

How stupid can you be? Pretty stupid . . . when you're a sheep. That is why the Bible says in Isaiah 53:6, "All we like sheep have gone astray; we have turned, every one, to his own way."

So in His love, God allows those correcting storms to come into our lives.

2. Protecting Storms

The gospel of John gives an account of Jesus' performing His most popular miracle: the feeding of the five thousand. With five loaves and two fish borrowed from a little boy's lunch, Jesus fed a multitude, with twelve baskets left over.

The people loved that miracle — so much so that they were talking about taking Jesus by force and making Him their king. Jesus, however, got His boys out of Dodge as quickly as possible. Why? Because He knew the hearts of those people were dead wrong. They didn't want Him to be their Lord and Master; they just wanted a free lunch from then on. And knowing that His disciples already were caught up in visions of grandeur and speculation about an earthly kingdom (with each of them in some prominent position), He wanted to remove them from that entire scene.

So what did He do? Matthew 14:22 says, "Immediately Jesus made His disciples get into the boat and go before Him to the other side, while He sent the multitudes away." And out in the middle of that lake, they encountered a storm.

It was a protecting storm. Protecting them from what? Themselves.

Sometimes God will bring difficulty in our lives to keep us from something worse! Be thankful God doesn't answer all of your prayers in the affirmative. Think back over some of your spontaneous prayers in unguarded moments:

Lord, if You really love me, You'll convince that girl to marry me.

Lord, I'm begging You for that promotion at work.

Lord, please help me to win the lottery, just this once.

The fact is, the Lord may know that answering those prayers with a yes might destroy you. The woman or man you wanted to marry might have ruined your life and brought you great unhappiness. That promotion at work might have given you ulcers and a heart attack. Winning the lottery might have been the worst thing that ever could have happened to you and your family.

Sometimes God says no for our own good. And sometimes He sends a protecting storm to get us back on track.

3. Perfecting Storms

These are probably the most common storms we face in life, coming to those who truly desire to follow Jesus. God has a work that He wants to accomplish in these storms, and He seeks to produce a desired result. In his second letter to the church at Corinth, the apostle Paul wrote,

> For our present troubles are small and won't last very long. Yet they produce for us a glory that vastly outweighs them and will last forever! So we don't look at the troubles we can see now; rather, we fix our gaze on things that cannot be seen. For the things we see now will soon be gone, but the things we cannot see will last forever. (2 Corinthians 4:17-18, NLT)

Yes, the storms will come, and God is doing a work in our lives. Sometimes you will be aware of that work and begin to see the results; at other times, you will struggle to see anything good come from those storms. Nevertheless, we can know God's intended outcome right from the get-go. Romans 8:29 says, "For those God foreknew he also predestined to be conformed to the likeness of his Son, that he might be the firstborn among many brothers" (NIV).

First and foremost, God's work in our lives is to conform us to the image of His Son, Jesus. When we cross over to the other side, in heaven, we will understand why God allowed certain storms to enter our lives and to last as long as they did.

You and I can't control our universe. I know. I've tried, and it doesn't work. We can't determine when a storm will start or when a storm will stop. All we can do is respond to the storm.

To me, one of the greatest examples of faith in today's world is the life of a woman named Joni Eareckson Tada. She has faced amazing obstacles — more than you or I could imagine — with her faith remaining intact. In fact, she has been a constant source of encouragement to millions of people all over the world. Back in 1967, as a vivacious, active seventeen-year-old, Joni dove from a raft into the shallow waters of Chesapeake Bay and broke her neck. As a result, she suffered a spinal cord fracture that has paralyzed her from the neck down. Despite this severe, lifelong disability, Joni has remained a shining light of hope and faith and encouragement to generations of people, both able-bodied and disabled. Through her books, her movie, her art (painted with a brush between her teeth), and her radio program, she has spread a message that says God can sustain us and use us in the midst of the worst storms of life.

Just recently, after forty-plus years in a wheelchair, Joni found out that she has breast cancer. So in addition to being a quadriplegic, Joni now has to deal with surgery and weeks of chemotherapy. Now if she were to just say, "I am really struggling with doubt right now . . . I don't know where God is," we would understand that, wouldn't we? But in an interview she did with *WORLD* magazine, she said that she sees herself in a battle against powers and principalities who want her to despair and emotions that take her down dark, grim paths.

Joni quotes Hebrews 10:38: "My righteous one will live by faith. And if he shrinks back, I will not be pleased with him" (NIV). In the interview she said, "I do not want to be one of those who shrink back. I don't want to tarnish His name."

So she memorizes Scripture, and she spends time ministering to others who are disabled or in pain, weeping with those who weep. She said, "God's up to something big. How can I showcase Him to others?"[1]

Joni knows that her life is on display before multitudes of people and before the angels and that others are learning by the way she responds to the heartbreaks and difficulties in her life. Acknowledging that she's in the middle of a battlefield, she asks, "How can I glorify God in this?"

Joni is a person just like we are, and she certainly has her moments of struggle, disappointment, and doubts. But for forty-plus years, she has made it her goal to use her disability as a platform to glorify God.

You and I can do this too in the storms that hammer our lives. We need to say, "How can I bring glory to God through this? How can I point people to the Lord through this?"

For most of us, a storm will have a beginning, a middle, and an end. A child raised in the way of the Lord rebels against the Lord, then comes back to the Lord. A person faces a serious illness, gets treatment for the illness, and then recovers from the illness. It's beautiful when it happens that way, and we get to tell the story of God's goodness and kindness toward us in keeping us through the storm.

For others (Joni included), life itself can be a storm. In other words, the trial comes and never leaves, and the storm doesn't end until that man or woman steps into heaven. Yes, the storm will end for every child of God . . . but it may not end on this side of eternity. In heaven, we will see the big picture and begin to understand God's ultimate plan and purpose for our lives.

SOMETIMES JESUS STOPS THE STORM, BUT HE IS ALWAYS WITH US IN THE STORM

In the frightening storm out on the Sea of Galilee, Jesus chose to stop the storm altogether. First He rebuked the disciples, saying, "Why are you fearful, O you of little faith?" (Matthew 8:26). And then He simply stopped the storm in its tracks, and the sea instantly became like glass.

In Mark's version of the story, we have this interesting detail. At the very beginning of that journey across the sea, Jesus had said to His disciples, "Let us cross over to the other side" (Mark 4:35).

Now if He had said to them, "Let's drown today in the middle of the Sea of Galilee," I don't know if I would have boarded that boat. But He didn't say that. He said, "Let us cross over to the other side." *He didn't promise them smooth sailing, but He did promise them a safe arrival.*

If Jesus says to you, "Let's go together to such and such a place," you will get there. Jesus gets to wherever He's going, and if we're with Him, we will too.

In Isaiah 43:2, we read,

When you go through deep waters,
    I will be with you.
When you go through rivers of difficulty,
    you will not drown.
When you walk through the fire of oppression,
    you will not be burned up;
        the flames will not consume you. (NLT)

Are you in a storm right now?
Know this: He is walking through it with you.

"BE MUZZLED!"

What could be more human than Jesus' falling asleep in a boat after a day of hard work? And what could be more divine than rebuking a storm?

"Peace, be still!" (Mark 4:39).

In the original language, the Greek term translated *be still* literally means "be muzzled," as you would muzzle a hostile or unruly dog. But who was Jesus talking to? The storm itself? The clouds and rain? No, He was speaking to the power behind that storm: the devil himself. God did not initiate this storm, but He did allow it. Satan was behind the storm, and it was Satan who needed to be muzzled.

The storm stopped in an instant, and they made it to the other side, just as Jesus had told them they would.

Sometimes in our lives, the devil will whisper in our ear, "You're never going to make it as a Christian. You're going to fail. You're going to crash and burn. You think you're going to heaven when you die? No, you'll never make it."

These are lies from the Father of Lies. If you have

committed your life to Christ, you will make it to the other side — *if you want to.*

In the book of Acts, Paul was on a ship, being driven along by a huge storm. One night the Lord revealed to Paul that although the ship would be destroyed, not one soul would be lost. In other words, if they stayed with the ship until God brought it close to land, they would be saved. But if they chose to jump overboard during the middle of the storm, they wouldn't be safe at all.

In the same way, if you exercise your free will to turn against God and abandon your faith, you won't make it to heaven. However, if you want to make it to heaven, you will — not through your own effort, but because God will give you the strength to make it.

In Jude 24 we read, "Now to Him who is able to keep you from stumbling, and to present you faultless before the presence of His glory with exceeding joy." God Himself will keep you from falling!

In Philippians 1:6, Paul wrote, "Being confident of this very thing, that He who has begun a good work in you will complete it until the day of Jesus Christ."

In Hebrews 12:2, the writer describes Jesus as "the author and finisher of our faith."

As we have said, storms will come into every life, for the believer and the unbeliever alike. The rain will fall and the wind will blow. But it is only the children of God who have the promise that God will be with them and that "in all things God works for the good of those who love him, who have been called according to his purpose" (Romans 8:28, NIV).

You will get through the storm, and you will get to the other side. You might have a rough voyage, but you will get there because Jesus says that you will.

3

SATAN, SOCIETY, AND THE SAVIOR

We all like power, but in different ways.

Most guys are really into horsepower. The era of the muscle car may have come and gone, but there are still some pretty fast, street-legal cars out there. (Not everyone is driving hybrids.) The Dodge Viper, for instance, has 600 horsepower, the Ferrari has 612, the Bentley has 621, and the Lamborghini, 632.

Just recently, I read about a new entry into the sweepstakes that is being called the world's fastest street-legal car: the Maxximus G-Force, with 1,600 horsepower. It will go from zero to sixty in two seconds. (And it will only set you back seven figures or so.)

If you happen to have one of those parked in your garage, then you have the ultimate bragging rights.

But maybe you're not into cars. In fact, you may be a nerd, and power for you is all about processors, gigahertz, and storage gigs.

Our culture today is all about the biggest, the fastest, the strongest, and the mostest.

In fact, the history of humanity has been all about power—using it and sometimes exploiting it. First there was man power, then there was horsepower (the kind with real horses), and then there was steam power. Now we have nuclear power. The only thing we seem to lack today is willpower. Humanity is able to harness the powers of the universe, but we can't seem to control ourselves.

But here is the good news: We serve a mighty God who will give us all the power we need to live the Christian life. Sometimes people will say, "I think it's hard being a Christian."

I completely disagree with that. I don't think it's hard being a Christian, I think it is *impossible* to be a Christian—without the help and power of the Holy Spirit in my life. But fortunately, I serve a God who has all power. In Psalm 62:11, the psalmist tells us, "Power belongs to God." Psalm 79:11 speaks of the greatness of God's power. And Jesus said, "All power is given unto me in heaven and in earth" (Matthew 28:18, KJV). The apostle Peter wrote, "His divine power has given us everything we need for life and godliness" (2 Peter 1:3, NIV).

All the power we need to live the Christian life is available to us through Christ.

That's an important fact to know, because we have an adversary, Satan, or the devil, who also has power—and it is power he wants to use to harm us or destroy us. In fact, the moment we put our faith in Jesus, we entered into a spiritual battle that will continue through all our days on earth.

It has been said that conversion has made our hearts a battlefield. The J. B. Phillips New Testament translates Ephesians 6:12 with these words: "For our fight is not against any physical enemy: it is against organisations and powers that are spiritual. We are up against the unseen power that controls this dark world, and spiritual agents from the very headquarters of evil."

Just as our God has angels doing His bidding, Lucifer, a fallen angel, has demons doing his dirty work. Lucifer, once a high-ranking angel, rebelled against God in heaven and, in that rebellion, took one-third of the angels with him. Those fallen angels are what we know as demons today. The purpose of demons seems twofold: They seek to hinder the purpose of God, and they seek to extend the power of Satan.

The story before us in this chapter gives the account of two men who fell under the power of the evil one, the devil—until they encountered an even greater Power that set them free.

THE CONFRONTATION

When He had come to the other side, to the country of the Gergesenes, there met Him two demon-possessed men, coming out of the tombs, exceedingly fierce, so that no one could pass that way. And suddenly they cried out, saying, "What have we to do with You, Jesus, You Son of God? Have You come here to torment us before the time?"

Now a good way off from them there was a herd of many swine feeding. So the demons begged Him, saying, "If You cast us out, permit us to go away into the herd of swine."

And He said to them, "Go." So when they had come out, they went into the herd of swine. And suddenly the whole herd of swine ran violently down the steep place into the sea, and perished in the water.

Then those who kept them fled; and they went away into the city and told everything, including what had happened to the demon-possessed men. And behold, the whole city came out to meet Jesus. And when they saw Him, they begged Him to depart from their region.

So He got into a boat, crossed over, and came to His own city. (Matthew 8:28–9:1)

The story begins with two pathetic, demented men who had come completely under the power of the devil. In Luke's account, he zeroes in on one of these men in particular, because he was probably the more extreme of the two. In Luke 8:27 we read that this man wore no clothing and lived among the tombs, where he would shriek and howl and cut himself with sharp stones. Although the authorities apparently captured him on several occasions, putting him in chains, he would simply break the chains with his superhuman strength and go on his way.

It paints a weird, frightening scene, doesn't it? How did this man end up in this tragic state? The Bible doesn't give us his biography. We're simply presented with a snapshot of two men who had fallen completely under the control of the devil, and it wasn't a pretty sight.

That's the trouble, of course, with all of Satan's offers. He comes to us with some very enticing, attractive offers right up front, but once he gets us where he wants us, he chews us up and spits us out. Jesus summed it up well: "[Satan] does not come except to steal, and to kill, and to destroy" (John 10:10). And that is what he had done in the lives of these two men in Matthew 8. He had stolen their lives and was in the very process of destroying them.

You might describe these two guys as "dead men walking." They were like spiritual zombies. It is the condition all of us were in before we received salvation in Jesus Christ. The Bible says when you are not a believer in Jesus Christ, you are dead in trespasses and sin (see Ephesians 2:1,5). Speaking of a widow who lives for pleasure, the apostle Paul said that she is "dead while she lives" (1 Timothy 5:6).

In the prison system in the old days, when a person would be marched to their execution, the prison guards would call out "Dead man walking!" as they were going down the hallway. In our world today, we have a great many dead men and dead women walking. And they are walking in the wrong direction.

How do you reach a person like one of these demon-possessed men in the book of Matthew? How do you break through to someone who harms himself, is suicidal, and has completely fallen under the devil's sway?

Is it hopeless?

No, it isn't. But the only way it can happen is through the power of Jesus Christ.

A number of years ago, our Harvest team held a crusade in North Carolina. On our youth night, a girl named Jennifer came. Sometime later, she sent me a letter. "The night before Harvest, I was depressed about everything," she wrote. "I wanted to give up on life altogether. I even thought about suicide. I was feeling unloved and began to look for love in all the wrong places, trying to fill the empty place in my heart. But I went that night with friends."

That night, when she heard the message of Christ's love for her, she was changed on the inside. "It's something I've never felt before," she told me. "I don't feel empty anymore. It's like being able to see for the first time."

Another teenage girl named Nikki, who was also suicidal, went to the same event. She later told us, "My life has been in the slumps. I have been having trouble at school, boyfriend trouble. I have been cutting myself, and it is just hurting me. And I can't stop because I am addicted. Then I heard that Christ saves lives, so I decided to give it a chance. My life has made a complete turnaround. I have given my life to Jesus. And I never thought God would forgive me for the things I had done to myself and the sins I had committed, but after hearing what Greg had to say, it opened my eyes. I am now living as a Christian."

The power of Christ reached these girls, who had been falling more and more under the devil's influence and control—to the point of wanting to destroy their own lives.

And that is the very thing that happened two thousand years ago for two demon-possessed men who seemed beyond all human hope or help.

AFTERMATH OF THE STORM

In the previous chapter, we read how Jesus and His men were hit with a huge storm on the Sea of Galilee. Jesus had been sleeping in the boat's stern, but when the waves grew so huge that they were actually crashing over the boat, the disciples woke Him up, crying out, "Lord, save us! We are perishing!" (Matthew 8:25).

You'll remember that Jesus stood up in the boat and stopped the storm with a loud command, saying, "Peace, be still!" His literal words were, "Be muzzled!" as though He were speaking to a wild animal. In effect, that's just what He was doing. He was talking to the power behind that storm, which was Satan.

Why did Satan send such a storm at a time like that? I believe the evil one didn't want Jesus to get to those men. Jesus, however, wouldn't let hell or high water stop Him. There were two lonely, tortured souls who needed help, and He was the only One who could help them.

It reminds us of when the Lord went to Samaria. We read in John 4:4 that "He needed to go through Samaria." Why was that? Most Jews would walk miles out of their way to avoid going through Samaria. But Jesus knew there was a burned-out, immoral woman who had been married and divorced five times who would come to the well at noon to draw water. So Jesus wanted to be at that well, waiting for her.

When He went to the town of Jericho, He found the little tax collector, Zacchaeus, up in the branches of a sycamore tree and invited Himself over to the man's house for a meal. Whenever there was a hurting person in a room, it wouldn't be long until Jesus made His way to that person.

In the account before us, Jesus had made His way through a killer storm to seek out two tortured, suicidal souls who roamed a graveyard, howling like animals.

As the story unfolds, we learn several interesting things about the activity of the devil and demons in our world.

A FEW OBSERVATIONS ABOUT DEMONS

1. Demons, though wicked, are orthodox in some of their beliefs.

In Matthew 8:29, the two demon-possessed men screamed out a bizarre question: "What have we to do with You, Jesus, You Son of God? Have You come here to torment us before the time?"

By addressing Jesus as the Son of God, they immediately acknowledged that they knew who He was.

Mark's version of this same story tells us that one of the demon-possessed men ran up and bowed down before Him. And the word used there for *bowed down* is the Greek word *proskyneo,* which means to bow down and worship. So the demon-possessed guy ran up to Jesus, acknowledged He was the Son of God, and bowed down to worship Him. It's a reminder to us that even though demons hate and loathe everything about God, they are powerless to do anything but worship. "I hate You, but You are God. I have to acknowledge it; Your power is greater." That is what was happening here.

If I were able to interview the devil (and I'm not applying for that job), I think we might be surprised at some of the things he would say.

I would ask him, "Do you believe in the existence of God?"

And he would say, "Yes, I do."

"Do you believe in the deity of Jesus Christ?"

"Yes, I do."

"Do you believe that the Bible is the Word of God?"

"Yes. I hate every word of it, but I believe it."

"Do you believe that Jesus Christ is coming back again?"

"Yes, I do."

"Do you believe there is a final judgment for you and your demons that follow you?"

"Yes, I do."

Just because you believe something is true, however, doesn't mean you have submitted your life to that truth. Demons are in open rebellion against God, but they know truth. Satan and his fallen angels certainly believe. Evil spirits may number in the millions, but there isn't an atheist or an agnostic in the bunch. They *know*. The apostle James wrote, "You believe that there is one God. Good! Even the demons believe that—and shudder" (James 2:19, NIV).

Actually the word *shudder* could also be translated "to bristle." It conveys the picture of some horror that causes the hair to stand on end. That is how the demons feel around Jesus. He is so powerful, great, and holy that they bristle. They're helpless to do anything but fall before Him and worship, affirming His authority. The fact is, wherever Jesus went, the demons affirmed His authority. Mark 3:11 says, "Whenever those possessed by evil spirits caught sight of him, the spirits would throw them to the ground in front of him shrieking, 'You are the Son of God!'" (NLT).

The demons in these possessed men asked a question: "Have You come here to torment us before the time?" That tells us the devil and his demons know that a day of judgment is coming. Some liberal theologians who call themselves Christians may not believe that Jesus Christ is coming back again soon, but the devil does. The book of Revelation speaks of him as being "filled with fury, because he knows that his time is short" (Revelation 12:12, NIV).

Obviously, Satan's agenda is very different from the Lord's agenda, but he knows that Jesus will return, and he knows that his own judgment is coming.

That is why the devil is pulling out all the stops, doing

as much damage as he possibly can and trying to stop us from reaching our world with the Good News.

In Luke's account of this story, we read that Jesus asked one of the men, "What is your name?" His response was "'Legion,' because many demons had entered him" (Luke 8:30). The man was so wrapped up in demonic power that he couldn't even answer for himself.

What is a legion? We know that a Roman legion consisted of six thousand soldiers. Does that mean this man was possessed by six thousand demons? We really have no idea. But judging by the effect the demons had when they were cast out of that man and into the herd of pigs grazing nearby, it must have been a large number. In effect, this man was occupied by a small city of fallen angels.

Someone might ask the question, "Can people be demon-possessed today?"

Yes, they can.

Can Christians be demon-possessed?

No, they can't be. Once you put your faith in Jesus Christ, it's as though a sign is hung around your neck that says, "Under new management." You belong to the Lord now, and Jesus isn't into a timeshare program. Isn't that nice to know? It's not as though He says, "Okay, devil, I've got Greg Laurie for six months, and then you can have him for the next six months."

No, once the Lord came into my life, He became the sole proprietor.

However, although the devil can't occupy us from the inside, he can still harass us from the outside. Demons can tempt, oppress, and even torment believers. The apostle Paul affirmed this when he wrote, "I was given a thorn in my flesh, a messenger from Satan to torment me and keep me from becoming proud" (2 Corinthians 12:7, NLT). Paul's torment was allowed by God but orchestrated by Satan.

The good news is that God will never give us more than we can handle. In 1 Corinthians 10:13, Paul wrote, "No test or temptation that comes your way is beyond the course of what others have had to face. All you need to remember is that God will never let you down; he'll never let you be pushed past your limit; he'll always be there to help you come through it" (MSG).

People who don't have the Lord in their lives, however, live in danger of demonic attack. If they begin to allow demons to gain a foothold in their lives, they can be taken over completely.

The only thing that will stop Satan in his tracks is the power of Jesus Christ. He is our only protection, and He is the One we need.

2. Demons, though wicked, have some spiritual insight.

In Matthew 8:30-31, we read, "A good way off from them there was a herd of many swine feeding. So the demons begged Him, saying, 'If You cast us out, permit us to go away into the herd of swine.'"

The demons knew that Jesus was about to cast them out of the men they had been tormenting. They understood that Jesus was compassionate and that He would rescue the men. They also knew that a time of judgment and torment awaited them in the future, and they wanted to put that off for as long as they possibly could. So they essentially said, "Just let us go into the pigs, and then we'll be out of Your way." And Jesus complied with their request.

3. Demons, though powerful, can't stand against the power of Christ.

The pigs couldn't tolerate the presence of a legion of demons in their midst, and they immediately plunged over a cliff to their deaths. Jesus Christ has power over the devil and his demons, and they must bow before Him. Philippians 2 declares, "God elevated him to the place of highest honor and gave him the name above all other names, that at the name of Jesus every knee should bow, in heaven and on earth and under the earth, and every tongue confess that Jesus Christ is Lord, to the glory of God the Father" (verses 9-11, NLT).

ENTER . . . THE SAVIOR

We see three forces at work in this account: Satan, society, and the Savior.

What did Satan do when he controlled these men? He ruined their lives. He drove them from their families, their friends, and their homes, pushing them to the very edge of suicidal despair.

So what did society do for these men? Not much, beyond making several attempts to chain them up. The fact is that society doesn't really have answers for all of the problems we face in our country today. But here is the irony. Even though society doesn't have any answers for our nation's deep problems, it seems to do everything in its power to shut down or undermine the one thing that could actually help us: Christ Himself.

Those in law enforcement see it every day. You have people who are repeat offenders in our legal system, breaking the law, being sent to jail, getting out, committing a crime, and being sent back to prison again. You have overworked police officers who are trying to keep a lid on dangerous, explosive situations. Oftentimes, you have activist judges who make wrong decisions based on faulty premises. You have the breakdown of the family. All of these elements together produce a society that can do very little, if anything, to change a person's heart. Rehabilitation efforts largely fail. In fact, the only programs that seem to offer long-lasting effects are faith based. More specifically, the most effective programs are being operated by evangelical Christians who are calling people to faith in Jesus Christ.

Satan trampled these men, driving them to the brink of destruction. Society attempted to chain these men and put them out of the way.

Enter . . . the Savior.

What did He do? He sought them out in their spooky graveyard haunts and offered them hope. In fact, Luke's account of the same story tells us what happened to one of the men who was delivered. After the demons left him, he was a changed man.

When the locals came by to see what in the world had happened, "they were afraid" (Luke 8:35). Why were they afraid? Because they couldn't understand what had just happened. They didn't know how to process it all, and they were simply stunned.

It's such a glorious thing when Christ so transforms a life that you can't even imagine that person as they used to be. Sometimes I'll be talking to a Christian who seems so "together"—successful on the job, a solid marriage, a happy family, and joy written across their face.

Maybe I will ask that person, "How did you come to Christ? Were you brought up in the church?" And then they will tell me about their previous life, where they came from, what they were involved in, and what used to mark their life.

Sometimes I'm just incredulous. Even though my eyes are giving me evidence of God's power to change a life, I find myself saying, "Are you kidding me? You used to be *what*? You used to do *what*?"

And the person will smile and say, "Yes, that's the way I was. But Jesus changed me."

That is what God can do. No one is beyond the reach of God. It doesn't matter how wicked they are, how vocal they are in their atheism, or how radical or far out their lifestyle may be. Beneath that exterior is a man or woman whom God could change. That's why everyone outside of Christ needs our prayers. We should never write people off in our minds, imagining they would never turn to the Lord. The fact is, we just don't know.

"PLEASE GO AWAY"

You would think that after such a mighty display of God's power, the people of that area would have said, "Jesus, You are the man! We love what You did! Now we can go back to the cemetery and pay our respects to our loved ones and put flowers on their graves. We wouldn't even go near that place before, because those guys were scary! Oh Lord, thank You for coming to our community."

But no, that is not what happened. Here is what did happen:

> The whole city came out to meet Jesus. And when they saw Him, they begged Him to depart from their region. (Matthew 8:34)

What? The whole city came out and did what?

They asked Jesus to leave. In fact, they *begged* Him to leave. Why? Because not only were they frightened by the radical change in the formerly demon-possessed men, but they were also upset over lost business—all those hogs that drowned when they plunged over the cliff.

If these people were Jewish, they were doing a very nonkosher thing by raising a herd of swine. But there was no more "bringing home the bacon" after the whole herd of pigs had committed swine-i-cide.

Apparently, Jesus was bad for business.

Here is what I would say to that: If Jesus is bad for your business, then get another business. Go work somewhere else. The truth is, Jesus is bad for some people's business—when that business preys on or contributes to human suffering.

So what did Jesus do when they asked Him to leave?

He left.

Jesus won't force His way into anyone's life.

STAY ... OR LEAVE?

In the final analysis, it's the same choice for every one of us. We can either ask Jesus to stay, or we can send Him away from our lives. We can say either, "Jesus, please come into my life and take control," or "Jesus, stay out of my life. I don't want any of Your control."

There are no other options. Ultimately, people will either come near to Jesus and open their lives to Him or deliberately keep Him at arm's length.

I love the story in the gospel of Luke where two discouraged, disheartened disciples are slowly trudging back home to Emmaus after witnessing the Lord's crucifixion in

Jerusalem. Their world seemed shattered beyond repair. The Jews and the Romans had killed Jesus! What did they have to live for now?

As they walked along, the resurrected Jesus caught up with them on the road and walked with them. But they didn't know it was Jesus; He was incognito. As they continued down the road, Jesus opened the Word of God to them. When they finally reached Emmaus, the Bible says that Jesus acted as though He would go farther — that He would keep on going down the road.

But the two men constrained Him. The text says, "But they urged him strongly, 'Stay with us, for it is nearly evening; the day is almost over.' So he went in to stay with them" (Luke 24:29, NIV).

Have you ever said something like that to the Lord? *Stay, Jesus. Don't go. Don't walk away. Stay right here. You're wanted. You're needed. Hang out with me all day . . . please don't move on.*

The account says that when these two disciples asked Jesus to stay, He did! He went inside their home and sat down to a meal with them.

Jesus won't force His way into a place where He is not wanted. But if He is invited, if He is deeply wanted, then He will come and He will stay.

As the Lord told Jeremiah, "You will seek Me and find Me, when you search for Me with all your heart. I will be found by you, says the LORD" (Jeremiah 29:13-14).

Don't send Him away as the townspeople in Matthew 8 did.

Invite Him to spend the day with you, and that is exactly what He will do.

4

THE WHOLE STORY

Have you heard a good story lately?

We all like a good story, whether in a book or a movie. For a story to be effective, there are usually certain elements present: a clear plot, characters you can relate to, and some kind of conflict that emerges that engages and holds your interest. Ultimately, everything comes to a point of resolution—or perhaps even a surprise ending.

Some Hollywood movies are driven by special effects to make them visually appealing. But the best movies are the ones with an engaging story line and appealing characters.

On more than one occasion, filmmakers have done a limited screening before a major release to see how people react to a movie. If they find that the audiences don't like the ending (the hero dies or the couple never gets together), they may even rewrite those last scenes and shoot them over again.

In other words, they redo the ending.

Wouldn't it be nice if we could do that in real life? We might say, "I didn't like this last week. I've had some hurts, I've had some disappointments, and I've been depressed. Let's reshoot that one more time."

The Bible tells us that our life is a lot like a story. Psalm 90:9 says, "We spend our years as a tale that is told" (KJV).

Real life, however, isn't a Hollywood story. There are certain things that happen in movies that never happen in real life, and vice versa. Someone took the time to write down some unique things that are true of every movie.

Think about this for a moment. Every movie you have seen probably has at least one of these elements. If someone walks out of a supermarket with a shopping bag, they always have one loaf of French bread in it. (It's apparently mandatory.) The ventilation system of any building is a perfect hiding place, and no one will ever think of looking for you in there. Besides that, you can travel to any other part of the building you want to without difficulty.

In the movies, if you happen to be in France, you will be able to see the Eiffel Tower from every window. If you are being chased by someone, you can always take cover in a passing Saint Patrick's Day parade, no matter what time of year it is. When someone in a movie gets into a taxi, they never have to pull out their wallet, because they always have the exact amount for the fare. It randomly happens to be in their back pocket.

Also in the movies, all bombs are fitted with electronic timing devices with large, red readouts so you know exactly when they will go off. And you can always park directly outside the building you are visiting, even if you are in the middle of New York City. Here is another thing true only of movies: It doesn't matter whether you are heavily outnumbered in a fight involving martial arts, because your enemies will patiently wait to attack you one by one, dancing around in a threatening manner until you have knocked out their predecessors.

And finally, in the movies, bad guys can spray machine-gun fire everywhere, hitting everything but the hero. Then the hero pulls out his five-shot revolver, hits all the bad guys, shoots more than twenty times, and never has to reload.

That is how it is in the movies.

But that is not real life.

Real life has twists and turns that don't make sense. Sometimes you are in the middle of something that makes no sense and doesn't seem to fit, and you find yourself wondering why in the world it's happening to you.

PLOT TWISTS

Imagine how Joseph from the book of Genesis felt mid-story. His life had started well, raised as he was in a loving home with a doting father. One night he woke up in the comfort and security of his own bed, and the next night he was in chains, in a caravan headed for Egypt, where he would be sold as a slave — by his own brothers!

Eventually he was bought by a wealthy Egyptian, who ended up putting Joseph in charge of his whole household. Joseph was so diligent and hardworking that he was elevated to a position of complete control over this man's finances. However, the Egyptian had an attractive, attention-starved wife who immediately began trying to seduce Joseph. Far from subtle, she would saunter up to him as he was walking through the house and say, "Have sex with me." Joseph resisted, but it must not have been easy. He was a red-blooded young man with a normal, God-given sex drive. When he kept resisting her advances, she got so mad at him that she falsely accused him of rape, and he was sent off to prison to do hard time.

Imagine how he felt sitting in that prison cell. He'd done nothing wrong in Israel to get sold as a slave. He'd done nothing wrong as a slave to be sent to a dungeon. We might imagine him thinking, *So this is what I get for obeying God? Maybe I should have just given in to that woman.* But as readers of Genesis know so well, the story took an amazing, supernatural twist, and Joseph ended up being the second most powerful man in the world.

Or consider Job's story. He woke up in the morning, had his breakfast, and everything seemed to be blue sky, sunshine, and roses. His large family was happy, the bills were paid, his health was strong, and he had more money than he knew what to do with.

And then . . .

In a matter of moments, everything changed. He lost his children, his wealth, most of his possessions, and eventually his health. Unfortunately, he still had his wife. Why do I say that was unfortunate? Because after all those calamities — one after another — had fallen on Job's head, his wife turned to him and basically said, "Why don't you just curse God and die?" (see Job 2:9).

Thank you for those encouraging words, dear.

But you know how the rest of his story turned out, as God restored everything to him and more.

In the beginning, however, Job didn't know that. He didn't know he would have more wonderful children. He didn't know that his wealth and health and possessions would all be restored. He was still in the middle of the story.

And so are we.

You and I are in a story authored by God Himself. There is a plot, you are the main character, and there certainly will be conflict. But here is the good news: If you belong to Jesus Christ, there will be a happy ending to your story. Why? Because the Author of your story is the almighty God, whom Scripture calls the author and finisher of our faith.

He Is the Author of our lives, and He will finish what He has begun.

In his letter to the Philippians, Paul wrote, "There has never been the slightest doubt in my mind that the God who started this great work in you would keep at it and bring it to a flourishing finish on the very day Christ Jesus appears" (Philippians 1:6, MSG).

In the book of Matthew, chapter 9, Scripture gives us two powerful, interwoven stories — two plot lines that intersect and somehow, for a moment, become one.

TWO IN DISTRESS

One of these stories is a snapshot of a poor, broken woman on the ragged edge of despair. Her life had been miserable for years, with no end to her misery in sight. She had lost her health and spent all of her money to get better, but to no avail. Then she found what she needed in the person of Jesus.

In contrast, the other person in the story was a man of great importance. While she was low, he was high. She was pitiful; he was powerful. She was insignificant; he was in high demand.

But he also had a problem and a crisis. His beloved young daughter was dying, and there was seemingly nothing he could do to save her. This reminds us that tragedy levels social topography. Pain visits every life, without exception. So these two suffering, despairing people—though they would have likely never met and didn't know one another—found themselves in the same path in the same village on the same page of the Bible.

Here is how it reads in Scripture:

> A ruler came and worshiped Him, saying, "My daughter has just died, but come and lay Your hand on her and she will live." So Jesus arose and followed him, and so did His disciples.
>
> And suddenly, a woman who had a flow of blood for twelve years came from behind and touched the hem of His garment. For she said to herself, "If only I may touch His garment, I shall be made well." But Jesus turned around, and when He saw her He said, "Be of good cheer, daughter; your faith has made you well." And the woman was made well from that hour.
>
> When Jesus came into the ruler's house, and saw the flute players and the noisy crowd wailing, He said to them, "Make room, for the girl is not dead, but sleeping." And they ridiculed Him. But when the crowd was put outside, He went in and took her by the hand, and the girl arose. And the report of this went out into all that land. (Matthew 9:18-26)

Twelve years is a significant period of time in the lives of both of these hurting people. The woman with the hemorrhage had been experiencing a living hell for twelve years. The girl, as we will find in another gospel, was sick and near death at the age of twelve. So while this girl had experienced twelve years of relative happiness, this sick woman had experienced twelve years of pain, rejection, loneliness, and tears. And yet on the same afternoon, both were impacted by Jesus.

WHERE THE STORY BEGINS

In the gospel of Mark, the father of the girl is identified as Jairus, who was "one of the rulers of the synagogue" (5:22). This meant that he was a powerful and respected man. And on the day where Scripture began to record his story, he did something he probably never expected to do: He got down on his knees in the dust before Jesus Christ and begged for help. That wasn't the normal thing for a man of his position and stature to do. He was a leader in the community, a person of great influence, and someone whom others looked up to.

But he also loved his little girl with all his heart and was willing to humble himself before Jesus to ask for help. He was pleading with Jesus to come and touch his daughter so that she might live. He was pleading with Jesus to come and touch his daughter before it was too late. And much to his relief, Jesus heard his request. Matthew's account says that "Jesus arose and followed him" (verse 19).

THE PLOT THICKENS

It all started with an interruption and a change in direction.

Jesus had been having a discussion with the disciples of John the Baptist when Jairus fell on his knees before the Lord and begged Him to intervene in his little daughter's illness. But then, even as the crowd began to head for Jairus's house, the woman in the story seemed to come out of nowhere, reaching out to touch the hem of Jesus' garment.

This proved to be an interruption of the interruption, as Jesus stopped to confront the despairing woman. In a moment of confusion, she suddenly reached out to Jesus and was made whole.

That's the way it works sometimes. In God's economy, interruptions can become opportunities. Disappointments can become His appointments. And sometimes when things seem to be going very wrong, they are actually going right. God can use interruptions to intervene in your life for good.

So Jairus's young daughter, the apple of this man's eye, hovered near death. Actually, Luke's gospel tells us that when he initially approached Jesus, the girl was still alive (see Luke 8:42), but she apparently died while he was trying to get Christ to his home—which adds even more pain to the story.

She was so young. In Jewish culture, a boy becomes a man at thirteen. He has his Bar-Mitzvah and says, "Today I become a man." A girl, however, officially becomes a woman at age twelve. So here was a young woman in the flower of her womanhood, and her life was about to slip away.

We read in the gospel of Mark that as they were on their way, "messengers arrived from the home of Jairus, the leader of the synagogue. They told him, 'Your daughter is dead. There's no use troubling the Teacher now'" (Mark 5:35, NLT).

Hearing those words is beyond comprehension for a father. I have been with fathers on two occasions when they have heard those words from a doctor. Both of their daughters had been in accidents, and they were in the emergency room. On both occasions, I was with the father, waiting for news, hoping his daughter would survive. And then we got the horrific news. The pain in that moment is unimaginable. Indescribable.

And, of course, I have been in that place too, when I got news about my own son Christopher being killed in a traffic accident. There is just no way to explain what it feels like. It's as though your life has just ended — but even worse because you wish it *had* ended.

Because of my own experience, I have a sense of what Jairus was going through when he got this message: "Don't bother Jesus anymore, Jairus. It's over. She just died."

I love how the gospel of Mark records what happened in that moment:

> As soon as Jesus heard the word that was spoken,
> He said to the ruler of the synagogue, "Do not be
> afraid; only believe." (Mark 5:36)

I can imagine Jesus laying a hand on this grieving father's shoulder and looking him straight in the eyes. "Don't be afraid, Jairus. Keep trusting in Me. Even now."

I'm sure that Jairus was feeling like a failure for not getting to Jesus more quickly. But Jesus was saying to him, "Just wait and believe, and keep believing."

So while this tragedy was unfolding for Jairus, while this distraught dad wanted to get Jesus to his little girl's bedside as quickly as possible, wouldn't you know it, there was an interruption! A woman burst onto the scene, bringing the whole group to a standstill.

How easily Jairus could have said, "Hey, excuse me! No cuts!"

Don't you hate it when people cut in line? If I'm driving on the freeway and someone tries to cut into the little space in front of me, I feel like stepping on the gas a little and closing that gap so they can't get in. If they're stuck in a bad position or have their turn signal on, that's okay; I don't mind letting them in. But when people suddenly cut in, well, I don't like that.

It's the same when you're waiting in line for a movie. If you've been waiting for a while in a big, long line and someone comes along and steps in front of you, that is a little offensive.

Imagine how Jairus felt: "Excuse me, but I have an emergency here, ma'am. I don't know what your problem is, but you need to wait your turn."

I think this was a test in the life of Jairus. How would he fare? Maybe Jairus had heard how Jesus always had time for the underdogs of the world. Maybe he'd been told the story of how Jesus called the hated tax collector, Matthew, to be one of His followers. Or perhaps he'd heard about the way Jesus had touched a demon-possessed man and delivered him. Maybe he considered those things in that moment and said to himself, *I don't like this interruption, but I know this is the way Jesus is. He takes time with needy people. I'm not going to create any trouble here. I'll just wait on Him. He knows what He is doing.*

If this really was a test, then Jairus passed it with flying colors. As anxious and distraught as he was, he waited on the Lord and kept trusting in Him.

Sometimes you and I are being tested at different points in our lives, and we aren't even aware of it. God usually doesn't tell us when we're being tested.

Sometimes "waiting on the Lord" isn't easy.

By nature, I am an impatient person and hate waiting

THE WHOLE STORY • 75

on anything. If I have to wait, I'm always doing something else — maybe checking my e-mail on my phone or fiddling around with something else. When I go to pick up a pizza, it's virtually impossible for me to get the whole pizza home intact. On more than one occasion, I have eaten the pizza while I am driving, because it smelled so good and I didn't want to wait. I'll grab a piece out of the box, burn my mouth, and get tomato sauce and grease on my shirt.

I will get home, and my wife will ask, "What happened to half the pizza?"

Sometimes people don't like to wait on the Lord, either. We'll complain to Him and say, "Lord, what's going on here? Are You paying any attention to this situation? When are You going to provide me with a husband (or wife)? When are You going to open a door of ministry for me? When are You going to help me find a better job? How long are You going to let that person get away with his sin?"

Or how about this one: "Lord, how long will it be until You come back to this earth? Have You noticed how bad things have gotten? How long, Lord?"

In spite of our complaining and fretting, God is certainly aware of our needs and hears our prayers. But He will act according to His timing, not ours.

Difficult and heartbreaking as it must have been, Jairus was willing to wait on the Lord for His timing.

A DESPERATE WOMAN

In Matthew 9:20, we read that "suddenly, a woman who had a flow of blood for twelve years came from behind and touched the hem of [Jesus'] garment."

She apparently had some kind of chronic hemorrhage that had caused continual bleeding for twelve painful years.

Blood simply wouldn't stay in her body, and in that culture, the stigma and humiliation of this condition was second only to leprosy. Her hemorrhage caused her to be declared ceremonially unclean, which meant that she was rejected from the synagogue and not allowed to worship with God's people. As a result, she was isolated and lonely.

The synagogue was the center of both spiritual and social life in the city. Cut off as she was from her neighbors, friends, and fellow citizens, she had really lost everything. Mark's version of the story tells us that she had "suffered many things from many physicians. She had spent all that she had and was no better, but rather grew worse" (Mark 5:26).

The truth is, first-century medicine was very primitive. Among the so-called remedies of the day was an instruction to carry the ashes of an ostrich egg in a linen bag in the summer and a cotton bag in the winter, and you would be healed. Really?

Another superstitious remedy involved carrying around a kernel of barley corn that had been found in the dung of a white female donkey. How would you like to take a prescription for *that* to your local pharmacy? It's craziness.

Then this woman heard about Jesus, the rabbi from Nazareth. She heard amazing stories of how He could heal any disease with a word or a touch. So she reasoned to herself, "If only I may touch His garment, I shall be made well" (Matthew 9:21). Maybe no one would even notice!

Back in those days, rabbis would have a strip of blue at the very hem of their garments. That is what she would have been aiming for as she reached out her hand that day.

It might have been a risky maneuver for her, but she had become so desperate that she was willing to chance it. What did she have to lose? She was already rejected and shunned by everyone. So when she saw Jesus walking with Jairus, she slipped up as inconspicuously as she could and touched her finger to His robe. Instantly, the healing power of God was released, and her disease was completely cured. She had no doubt of it. The hateful disease that had dogged her steps for twelve long years was *gone.*

One of the reasons she perhaps had thought she could escape unnoticed was the large crowd that followed Jesus in those days. There were all kinds of people milling around, trying to get a glimpse of Him, pushing and pulling and creating a commotion. There was always lots of noise and general chaos wherever He went in the city.

So there was Jesus, making His way through that gaggle of people, when He suddenly stopped and said, "Who touched Me?"

Peter must have looked at John, and John looked at Andrew, and everyone just shrugged. What kind of question was that? *Everyone* was touching Him. He was being pushed on from all sides.

Jesus, however, was insistent. "No," He was saying, "I know that something happened. I know that power has gone out of Me."

I can just imagine the crowd parting as the woman, trembling and afraid, pushed her way forward. But when she saw the Lord's face, it must have set her heart at ease. He didn't want to single her out to scold her or humiliate her but to commend her and acknowledge her faith. I can picture Him smiling at her and speaking gently to her, saying, "Be of good cheer, daughter; your faith has made you well."

In Mark's version of the account, we read that "the woman, fearing and trembling, knowing what had happened to her, came and fell down before Him and told Him the whole truth" (Mark 5:33).

Another translation says that she "gave him the whole story" (MSG). That's why I have called this chapter "The Whole Story."

It had probably been a long time since someone had actually listened to her story. People had avoided her for years, crossing over and walking on the other side of the street when they saw her coming. Their actions said, "You're unclean. Get away from me."

But Jesus said, in effect, "Tell Me your story, dear lady. I'm all ears."

Have you ever tried to talk to someone who was distracted and wouldn't give you their full attention? Let me restate the question: Have you ever had a conversation with *me*? I have to admit that I'm very easily distracted and it's hard for me to focus on anything for more than a few seconds. I had ADD before ADD was cool.

It's frustrating to be pouring your heart out to someone, only to have him or her say, "Just a second, I'm getting a text." And they start fiddling with their smartphone.

You want to say, "Would you put that thing away and pay attention to me for a moment? You are with *me* now."

Jesus was there for this woman at what surely must have been the greatest moment of her life. He listened to her whole story as she poured out her heart to Him. He cared about her, comforted her, and commended her for her faith.

HOW TO BREAK UP A FUNERAL

Jairus, of course, was standing there, watching all of this unfold. He had been racing against time to find Jesus and persuade Him to come to his daughter's bedside. And now? Well, there was this woman, pouring out her life story, and Jesus was giving her His full, sympathetic attention.

In what must have seemed like an hour, but was probably only a few moments, Jesus turned His attention back to Jairus, and they made their way back to his home.

In the gospel of Mark, we read,

> And He permitted no one to follow Him except Peter, James, and John the brother of James. Then He came to the house of the ruler of the synagogue, and saw a tumult and those who wept and wailed loudly. When He came in, He said to them, "Why make this commotion and weep? The child is not dead, but sleeping."
>
> And they ridiculed Him. But when He had put them all outside, He took the father and the mother of the child, and those who were with Him, and entered where the child was lying. Then He took the child by the hand, and said to her, "Talitha, cumi," which is translated, "Little girl, I say to you, arise." Immediately the girl arose and walked, for she was twelve years of age. And they were overcome with great amazement. But He commanded them strictly that no one should know it, and said that something should be given her to eat. (Mark 5:37-43)

Arriving at the house, they encountered a scene of noise and great commotion. Back in those days, grieving and funerals were loud and noisy affairs. People would scream, wail, and shriek. In fact, the family would actually hire professional mourners, which seems completely bizarre to us today. They would come in with their musical instruments and would sing and wail the name of the deceased over and over again.

So Jairus and Jesus arrived to a room filled with fifty to one hundred shrieking, screaming people (the wealthier you were, the more mourners you could hire), along with the discordant sounds of multiple musical instruments.

It was chaos, but Jesus was just about to take charge.

Stepping into the middle of it, He raised His voice and said, "Why all this weeping and commotion? . . . The child isn't dead; she is only asleep!" (Mark 5:39, TLB).

At that, everybody started laughing. They went from mourning to laughing, which shows that it wasn't real grief at all.

The Bible says that Jesus "put them all outside." In other words, He said, "Get these people out of here," and He pushed them right out the door.

I love that.

This was not the kind of environment that God wanted to work in. The house was full of despair and empty tears and fake grief. Mostly, it was filled with unbelief. Elsewhere in the Gospels, we read that Jesus could do no mighty works in His own hometown, because the whole atmosphere reeked of skepticism and unbelief (see Matthew 13:58).

Sometimes we hinder the work of God in our own lives when we are filled with unbelief. We will say things like "I could never change," or "Jesus would never do that for me," or "This won't work for me."

If you keep saying such things, it may end up that way. What you need is a little bit of faith. You don't even have to have a lot. The woman who reached out to Jesus probably said, "What do I have to lose? I'm going to take a chance and reach out to Jesus with what faith I have."

Jesus went into the room where the little girl was lying. She had already passed to the other side; her spirit was in heaven, in the presence of the heavenly Father. And Jesus simply called her back—back to earth, back to her physical body, back to her home and her parents. When you are Jesus, you can do things like that.

Notice that He didn't shout. When Jesus summoned Lazarus from the tomb, He called out, "Lazarus, come forth!" And it's a good thing He called Lazarus by name. If He had just said, "Come forth!" every grave in the world would have been instantly emptied.

Here, however, in the now-quiet room with the dead little girl, He was very tender and sweet. He simply said, "Little girl, I say to you, arise." Her little eyes began to flutter, the color returned to her ashen face, and she opened her eyes and sat up. What an incredible joy that must have brought to the hearts of her dad and mom.

I love the fact that He also instructed them to give her something to eat. That was so thoughtful, and the little lady had been on quite a journey. I can imagine that dad saying, "Honey, you can have anything you want. Twinkies . . . Fruit Loops . . . whatever your heart desires!"

WHAT DO WE LEARN FROM THIS STORY?

1. If you have a need, reach out to Jesus.

If Jairus or that afflicted woman hadn't sought out Jesus, the next morning would have been very, very different for them. Jairus and his wife would have opened their eyes to the realization that their little girl was gone. The woman would have faced another day of illness, another day of rejection, loneliness, and depression.

But that's not what happened. Their lives had changed because they had sought out Jesus, believing He had the answers to their deepest needs.

I think there are many times, possibly more times than we imagine, when we continue to wrestle with problems and situations simply because we have neglected to cry out to God for help.

Have you prayed about your problem? Have you talked to the Lord about your medical condition? Your finances? Your marriage? Your seemingly mountain-sized problems?

God is still in the miracle business. He still heals, delivers, helps, and provides. The psalmist said, "The LORD is with me; he is my helper. I will look in triumph on my enemies" (Psalm 118:7, NIV).

Is there a decision you need wisdom on? Have you prayed for wisdom? The Bible says, "You don't get what you want because you don't ask God for it" (James 4:3, PH).

Whatever you may be facing in your life, call out to Jesus. Your need isn't too large, nor is it too small or trivial. And guess what? Jesus is a good listener. He will pay attention. He will hear you out. He won't cut you off.

He may give you what you ask for; He may say, "Not now," or He may say, "No, My child, that wouldn't be good for you now. You have to trust Me to do the best for you." Then again, He may give you abundantly above and beyond what you ask for.

The important thing is to call out to Him.

In Jeremiah 33:3, God says, "Call to Me, and I will answer you, and show you great and mighty things, which you do not know."

Call out to Jesus.

2. Your story isn't finished yet.

God finishes what He begins. It started out badly for Jairus, and it got even worse. But what had been the worst day of his life turned out to be the best and most joyous day of his life. It was the same for the woman who touched Jesus' robe. She was at the end of her rope physically, financially, and emotionally. Her story seemed to be coming to a close. But then Jesus intervened and gave her a happy ending.

3. If you trust in Jesus, your stories will have a happy ending.

You might say, "What are you talking about, Greg? Are you living in the same world I'm living in?"

Yes, as a matter of fact, I am.

And I've had my share of suffering and sorrow in life. So how can I come to the end of this chapter and tell you that your story will have a happy ending? It's because I believe in heaven.

Your story will not be over at the end of your life on earth. In fact, if you belong to Jesus Christ, your story will be just beginning in eternity, in the presence of God. This is where every follower of Jesus will have a happy ending.

Not so for the unbeliever. This life is as good as it gets for the non-Christian. It will only get worse — much, much worse — later. But if you are a Christian, life here on earth is as bad as it gets.

When Jairus went looking for Jesus, he realized that he was in a race against time and that death was drawing close. That's a good thing for all of us to remember. We live our lives on borrowed time, and there will come a day for all of us when we step out of this life and into eternity. Some of us will live long lives here on earth, but some of us won't. That's up to God. But what we want to do is live in such a way that when our day is done and our number is up, we will be ready to meet Him.

Only those who are prepared to die are really ready to live. I don't mean that in a morbid way. I think no one lives life more fully than a follower of Jesus Christ. No one can appreciate the joys of life more than a Christian. But at the same time, no one has a better perspective than the Christian, because we realize that this life is temporary and passing away.

Life here on earth — with all its happy moments and tears, all its struggles and blessings, all its setbacks and triumphs — is only a tiny part of our whole story.

The best is yet to come.

5

DEALING WITH DOUBT

Oswald Chambers once said, "Doubt is not always a sign that a man is wrong; it may be a sign that he is thinking."

Most of us, if we were honest, could admit to times when we doubted God and doubted our faith. Sometimes things happen in our lives that seem to make no earthly sense. In the midst of these experiences, we wonder where God is and why He permitted these things to happen in our lives. Or perhaps we come to a crucial crossroads where we desperately need an answer from God, but heaven seems silent and unresponsive to our cries.

We wonder, *Is God just sitting on His hands, watching me twist in the wind? Is He paying any attention to me at all?* And in such moments, we may (at least momentarily) entertain a few doubts.

Someone once said, "When the warm moist air of our expectations collides with the icy cold of God's silence, inevitably clouds of doubt begin to form."

And then, of course, we know that Satan loves nothing better than to pile on to those negative thoughts, encouraging us to slip even further into darkness. He will say, *I can't believe you're entertaining thoughts like that! You're such a failure, such a hypocrite. If you have doubts like this, you're probably not even a Christian.*

You may be surprised to learn, however, that some of the greatest men and women of God in the Bible and in history had their moments of doubt. This includes the prophet whom Jesus called the greatest "of all who have ever lived" (Matthew 11:11, NLT).

That's what we will talk about in this chapter. We will see how Jesus dealt with John in his hour of doubt and uncertainty.

IT BEGINS WITH CONFUSION

John's doubt began with confusion. From the beginning of his ministry, and perhaps for most of his life, John had cherished an idea of what the Messiah would be and do when He came. But as John watched Jesus' earthly ministry develop, he became more and more puzzled. Jesus simply wasn't doing what John had expected and anticipated Him to be doing. John had misunderstood what God was intending to do, and his perplexity and confusion pushed him into doubt.

We have that same problem sometimes. The doubts we feel might have their start with a misunderstanding. Sometimes we are simply confused about what we think God should be doing. In the following pages, let's take a closer look at Scripture and see how Jesus dealt with John's confusion and disappointment.

"MORE THAN A PROPHET"

Now it came to pass, when Jesus finished commanding His twelve disciples, that He departed from there to teach and to preach in their cities.

And when John had heard in prison about the works of Christ, he sent two of his disciples and said to Him, "Are You the Coming One, or do we look for another?"

Jesus answered and said to them, "Go and tell John the things which you hear and see: The blind see and the lame walk; the lepers are cleansed and the deaf hear; the dead are raised up and the poor have the gospel preached to them. And blessed is he who is not offended because of Me."

As they departed, Jesus began to say to the multitudes concerning John: "What did you go out into the wilderness to see? A reed shaken by the wind? But what did you go out to see? A man clothed in soft garments? Indeed, those who wear soft clothing are in kings' houses. But what did you go out to see? A prophet? Yes, I say to you, and more than a prophet. For this is he of whom it is written: 'Behold, I send My messenger before Your face, who will prepare Your way before You.'

"Assuredly, I say to you, among those born of women there has not risen one greater than John the Baptist; but he who is least in the kingdom of heaven is greater than he." (Matthew 11:1-11)

We need to understand who John was. In another translation, Jesus said of him, "No one in history surpasses John the Baptizer" (verse 11, MSG). At the time Jesus spoke those words, John was highly significant in Israel, a man of national prominence and renown, greatly admired and followed by thousands. You might say that John was a first-century rock star. He was someone whom people looked up to and loved because he was a prophet of God.

This was a big deal — a *very* big deal. Israel hadn't heard from the God of Israel for four hundred years, from the death of the prophet Malachi to the angelic announcement of John's birth. For four hundred years, heaven had remained silent, without a single prophet, angelic appearance, or miracle. And then suddenly a colorful prophet burst onto the scene out of the wilderness, dressed in the skins of wild animals, subsisting on a diet of locusts and wild honey.

He captured the imagination of the people, and they loved him. So significant was John in his day that the ancient historian Josephus wrote more about him than he did about Jesus. In fact, John was so popular that some thought he might be the Messiah. But that was never his role; it was his God-given task to prepare the way for the Messiah, to go before the Lord and blaze a trail.

Famous as John may have been, his motto as time went on became, "He must become greater and greater, and I must become less and less" (John 3:30, TLB).

John had no doubt about his job description: It was to point people to the Messiah. One day Jesus was walking toward John and his followers, and John declared, "Behold! The Lamb of God who takes away the sin of the world!" (John 1:29).

Though John had his own followers, he was essentially

saying, "My work is done. You guys need to follow Jesus now." Almost overnight, he walked away from a huge national ministry because his mission was completed. The Messiah had now come, and John had done his best to prepare His way.

Herod, Israel's puppet king, had been impressed by John's preaching. John was maybe one of the only men in Herod's life who would look him eyeball to eyeball and tell him the truth about life. Herod no doubt found that shocking—but maybe also a bit refreshing.

It was something of a strange relationship. We read that Herod imprisoned John, yet he feared and protected him while he was in custody. Mark 6:20 tells us that when John spoke to Herod, the king was "greatly puzzled; yet he liked to listen to him" (NIV).

What Herod didn't appreciate hearing was John's straightforward rebuke regarding the king's immoral relationship with a woman named Herodias. As it turns out, she was already married—to Herod's brother Phillip. She also was the daughter of Aristobulus, another half-brother of Herod, meaning that Herod had taken up with his own niece and sister-in-law.

John called him on it, and Herod didn't like it one bit.

Herodias liked it even less.

While Herod might have been perturbed, Herodias was coldly furious. She hated John and wanted him silenced, ASAP.

Herodias finally had her chance in the course of a drunken banquet, when she had her daughter Salome perform a seductive dance in front of the leering king and his guests. In the fog of his drunkenness and the excitement of the moment, Herod made an oath to give the girl whatever she wanted, up to half his kingdom. Salome hurried back to her mother, but there was never any real question about what the girl would ask for. Herodias said, "You tell the king I want the head of John the Baptist on a platter *right now*." Because the king had made an oath in front of all of his guests, he felt he had to comply and John was executed.

But in Matthew 11, John was still alive and in prison. How difficult it must have been for an outdoorsman like John, used to roaming far and wide and sleeping under the stars every night, to be locked away in a dark, smelly dungeon. How strange it must have been to be a national news story and phenomenon one moment, only to be plunged into total obscurity the next.

For John, however, that wasn't the worst of it.

There in confinement in Herod's jail, he began to wonder if he had misunderstood the Lord or missed the boat somehow. *Was Jesus Christ really the Messiah?*

MISUNDERSTANDING GOD

The fact was, Jesus simply wasn't doing what John had thought, anticipated, or imagined He would be doing. It didn't make sense to John, and he felt perplexed—and probably disappointed. John's problem was that of many others when Jesus first came on the scene: He thought Jesus would overthrow Rome and establish His kingdom then and there.

After a while, however, it became evident that Jesus wasn't going to do those things—yet. The situation in Israel was as bad as ever, and John had seemingly been left to languish in Herod's dungeon.

Besides those things, John was hearing rumors that Jesus had been hanging out with some pretty unsavory characters. What was that all about? Maybe the reports sounded something like this: "Say, John, did you know that your cousin Jesus—the one you said was the Lamb of God—was just at a big party with a bunch of tax collectors and prostitutes? I kid you not!"

John, in his humanity, began to wonder if he had made a mistake.

"After all," John might have reasoned, "when the Messiah comes, isn't He supposed to bring deliverance to the captives and hope to the brokenhearted? But here I sit in this dungeon. This isn't working out the way I thought it would."

In fact, events were developing exactly as God intended. The Lamb of God was headed toward a cross to give His life as a ransom for all people, for all time. The restored kingdom of Israel, with Jesus on the throne, had to await His Second Coming. This time, He had to suffer and die. Before Jesus would wear a crown of gold, He would first have to wear a crown of thorns. Before He would sit on a throne, He would first be nailed to a cross.

The Scriptures, of course, taught this all along. Passages such as Psalm 22 and Isaiah 53 speak extensively about the suffering of the Messiah. But because John didn't understand this—or possibly because he longed with all his heart to see Rome overthrown and the kingdom of God arrive—he felt confused by the Lord's actions. That's how he ended up sending Jesus a message that basically said, "Are you the One? Did we misunderstand this?"

This can happen to us as well. Sometimes we misunderstand God and His Word. This might happen to us when a tragedy hits, when a child goes astray, when a loved one dies, or when there is a sudden cancer diagnosis. A shocking event like that just doesn't fit in with what you had planned for your life or how you believed things would work out. And perhaps you find yourself saying, "God, are You really paying attention? Why did You let this happen to me?" Our problem is that we tend to interpret God in light of the tragedy, instead of the other way around.

In Matthew 11, John was essentially crying out to Jesus, saying, "Why haven't You helped me?" And he found himself wrestling with doubt.

CRY OUT TO GOD

Doubt is not necessarily a sin.

It has been said, "He that knows nothing doubts nothing." Sometimes doubt is not the opposite of faith; it is rather an element of faith. It means you are thinking some things through and grappling with the issues. It means you are trying to process certain events or information, wondering how it all fits in with life as you understand it.

Sometimes you and I have to pass through the foyer of doubt to enter the sanctuary of certainty. That's something to keep in mind if your kids come to you and say, "Mom, I'm struggling with this. How can you say that God created the world?" Or, "Dad, I'm having a hard time with what the Bible says about living morally." Or, "My teacher says there are lots of contradictions in the Bible." Don't panic. That can be a good sign. It means they are starting to grow up and think for themselves, and you need to be available to help them through this process of finding their own faith. They can't live off the faith of their parents.

The key, however, in this matter of dealing with doubts is to cry out to God.

British pastor G. Campbell Morgan put it like this: "Men of faith are always the men that have to confront problems. Blot God out, and your problems are all ended. If there is no God in heaven, then we have no problem about sin and suffering."

Doubt, then, is a matter of the mind. Unbelief is a matter of the will. Doubt says, "I don't get it. Help me understand this. Work with me through this."

Unbelief says, "I do get it, I don't like it, and I refuse to accept it."

John the Baptist, closed up in his lonely prison cell, was simply doubting. But it wasn't unbelief.

Even the great men and women of God had their moments of despair. Moses was ready to quit on one occasion after listening to the Israelites complain for the umpteenth time. He said, in essence, "Lord, if this is the way it's going to be, then I'd prefer that You just kill me right now."

And Elijah? He said pretty much the same thing after hearing that Queen Jezebel had put out a contract on his life. He basically prayed, "Enough of this, Lord. Please take my life. I've had it."

Even the great apostle Paul was discouraged. Listen to this passage from his life journal, recorded in 2 Corinthians 1:8-9:

> We think you ought to know, dear brothers and sisters, about the trouble we went through in the province of Asia. We were crushed and overwhelmed beyond our ability to endure, and we thought we would never live through it. In fact, we expected to die. (NLT)

So then, if you find yourself struggling with some doubts right now, take heart. You are in very good company.

When you think about it, John wasn't asking for information as much as confirmation. He was saying, in effect, "Lord, explain this to me again. Did I get this right? Are You the Messiah? Are You the One we've been looking for?"

In consequence, he sent two messengers to Jesus with his honest question: "Are You the Coming One, or do we look for another?" Notice how Jesus responds:

> "Go and tell John the things which you hear and see: The blind see and the lame walk; the lepers are cleansed and the deaf hear; the dead are raised up and the poor have the gospel preached to them. And blessed is he who is not offended because of Me." (Matthew 11:3-6)

In His answer, Jesus refers to Old Testament passages that John would have been familiar with, including Isaiah 35 and 61. He was effectively saying something like this: "No, John, I'm not leading a revolt, and I'm not going to overthrow Rome. That's not in the program right now. But I am removing disabilities wherever I encounter them, and I am bringing men and women into a right relationship with God. When that is right, everything else will change as well."

To borrow the current popular expression, Jesus could have thrown John under the bus in that moment. He could have said, "It's disappointing that John is doubting Me. I'm sorry to see him cave under pressure like this." Instead, He stuck up for John, giving him high praise.

Do you do that? When someone criticizes one of your friends in your presence, do you stick up for him? Do you defend her? "Wait a second. That's my friend you're talking about. I happen to know that this person is a godly man (or godly woman). Where did you get that stuff?"

Or, do you give a listening ear to gossip instead of challenging it? Stick up for your friends as Jesus stuck up for His friends.

John the Baptist was a loyal man of God, and the Lord spoke well of him before the people. In verse 6, He used the occasion to make a point about persevering in faith: "Blessed is he who is not offended because of Me." Or literally, "Blessed is the man or woman who is not annoyed or repelled or made to stumble, whatever may occur." In essence, Jesus was saying, "Look, you may not understand My methods or My ways or My timing. But I am asking you to trust Me, even when you are unable to see why I am doing what I am doing—or why I'm *not* doing what you think I ought to be doing. Just trust Me, hang in there, and hold your course."

Jesus was telling the people, "What were you looking for when you went searching for John out in the desert? A reed blowing in the wind? Someone who was unstable, with no courage? Listen, John the Baptist is a great man. And even though he's in a tight place right now and wrestling with some doubts, I love him."

Then He makes this amazing statement in verse 11: "Assuredly, I say to you, among those born of women there has not risen one greater than John the Baptist; but he who is least in the kingdom of heaven is greater than he."

Why would Jesus say that John was the greatest of all men—or maybe the greatest of all the Old Testament prophets? After all, we have no record of John's performing any miracles, as Elijah and Elisha did. John never wrote a prophetic book like Isaiah, Jeremiah, or Ezekiel. So why would John be the greatest of the prophets?

First of all, he was the greatest because he was the last of them. Yes, he was the final prophet of the Old Testament economy or system. But beyond that, John was the greatest because he, and he alone, was the direct forerunner and herald of the Messiah. His greatness was a direct result of his nearness and connection to Jesus. His story is in the New Testament, but his life and ministry were actually part of the Old Testament system. The New Testament system didn't really begin until Jesus inaugurated it and fulfilled the Old.

John was the greatest of the greatest, the best of the best, and the finest of the prophets. Jesus was saying, "This is My man, John. Don't even think about criticizing him!"

What, then, does the last phrase in verse 11 mean? Jesus concludes, "But he who is least in the kingdom of heaven is greater than he."

This speaks to the incredible privilege you and I experience now as believers in Jesus Christ, with Christ actually taking up residence within our very lives. Jesus is saying that the least among us, the most timid, least visible Christian you can imagine, is greater than John the Baptist. John, still living under the Old Testament economy, hadn't experienced that.

But we have.

Jesus said, "Look! I have been standing at the door and I am constantly knocking. If anyone hears me calling him and opens the door, I will come in and fellowship with him and he with me" (Revelation 3:20, TLB).

We really have no idea what an awesome privilege that is. To have the Son of God actually enter our lives, live inside us, and be our constant companion and friend—what an incredible opportunity! John was a herald of the King; you and I get to be friends of the King. John was a friend of the Bridegroom; you and I are the bride of the Bridegroom. You can't find a higher privilege than that.

John the Baptist lived and died on the other side of the cross, resurrection, and ascension of Jesus. We live in the New Covenant, with Christ living in our hearts. As great as John was, he didn't have that kind of privilege and closeness to Jesus.

HOW DID THE LORD DEAL WITH JOHN'S DOUBT?

In fact, the Lord dealt with John's season of doubt in the same way He will deal with doubt and uncertainty in our lives.

1. Jesus refocused John's priorities.

John had some unbiblical and unrealistic expectations of the ministry, purpose, and timing of Jesus. And that was true pretty much of all His disciples. He didn't rebuke John for that, but He didn't release him from prison, either. Instead, He just corrected his thinking.

All of us need that sort of correction and refocusing in our lives at times because we tend to get things out of perspective.

An unexpected bill comes due, you can't imagine how you will ever pay it, and . . . you panic. What do you need to do? You need to remember the Word of God that tells you, "God shall supply all your need according to His riches in glory by Christ Jesus" (Philippians 4:19).

Maybe some crisis slams into your life, and you feel like events are spinning out of control. You need to remember that the Word of God says, "God is our refuge and strength, a very present help in trouble. Therefore we will not fear, even though the earth be removed, and though the mountains be carried into the midst of the sea" (Psalm 46:1-2).

We have to allow the Word of God and God's Holy Spirit to correct our thinking. It's like being in a car that has run into a curb and knocked itself out of alignment. Unless you get the car's steering realigned, it will pull to the left or pull to the right, and it will be difficult to keep it on the road. In the same way, taking time to meditate on the Scriptures will realign our thoughts and our emotions.

In the interest of full disclosure, I have to do this myself. There are times when unexpected, stressful events can send me into a tailspin. Even though my son Christopher went to heaven back in 2008, the terrible finality of that will sometimes just hit me: *My son is no longer here with me. I will never see him again in this life.* In those moments, I will sometimes feel gripped by a panic, thinking, *No! This can't be true!* Even though four years have gone by, Christopher's death is very hard for me to accept at times, and I will have to correct my thinking with biblical truth. I will quote Scripture to myself, and I will say, "Now, Greg, you listen. The Bible says that your son is still alive. He is in heaven, and you're going to see him again. Jesus is the resurrection and the life, and both you and Christopher belong to Him."

I allow God's Word to realign my thinking and to refocus my priorities, clearing away the fog and barrage of emotions. God does this for me, and He uses His Word to accomplish it.

2. Jesus brought John back to the Word of God.

In the message Jesus sent back to John, He quoted prophecies in the book of Isaiah, reminding John what the Word of God said about the ministry of the coming Messiah. It was a firm but kind way of saying, "John, remember the Word of God. I am fulfilling the Scriptures."

When you're going through difficult times, you don't need pious platitudes, empty human wisdom, silly sayings, or greeting card verses. You need the Word of God. That alone resonates. That alone gives hope. That alone resounds in our soul. Advice from other sources or humanist philosophies not only fails to help us but might actually hurt us.

People in crisis need the Word of God. We might try all day to think of something clever or insightful to say to someone who is in distress or pain, but if it isn't based on God's eternal Word, it might do more harm than good.

Even those of us who have been Christians for years, who have studied the Bible and perhaps even preached the Bible, still need to be reminded from time to time of what the Bible *says*.

The apostle Peter stated right up front that reminding believers of what they already knew was one of the main goals of his New Testament letters. One translation records Peter's words like this:

> Because the stakes are so high, even though you're up-to-date on all this truth and practice it inside and out, I'm not going to let up for a minute in calling you to attention before it. This is the post to which I've been assigned — keeping you alert with frequent reminders — and I'm sticking to it as long as I live. (2 Peter 1:12-13, MSG)

I find that I often forget what I ought to remember, and then I remember what I ought to forget. I have reams of worthless information permanently embedded in my mind that I can call up at a moment's notice, while other things — including some very, very important things — are fuzzy to me at times. How do I overcome this short-term spiritual memory? By constantly going over those things I have read and reread in Scripture, recalling to memory those truths that really matter in life and are eternal.

3. Jesus encouraged John to hold his course.

In essence, Jesus was saying to John, "Hold your course! I know it's hard, and I know you don't get it right now. I know it isn't making sense to you. But I am asking you to hold your course."

That is what we need to do in our times of heartache and trial. We can honestly pray, "Lord, I don't understand this at all right now. These things don't make any sense." But the Lord says to us, "I know you can't understand right now. But remember that I am in control, remember that I love you, and remember that I am working all things together for your good. You just stay on course, and don't let this situation throw you. Keep trusting Me, and keep doing what you know to do."

In the book of Hebrews, the author says this to a group of hurting, under-pressure believers:

> Take a new grip with your tired hands, stand firm on your shaky legs, and mark out a straight, smooth path for your feet so that those who follow you, though weak and lame, will not fall and hurt themselves but become strong. (Hebrews 12:12-13, TLB)

One day everything will come into focus when we see the Lord, and we will realize that the Lord wasn't sitting on His hands during our hard times. As a matter of fact, those hands were nailed to a cross. One day we will understand why God did or did not do what we thought He should do.

And until that day, Jesus wants us to simply trust and follow Him.

A REED IN THE WIND

"What did you go out into the wilderness to see? A reed shaken by the wind?" That wasn't John. He didn't flip-flop or follow the latest fads. John knew who he was, understood his God-given role, and held to his course.

As Christians, we experience many different cross-currents of wind that blow into our lives.

1. Winds of Adversity

It's like a strong, cold wind that cuts through everything and everyone in its path. Where I live, in Southern California, we don't experience those frigid winter winds very much. On the East Coast or in the Midwest, however, you had better wear layers in the winter and make sure you have a scarf, gloves, and something over your ears, because the icy, biting wind will sometimes make you feel like you're not wearing anything at all. The winds of adversity can swoop down upon us unexpectedly and with great and devastating force. We really can't avoid those winds. John the Baptist faced them too, but he held to his course in spite of them. He was no spineless reed, bowing before every breeze. John stood strong in his faith, and so should we.

I heard a story about a traveler who was visiting a logging area in the Pacific Northwest. He watched with great interest as a lumberjack walking alongside a mountain stream would periodically jag his sharp hook into a log, separating it from the others. The traveler asked the logger what he was doing, and the man replied, "These logs probably all look alike to you, but I recognize that some of them are quite different. The ones I let pass are from trees that grow in a valley, where they're always protected from the storms. The grain on those logs is rather course. But the logs I pull aside come from high up in the mountains, where they're beaten by strong winds from the time they're seedlings. This toughens the trees and gives them a fine grain. We save them for choice work. They're too good to be used for ordinary lumber."

So maybe you are facing the winds of adversity right now, and you wonder why. Could it be that God is saving you for a choice work? Could it be that the Lord is allowing this to toughen the grain of your life, letting you go through hardship so that you'll be able to do something unique that He has in store for you?

2. Winds of Temptation

Here in coastal Southern California, we have to deal with the hot, dry Santa Ana winds, justly called "devil winds." They come roaring out of the deserts to the east and instantly change the temperature. Any small spark in the dry hills can turn into a raging fire. If an arsonist gets involved to exploit the situation, these winds can create devastating property damage and even loss of life.

Temptation can be like that in our lives. Those hot winds can suddenly blow across our lives, and Satan, the master arsonist, will seek to exploit those temptations to lead us down a destructive path. But we have to stand strong in those winds, not bowing to them or giving way before them. We need to be like John the Baptist and stand our ground.

3. Winds of Compromise

In contrast to the winds of adversity or the hot blast of temptation, the winds of compromise feel more like a soft summer breeze, lulling you to sleep. Can you picture it? The ukuleles are playing, the soft trade winds are blowing, and the palm trees are gently swaying. You're half asleep and at your ease, and in that state of mind, compromises don't seem like such a bad thing.

Temptations to compromise your honesty, your purity, and your integrity will blow your way every day. If Satan can't get us to fall into the "big" sins, he will encourage us to simply cut the corners a little, perhaps dabbling with sin or playing around the edges of immorality or dishonesty.

Jesus said that John wasn't that kind of man. He wasn't a reed swayed by the wind. He didn't adapt his message to please people or ingratiate himself to those in power. He stood his ground and spoke the truth, even to the enemies who wanted to destroy him.

WHATEVER YOU ARE FACING . . .

Doubts will come into our lives, as surely as the wind will blow. We need to remember, however, that no matter how the wind howls and tries to shake us, God is in control and has His purposes in all of these things. We need to stand our ground, like John did, trusting the Lord and remembering that He will never give us more than we can handle (see 1 Corinthians 10:13). Remember that amazing statement Jesus made? "He who is least in the kingdom of heaven is greater than [John the Baptist]." As I mentioned, this refers to all of us who have put our faith in Jesus Christ.

We who have Jesus Christ actually living at the core of our lives have even greater resources than John the Baptist had available to him. Whatever you may be facing in your life, you don't have to face it alone. There is a God who cares, a God who loves you, a God who will forgive you of your sins and give you the strength to get through your circumstances and challenges.

The kingdom of heaven doesn't begin for us when we die; it begins the moment we yield our lives to Jesus Christ.

He is with us, and He is in us.

There is no greater privilege than that.

6

COME AND FIND REST

Tattoo the Basset Hound was having a very bad day.

According to a Tacoma, Washington, newspaper account, the hound had not planned on going for a swift run. But when his owner inadvertently shut the dog's leash in the car door and took off for a drive—with Tattoo still outside the vehicle—the dog had no choice.

A motorcycle officer noticed a passing vehicle with "something dragging behind it." The policeman said the poor Basset Hound was "pickin' 'em up and layin' 'em down as fast as he could."

As you may know, Basset Hounds are built close to the ground, with very short legs. They're not built for running—especially at 20 to 25 miles an hour, trying to keep up with a car. Fortunately for all concerned, the officer chased the car down, and Tattoo was rescued without serious injury.

But he was really tired and had been dragged around a bit.

Have you ever felt that way—dragged through life? On some days, maybe we feel like Tattoo the Bassett Hound, running as fast as our little legs will carry us but still unable to keep up.

In his classic book *Through the Looking-Glass,* Lewis Carroll put these words in the mouth of the Red Queen: "Now *here*, you see, it takes all the running you can do, to keep in the same place. If you want to get somewhere else, you must run at least twice as fast as that."

Can you identify with those words? Do you feel like you are always running but getting nowhere?

Take a minute to fill in the blanks on this little quiz.

"I'm ready to throw in the _____."

"I'm almost at the end of my _____."

"I'm just a bundle of _____."

"My life is falling _____."

"I'm at my wit's _____."

The epitaph "Hurried, worried, and buried" could be written on countless American tombstones today.

The fact is, sometimes we just feel weary with life itself and don't know where to turn for relief. If that's where you find yourself as you read the words of this chapter, consider the words of Jesus in Matthew 11. To me, these are some of the most encouraging, hopeful words in all of the Bible—or anywhere else.

"COME TO ME"

"Come to Me, all you who labor and are heavy laden, and I will give you rest. Take My yoke upon you and learn from Me, for I am gentle and lowly in heart, and you will find rest for your souls. For My yoke is easy and My burden is light." (Matthew 11:28-30)

These verses are often quoted when we want to tell someone how to come to Jesus, and that is a completely appropriate use of them. But Jesus wasn't speaking only to unbelievers; His words are for anyone who is under pressure, stressed out, or carrying a heavy load.

An expanded translation of this statement of our Lord from the Greek reads like this: "Come here to Me, all of you who are growing weary to the point of exhaustion, loaded with burdens, and bending beneath the weight. I alone will cause you to cease from your labor, take away your burdens, and refresh you with rest."

It's an amazing, unprecedented invitation from the Son of God Himself. But to whom was He speaking? Who should respond to this invitation?

AN INVITATION FOR EVERY WEARY PERSON

These words from Jesus are for every person in every place with any problem. They're for men and women, young and old, rich and poor, healthy and sick.

Nevertheless, this isn't an invitation to lazy people. He's speaking to people who labor and are heavy laden. To be weary implies that you've worked very hard—even to the point of exhaustion. I personally believe that Christians should be the hardest workers of all, no matter what the task. In 2 Thessalonians 3:12-13, the Bible tells believers to "settle down and work to earn their own living. . . . Never get tired of doing good" (NLT).

The Lord isn't speaking to unmotivated people here. He is speaking to weary people. He is addressing those who feel loaded down—and nearly crushed—by the weights and burdens of life.

Is that a description of you as you read these words?

What will happen to the person who comes to Him? Matthew 11:28 holds out a clear promise. Jesus said, "I will give you rest." Rest doesn't mean taking a nap. It's a word that means "to be refreshed or revived." For starters, this would be the sort of rest that comes with the assurance of our salvation in Christ. If you have put your faith in Jesus Christ, you should never have to doubt the fact that you are right with God and that you will go to heaven and be in God's presence when you die. The book of Romans gives us these glorious words:

> Therefore, since we have been made right in God's sight by faith, we have peace with God because of what Jesus Christ our Lord has done for us. Because of our faith, Christ has brought us into this place of undeserved privilege where we now stand, and we confidently and joyfully look forward to sharing God's glory. (Romans 5:1-2, NLT)

In other words, we need to rest in the finished work of Christ that He accomplished on the cross. It was there that our Lord shed His blood for every sin that we have ever committed, assuring us that God's righteous demands have been fully met by Christ. We can rest in that.

We can rest in that finished work, accomplished for us.

With our eternal destiny settled by God Himself, you and I really don't have to sweat the small stuff. Yes, as Christians we will certainly face problems and challenges, tragedies and trials. But through them all, we can know deep, deep down that we are saved and safe in our Lord's protective care.

RELEASE FROM BONDAGE

The word Jesus uses here for *rest* is an interesting one. It is used elsewhere in the New Testament to describe chains falling off someone's hands. It carries with it the idea of being released from any kind of bondage. The child of God should not be under any kind of legalism, any kind of vice, or any kind of enslaving habit. Jesus said, "I will give you rest and relief."

This same word for *rest* also describes a person who has been released from financial debt. Yes, He can do that literally, helping us through our financial troubles and providing for our needs. But I think the principal impact of these words is that Jesus wants to release us from our debt of sin and all its life-destroying consequences and repercussions. If we have placed our faith in Christ, the Bible says we have been *justified*. Our sins have been forgiven, and the righteousness of Christ now has been placed into our account.

Finally, in Greek literature that same word used for *rest* is used to describe a door you can't quite open that suddenly flies wide open. It's like gaining access to an area you never were able to enter before. Maybe you have tried to get into a certain private event but didn't have the right ticket or the right pass or know the right people.

Once when I was speaking at a downtown mission, I had stepped out for a few minutes after finishing with my message and then wanted to get back in. There were hundreds of people, and I had my little granddaughter

Stella with me. We made our way through the crowds to the door, and they wouldn't let us back in!

Stella had sung "Jesus Loves the Little Children" at the service that night, and everyone loved it. So there I was, holding Stella, and somebody recognized her. He said, "Hey, it's that little girl that sings! Let them in!" They didn't know me from Adam's housecat, but I was holding "that little girl that sings." So I got backstage access through Stella.

Using that analogy, you and I have "backstage access" to God the Father through His Son, Jesus Christ. You can call upon Him at any time. If you wake up at three in the morning, the Lord is not asleep. He is ready to hear your cry and your prayer.

"GIVE ME THE STEERING WHEEL"

So once I have come to Christ, what should I do then? Jesus has already said, to paraphrase, "You who are exhausted, you who are weary, you who are burdened down with weight, come to Me, and I will give you rest. I will forgive you of the crushing spiritual debt that you owe and will deposit My own righteousness into your account. I will break the chains off you and give you free access into My presence."

What's next, then? Pay very close attention to Matthew 11:29:

> "Take My yoke upon you and learn from Me, for I am gentle and lowly in heart, and you will find rest for your souls."

If we were updating this verse, Jesus might be saying to us, "Give Me the steering wheel of your life."

In our family, I've gotten used to doing the driving. The

fact is, I'm not particularly fond of being driven by my wife. It's not Cathe's driving. She is an excellent driver and is always very careful. It's not her; it's me. I'm the worst backseat driver who has ever lived. *"Turn right. Get in the right lane. Get in the* right *lane! Get in it. Now! Now! Okay. Hurry! Go around that person. Oh—watch out!"* That's just how I am.

After a while, she will finally say, "Fine. You just drive the car."

And I will say, "Good. Yes."

Sometimes we can be that way with the Lord. We *say* that we have yielded the steering wheel of our lives to the Lord, but we still try to do a lot of backseat driving. *"Lord, speed up, speed up. Turn right. No, Lord, get us out of this lane—I don't like this lane. Oh . . . make a U-turn and go back, Lord. Let's not go this way."*

But He is saying, "Give Me the steering wheel."

With that in mind, let's come back to Matthew 11:29. Jesus said, "Take My yoke upon you."

What's a yoke? A yoke was made of wood, hand-hewn to fit the neck and shoulders of the animal that was to wear it, to avoid the animal's pain, discomfort, or injury. It follows, then, that back in the culture of the first century, a yoke was an expression used to describe submission. When you described yourself as yoked to something or someone, it communicated the idea that you were submitted to that something or someone. When the ox was yoked to the cart under the direction of the driver, he had submitted himself to that power.

When Jesus says, then, "Take My yoke upon you," it means submitting yourself to Christ every day in every way.

So some might say, "Are you serious, Greg? Are you suggesting that to really follow Jesus I have to serve Him and obey Him?"

That is exactly what I am suggesting. And that is exactly what Jesus was saying.

But before you bristle at that idea, consider this. Everyone is yoked to something or someone. Maybe another way to explain it would be to say that everyone is in sync with something. In your life, you are in sync with certain people, ideas, and relationships.

It then becomes a question of who or what do you want to yoke your life to? Some are yoked to the power of sin and live under its power and control all their days. I don't want to be under that power because I know it would shame me, wound my family and friends, shred my integrity, destroy my testimony for Jesus, and eventually kill me. Who wants to live like that? In Isaiah 10:27, however, we learn that the Lord can remove the bondage of His people and break the yoke of slavery: "In that day their burden will be lifted from your shoulders, their yoke from your neck" (NIV).

Some are yoked in a relationship with unbelievers. The Bible speaks very specifically to that situation, saying in 2 Corinthians 6:14-15,

> Don't team up with those who are unbelievers. How can righteousness be a partner with wickedness? How can light live with darkness? What harmony can there be between Christ and the devil? How can a believer be a partner with an unbeliever? (NLT)

This is why a believer wants to avoid becoming romantically involved with an unbeliever. Why? Because it is more likely the unbeliever will pull the believer down than the Christian will pull the unbeliever up.

After I became a Christian, I remember that for the

first week or so, I felt a very strong call by God to share the gospel with pretty girls. After all, someone needed to reach them, and maybe I was the guy.

It wasn't long before the Lord showed me that He hadn't called me to be a missionary to attractive young women, and He had other things for me to do.

Someone might say, "I'm only going to date this person to try to win him [or her] to Christ." But the reality is they will drag you down. Why? Because it's easier for you to go backward than it is for him (or her) to go forward.

Everyone, whether they admit it or not, will be yoked to something or someone in life. Why not be yoked to the Son of God, mighty in power, who loves you with an everlasting love?

"MY YOKE IS EASY"

Jesus says, "Take My yoke upon you and learn from Me."

How do I do that?

In Scripture, Jesus said, "Behold, I have come — in the volume of the book it is written of Me" (Hebrews 10:7). That's the answer: I will learn from Jesus by studying the Bible. You might have one of those Bibles where all the words of Jesus are printed in red. When you get to the Sermon on the Mount, it's just red page after red page, and it's a little hard to read. The truth is that *all* of the words in Scripture are inspired by God, New Testament and Old Testament, from Genesis to Revelation. So take His yoke upon yourself and set out to learn from Him.

Jesus goes on to say in verse 30, "For My yoke is easy and My burden is light."

Now, when I think of a yoke around my neck and shoulders, I don't think of something that is light. The word *light*, however, could be better translated as "well fitting" or "easy to wear." The carpenter would custom-design each yoke for the particular ox that would be wearing it. In the same way, when you are committed to the Lord and submitted to His plan for your life, the yoke He gives to you just fits! It isn't burdensome at all. In fact, 1 John 5:3 says, "For this is the love of God, that we keep His commandments. And His commandments are not burdensome."

I've heard people say, "The Christian life is a drag. It's just a bunch of rules and regulations. I don't like to live by the commands of God."

Really? Which ones are you struggling with? Are you bummed out that you can't steal, lie, and murder people? Was that something you would have done otherwise?

Don't the commandments make sense when you stop and think about them?

I remember looking out in our backyard years ago and seeing a brightly colored little bird, nestled in the grass, shaking and looking very afraid. That's probably because my fairly large German Shepherd was looking right at him, and that bird realized it was going to be curtains very soon.

So I sent my dog somewhere else, knelt down by the bird, put out my index finger, and the little bird hopped right on. It was obviously someone's pet bird that had escaped and ended up in a very bad situation in my backyard.

Cathe was cooking something in the kitchen, and I came through the door with the bird on my finger.

"Look at this little bird I found."

"Where did you find that?"

"It was in the backyard. Jumped right up on my finger. I think it's someone's pet."

"What do we do with it?"

"I don't know."

Our son Jonathan piped up and said, "There's a little girl down the street that has a birdcage. Her bird died. Shall I get it?"

"Yes," I told him. "Run, get it."

So Jonathan took off like a shot, ran down the street, and brought back the cage. We set it on the counter, and I opened up the little door of the cage, with the little bird still on my finger. When the cage door opened, the bird hopped right in and jumped up on the perch. Before long, he was swinging back and forth on his perch. *Happy days are here again!* He liked being in a cage.

That goes against conventional wisdom, doesn't it? Some would say, "Don't coop up animals in cages. Set them all free!"

This terrified little bird, however, was about to become an appetizer for my dog. He didn't see the bars of that cage as a barrier that kept him in; he saw those bars as walls of protection, keeping predators out.

It's not a perfect metaphor, but we might look at the commandments of God in the same way. Yes, a person could say, "God's laws and standards are too constraining. They would only make my life miserable."

Or, you can see His laws for what they really are: a wall of protection to keep your predators, your enemies, and your adversaries from attacking you and destroying your life. His commandments are not burdensome. He says, "My yoke is easy and My burden is light."

SIMPLY COME

When I am burdened, when I am overwhelmed with worries, I need to come to Jesus with them. There is really nowhere else to go. Jesus did not say, "You who are weary and burdened should go to counseling." Nor did He say that you should take a walk, go to church, listen to a sermon, or read a book. All of those things are good and helpful in their place. But the ultimate answer is to go to Jesus.

I remember talking to a father whose daughter died on the day before Thanksgiving.

Referring to the loss of my own son, he asked me, "What words helped you?"

"I don't know what *words* helped me," I said. "I just know *Who* helped me. I knew where I needed to turn . . . and I still do."

In times of disappointment and difficulty, in seasons of anxiety or pressure, you don't need words; you need the Living Word. You need Jesus. That is where you need to go.

Jesus simply said, "Come to Me."

He didn't say, "Study My teachings," though coming to Him includes that. He simply offered a wide-open invitation to approach Him, to be near to Him, and to have fellowship with Him.

Let me return to the literal translation of Matthew 11:28: "Come to Me, all of you who are growing weary to the point of exhaustion and have been loaded with burdens and are bending beneath their weight. I alone will cause you to cease from your labor and take away your burdens and refresh you with rest."

The psalmist cried out,

> From the end of the earth I will cry to You,
> When my heart is overwhelmed;
> Lead me to the rock that is higher than I.

For You have been a shelter for me,
A strong tower from the enemy.
I will abide in Your tabernacle forever;
I will trust in the shelter of Your wings. (Psalm 61:2-4)

It may seem like a small distinction, but notice that Jesus doesn't first say, "Learn from Me," or "Take My yoke upon you."

Before that, He just says, "Come to Me."

It's not as though He is saying, "Make changes in your life first, and then, when you have yourself cleaned up a little, come to Me."

No, just "Come to Me . . . and I will give you rest."

Our modern culture would say something very different. It would say, "Well, if you can just get that promotion . . . if you can just buy that house . . . if you can just get married . . . if you can just take that two-week cruise . . . if you can just lease that expensive sports car . . . then you will find rest and be happy."

Materialism says, "Build it up, and you will find rest."

Pleasure mania says, "Live it up, and you will find rest."

Religion says, "Keep it up, and you will find rest."

But Jesus says, "Come to Me . . . and you will find rest."

As Paul tells us in the book of Romans, "Therefore, since we have been justified through faith, we have peace with God through our Lord Jesus Christ" (Romans 5:1, NIV).

Corrie ten Boom once put it like this: "Look without and be distressed. Look within and be depressed. Look at Jesus and be at rest."

7

A PARABLE OF SPIRITUAL GROWTH

I heard the story of a father who was talking with his daughter and her five-year-old friend Kristin about birthdays. In their discussion, the dad had discovered that Kristin's birthday was on March 30, close to his own birthday on March 27.

"You know what?" he said to Kristin. "Our birthdays are only three days apart."

She looked at him for a moment and said, "Yeah, but you grew much faster than I did."

Why is it that some people seem to grow faster than others? Why does there seem to be more spiritual growth in the lives of some followers of Jesus and less in others? I think that question can be answered in the parable before us in this chapter. It is best known as "The Parable of the Sower," but considering its theme, I think a better title would be "The Parable of Spiritual Growth."

GROWING OR REGRESSING

When it comes to the spiritual life, there is really no such thing as standing still. You are either progressing spiritually or regressing, growing or drawing back, gaining ground or losing ground. Someone has likened the Christian life to climbing a greased pole: You are either climbing or slipping, but you never stay stationary.

What, then, is the determining factor in your spiritual growth as a believer in Christ?

You are.

It isn't up to God; it's up to you.

We already know that God wants us to grow in our faith, deepen in our knowledge, and blossom in our love for Him and others. But He has also given us a free will. Although He has provided us with mighty resources to enable us to grow and to help us grow, the ultimate decision on whether we *will* grow belongs to you and me.

The simple fact is, if you don't want to grow in the Lord or if you don't really care whether you grow in the Lord, you will find a million reasons why you can't do it.

Really, those "reasons" are just excuses. And what is an excuse? It's a fancy lie. As one person defined it, an excuse is the skin of a reason stuffed with a lie. The unvarnished truth is that we will make time for what is truly important to us.

What is the bottom line that God is looking for in our lives? He wants to see spiritual fruit. In fact, that is why God put you here on this earth. Jesus said in John 15:16, "You did not choose Me, but I chose you and appointed you that you should go and bear fruit, and that your fruit should remain." He also said, "By this My Father is glorified, that you bear much fruit" (verse 8).

In Colossians 1:9-10, the apostle Paul said,

> We . . . do not cease to pray for you, and to ask that you may be filled with the knowledge of His will in all wisdom and spiritual understanding; that you may walk worthy of the Lord, fully pleasing Him, being fruitful in every good work and increasing in the knowledge of God.

The enemy to spiritual growth is contentment. Yes, it's good to be content with what God has given us, but we should never be content with where we are in our walk with Christ. We should always want to learn more, grow more, love more, obey more, and hear God's voice more often and more clearly.

After years of walking with the Lord, the apostle Paul made this amazing declaration:

> I don't mean to say that I have already achieved these things or that I have already reached perfection. But I press on to possess that perfection for which Christ Jesus first possessed me. No, dear brothers and sisters, I have not achieved it, but I focus on this one thing: Forgetting the past and looking forward to what lies ahead, I press on to reach the end of the race and receive the heavenly prize for which God, through Christ Jesus, is calling us. (Philippians 3:12-14, NLT)

In other words, Paul was saying, "I am not satisfied with where I am in my walk with Jesus. I want to keep growing and progressing spiritually."

In His parable of spiritual growth, Jesus laid out the issues for us in a memorable way.

FOUR SOILS, FOUR RESPONSES

"Behold, a sower went out to sow. And as he sowed, some seed fell by the wayside; and the birds came and devoured them. Some fell on stony places, where they did not have much earth; and they immediately sprang up because they had no depth of earth. But when the sun was up they were scorched, and because they had no root they withered away. And some fell among thorns, and the thorns sprang up and choked them. But others fell on good ground and yielded a crop: some a hundredfold, some sixty, some thirty. He who has ears to hear, let him hear!" (Matthew 13:3-9)

It's a good story, but what does it mean? Thankfully, we don't have to wonder about that, because Jesus Himself explained the meaning:

"Therefore hear the parable of the sower: When anyone hears the word of the kingdom, and does not understand it, then the wicked one comes and snatches away what was sown in his heart. This is he who received seed by the wayside. But he who received the seed on stony places, this is he who hears the word and immediately receives it with joy; yet he has no root in himself, but endures only for a while. For when tribulation or persecution arises because of the word, immediately he stumbles. Now he who received seed among the thorns is he who hears the word, and the cares of this world and the deceitfulness of riches choke the word, and he becomes unfruitful. But he who received seed on the good ground is he who hears the word and understands it, who indeed bears fruit and produces: some a hundredfold, some sixty, some thirty." (verses 18-23)

Farming in the first century was far different than it is in the twenty-first century. We have sophisticated equipment, fertilizers, pesticides, herbicides, hybrid seeds, and high-tech irrigation methods.

Back in biblical times, it was pretty basic. A farmer with a big bag of seeds would simply walk through his plowed field, throwing out the seed in a relatively random manner.

In the process, the wind would pick up some of it and blow it away. Other seed would land on the road, where it would be trampled by people, animals, and cart wheels. Other seed would fall into ground that was embedded with stones or overgrown with weeds. Thankfully, some of it also would fall into receptive soil, where it would germinate, send down roots, and begin the process of growing and bearing fruit.

In His explanation of the parable, Jesus said the seed represents the Word of God, and we as believers are called to spread that seed as far as we can and reach as many people as possible with its life-transforming message.

Once you throw the seed out there in obedience and in faith, you really don't know where it will land. For instance, on any given day, our radio broadcast, *A New Beginning*, will be heard by two to three million people around the world. Every day, we receive letters from people in amazing places with incredible stories. Not long ago, I received a letter from a man who identified himself as an "outlaw biker." He heard our radio show, gave his life to Jesus Christ, and went on to become ordained as a pastor. Now he is ministering full-time to other outlaw bikers.

You may not have a radio program or some high-profile way to spread the seed, but your job description as a believer is just the same: to spread the message of the gospel to as many people as you can, wherever you are, and however you can. That's our responsibility. How the person hears or responds to that message is their responsibility. As Jesus said in His parable, "He who has ears to hear, let him hear!" In other words, "Listen up!"

President Franklin Roosevelt often endured long receiving lines at the White House and complained that no one ever really paid attention to what he was saying. So one day during yet another long, dreary reception, he decided to try a little experiment. To each person who walked by and shook his hand, he murmured, "I murdered my grandmother this morning."

A long line passed by, and the president made that startling statement to every individual. Guests responded with polite phrases like, "Wonderful to meet you, Mr. President," or "Oh, I appreciate your saying that," or "That is wonderful, Mr. President. Thank you."

Finally, as the reception line was almost at an end, one guest walked by, and President Roosevelt again smiled and said, "I murdered my grandmother this morning."

The guest replied, "I'm sure she had it coming to her."

So at least one person listened!

Those of us who aren't deaf hear all kinds of sounds all day long, but listening is something else altogether. You might say that listening is attention with intention.

Jesus was saying, "Don't just hear My words. Listen to what I am saying, and take these things to heart. You are the one who determines what sort of 'soil' your heart will be and how you will respond to the seed of God's Word."

In His parable, Jesus gave four categories of soil, or listeners.

Category 1: Highway Hearers

"When anyone hears the word of the kingdom, and does not understand it, then the wicked one comes and snatches away what was sown in his heart. This is he who received seed by the wayside." (Matthew 13:19)

It isn't that these people do not hear the Word; it's that they choose not to believe it. The effect, then, is like throwing seed on the asphalt. There is nothing for the seed to take root in.

In the parable, Jesus said the birds came and devoured the seed (see verse 4). You've seen birds like that. They hang out at fast-food restaurants, waiting for you to drop a French fry so they can swoop in and grab it.

Years ago, when our son Christopher was just a little boy, we went to visit Sea World. At the dolphin tank, you could buy little fish to feed the dolphins. I gave Christopher one of the fish and said, "Go ahead, feed the dolphins."

He took the fish, and out of nowhere, a seagull swooped down, grabbed the fish right out of his hand, and flew away.

"Stupid seagulls," he said.

We went to lunch and ordered chicken. Jonathan had been working on a chicken leg, set it down for a moment, and a seagull dropped out of the sky and flew off with it.

That really made Christopher mad. "Dad," he said, "I hate seagulls."

As we were leaving the park, a seagull flying overhead committed one final act of injustice. *Splat!* . . . a direct hit on Christopher.

I remember him looking up at the sky and yelling, "I hate seagulls!"

Those are the kind of birds Jesus described in His parable, and they symbolize the devil, who steals the Word away from people.

The people I call "highway hearers" are those who might hear the Word, but they have allowed their hearts to become cold and hard. Where is the easiest place to get a hardened heart? The answer might surprise you. It's not in a bar, and it's not hanging around godless people who are doing godless things. In fact, the easiest place to get a hardened heart is in church.

As I have said many times before, the same sun that softens the wax hardens the clay. If you go to a church service or a Bible study with an attitude that says, "I don't want to hear this," your heart will be become just a little bit harder and less responsive.

The Bible says, "He who is often rebuked, and hardens his neck, will suddenly be destroyed, and that without remedy" (Proverbs 29:1).

In other words, the person who keeps hearing truth and keeps rejecting it will develop a hard heart and become very unresponsive to the Lord.

In the book of Exodus, the pharaoh of Egypt is a good example of this. He heard the word of God from Moses and Aaron and saw them perform miracle after miracle before his very eyes. But what do we read? Pharaoh hardened his heart. Ultimately, after Pharaoh stubbornly refused to listen or believe, we read that God Himself hardened Pharaoh's heart. Some people are confused by that. How is it that Pharaoh hardened his heart, and then we read that God hardened his heart?

The answer is that both are true. God waits for us to make our move, and then He will confirm us in it. Pharaoh hardened his heart and, ultimately, God strengthened him in that decision, even though it was wrong.

The lesson for all of us is to keep our hearts pliant and receptive by remaining open to hearing the Word of God and quickly responding to the voice of God's Holy Spirit. Don't ever let your heart become hard by closing your ears to God's Word.

Category 2: Rocky Road Hearers

"He who received the seed on stony places, this is he who hears the word and immediately receives it with joy; yet he has no root in himself, but endures only for a while. For when tribulation or persecution arises because of the word, immediately he stumbles." (Matthew 13:20-21)

In contrast to the hard heartedness or indifference of the "highway hearer," there are those who seem to understand the Word and initially receive it with enthusiasm. But their response is a mile wide and an inch deep. The truth never really takes root.

These verses describe a seed that falls into shallow, rocky soil. Even though it germinates and quickly shoots up a plant, it's never able to take root and soon withers in the blazing sun.

This speaks of a person who seems to be converted but ends up walking away from the faith. You've no doubt seen people like this. They have an experience at church or at an evangelistic crusade and become very excited. They go out and buy a big Bible, start learning the worship songs, and sing louder and raise their hands higher than anyone else. They pray passionate prayers and talk about sharing their faith with others. Watching them, you might think, *This is one of the most amazing conversions I've ever seen.*

And then, in a month or six weeks, they suddenly disappear.

You call them up and say, "Hey, where are you? I didn't see you at church."

"Oh, I'm not into that anymore."

"What do you mean, you're 'not into that anymore'?"

"That was just a fad—a phase. I psyched myself into that. It wasn't real."

So what happened? Was this someone who was genuinely converted and then lost their salvation? I would suggest to you they were never truly saved to begin with.

Becoming a Christian isn't about the emotion of the moment; it's about the test of time. If someone is genuinely saved, they will continue on. No, they won't be flawless or perfect. None of us is. It's even possible that some Christians will go astray for a time. But if they are real believers, they always will come back.

If, on the other hand, they walk away and never return, they never were believers to begin with. As the apostle John noted, "They went out from us, but they did not really belong to us. For if they had belonged to us, they would have remained with us; but their going showed that none of them belonged to us" (1 John 2:19, NIV).

Why did they leave? It may be because they tried to build

their faith on an emotional experience. There certainly can be emotion when someone turns to the Lord, although that isn't always the case. When I asked the Lord to come into my life, I didn't have an emotional experience. But emotions did come later. The Bible certainly promises a peace that passes human understanding and a joy that is unspeakable. But you can't build your life on emotion, because emotions come and go.

Sometimes someone will come to the Lord out of a background of drugs or alcohol, and they will say, "I'm getting high on Jesus now. Jesus is the ultimate high."

I'm always concerned when I hear statements like that. Jesus isn't a drug, Jesus is the Lord. And He won't always be your ultimate high. A person who thinks that every day with the Lord will be a big emotional rush will sooner or later wake up disappointed, because the emotions won't be there.

That's a critical moment in the Christian life, because God is saying to us that it's time to grow up and start walking by faith rather than by feelings. As Scripture says, "The just shall live by faith" (Romans 1:17). Some people, however, try to build their entire relationship with God around an emotional experience. And when the emotions flatline for a while, as they inevitably will, they get discouraged and walk away. They have attempted to build their life on the wrong foundation.

The main reason that people with shallow roots fall away is because of tribulation and persecution. Matthew 13:21 says, "When tribulation or persecution arises because of the word, immediately he stumbles."

Notice that the verse above says *when*, not *if*. According to the Bible, all believers will experience tribulation and persecution. No one gets a pass. The word *tribulation* isn't speaking of the normal hardships of life, but those that come our way because of the Word of God. When you become a Christian, it won't be received well by everyone in your life. If you came from an unbelieving family as I did, you certainly will face opposition. If you have friends who aren't believers, they will question your motives, your intelligence, and even your sanity.

In Matthew 10:34 and 36, Jesus said, "Don't imagine that I came to bring peace to the earth! I came not to bring peace, but a sword. . . . Your enemies will be right in your own household!" (NLT). When you become a believer and really seek to begin living for the Lord, it will cause friction with some people, which will produce tribulation.

Sometimes that friction is more a result of our own foolishness or lack of tact than our faith in Christ. I think back to when I first became a Christian as a teenager and the tactless way I spoke about my faith to my mother. She was a big drinker at the time and very much into the party scene. I remember coming after her with my gospel guns blazing, telling her to repent.

There was nothing wrong with verbally sharing my faith with Mom. That wasn't the problem. The problem was that I was abrupt and harsh and should have eased into it a little bit more.

We should never forget that one of Jesus' nicknames was "Friend of Sinners." The religious leaders of His day tore into Him all the time for being friendly with tax collectors, thieves, prostitutes, and scoundrels. In the same way, we need to be friendly, caring, and winsome when we're among unbelievers.

Just make sure that when you're persecuted, it's for the right reasons. Be persecuted for being righteous, not for being obnoxious.

Category 3: Thorny Hearers

"He who received seed among the thorns is he who hears the word, and the cares of this world and the deceitfulness of riches choke the word, and he becomes unfruitful." (Matthew 13:22)

A "thorny hearer" is a person who receives the Word of God, but in time it is choked out by other things. This is a very different person from the first category of hearer, who has such an asphalt hard heart that the seed never takes root. It is also different from the second category of individual, who initially receives the message with joy but later walks away.

The problem with this soil is that it develops in slow motion. In this case, the stealing away of the potential fruit is a subtle and gradual process.

Do you remember the story of the frog in the kettle? This third category of hearer has more in common with that picture. As you will recall, if you put a frog into a kettle of cold water, he will sit there and not jump out. Then, if you heat the water ever so gradually, the frog still won't jump out, because he doesn't notice the change. By the time the water is boiling, it will be too late.

This is a gradual process.

Notice that Jesus didn't identify those choking weeds as "sins." He spoke of "the cares of this world and the deceitfulness of riches" that gradually strangle the once-healthy plant. *The Message* translates this as "weeds of worry and illusions about getting more and wanting everything under the sun."

The simple fact is that *good* things can occupy a person's time as well as bad things. And these worldly concerns may not be bad to begin with; they might be perfectly legitimate. They really only become "weeds" when they begin to crowd out and overshadow a man or woman's all-important relationship with God and get in the way of spiritual growth. The second best—even when that second best is legitimate and worthy—is often the worst enemy of the best.

This thorny hearer is not the person who deliberately says, "I won't pray" or "I won't read the Bible" or "I won't go to church." In fact, they will consider these to be good things. They may actually go out and buy a Bible, and they have every intention of going to church . . . unless something more interesting comes along. And then maybe they won't go.

It's a beautiful morning, there's a swell, and they decide to surf instead. Or a buddy calls and wants to get in a game of golf. Or there's something on TV they really wanted to see. Or there are some things they need to pick up for dinner. None of these are bad things. In fact, I'm in favor of all of them. It's just that this individual keeps allowing other interests, other priorities, and other activities to become more important than pursuing a relationship with the living God. These people aren't against the Bible. On the contrary, they respect and revere the Bible and insist that the Bible is the Word of God. They will talk it up and hold it up, but they just don't find time to *open* it up very often.

Life becomes busy, busy, busy, with a thousand things going on in every given day. It never stops. You have to get the kids to school, maybe go to work, pick up the dry cleaning, get in a workout, spend a little time with a friend, answer e-mails, check out Facebook, and—my goodness!—where did all the time go?

Again, none of these life activities are wrong or sinful.

They are simply out of balance if they begin to cut into a person's time with God. Ever so gradually, the physical becomes more important than the spiritual. TV or sports become more important than the Bible. Movies become more appealing than church. Talking about people to other people becomes more appealing than talking to God. Things on earth become more important than treasures in heaven.

Some people are drawn to the world like a moth is drawn to a light. Have you ever watched moths bouncing around a porch light or street light? It's like they get drunk on light and go just a little bit crazy.

In his New Testament letters, the apostle Paul would sometimes refer to particular people that he knew. He mentioned one guy, Demas, in two different letters. The first mention was in Philemon verses 23 and 24. Writing from prison, the apostle concluded his letter with this sentence: "Epaphras, my fellow prisoner in Christ Jesus, greets you, as do Mark, Aristarchus, Demas, Luke, my fellow laborers."

Wow . . . a "fellow laborer" with the mighty apostle Paul. I don't know about you, but if I had been mentioned in one of Paul's epistles, I would probably bring it up in every conversation. "Hello, my name is Demas. Oh, by the way, I was in the epistle to Philemon. You might have come across my name . . ."

Demas was also mentioned in Paul's final epistle. Only this mention wasn't anything to be proud of. In 2 Timothy 4:9-10, the apostle wrote, "Be diligent to come to me quickly; for Demas has forsaken me, having loved this present world, and has departed for Thessalonica."

Why did Demas leave Paul? Because he had fallen in love with the things of this life. Another Bible version translates the passage like this: "Demas has left me. He loved the good things of this life and went to Thessalonica" (TLB).

In 1 John 2:15-16 we read, "Do not love the world or the things in the world. If anyone loves the world, the love of the Father is not in him. For all that is in the world—the lust of the flesh, the lust of the eyes, and the pride of life—is not of the Father but is of the world."

When the Bible speaks of "the world," it isn't talking about our planet. It doesn't mean you can't enjoy the beauty of Planet Earth or all the blessings God has given us to enjoy. The world in this context speaks of a culture, a mentality, and a system that is hostile to God.

Another translation of these two verses puts it this way: "Don't love the world's ways. Don't love the world's goods. Love of the world squeezes out love for the Father. Practically everything that goes on in the world—wanting your own way, wanting everything for yourself, wanting to appear important—has nothing to do with the Father. It just isolates you from him" (MSG).

Going back again to Jesus' parable, what are the thorns, what are the weeds that threaten our spiritual lives? Jesus called them "the cares of this world and the deceitfulness of riches."

The fact is, a thorn or a weed is anything that crowds Jesus out of your life. The word used here for *care* means anxiety or worry. So this is a person who allows his or her anxieties and worries about life to crowd out a love for God and a walk with Jesus.

Life gives most of us plenty of things to worry about. We think about the future, our jobs, our health, our finances, and our families and their safety. We have no shortage of things that stir up anxieties and keep us awake at night.

Jesus also mentioned the deceitfulness of riches. It's not

wrong to have a successful career and enjoy your material possessions. What Jesus was talking about here is becoming *obsessed* with possessions.

Over in 1 Timothy 6:17-18 we read,

Teach those who are rich in this world not to be proud and not to trust in their money, which is so unreliable. Their trust should be in God, who richly gives us all we need for our enjoyment. Tell them to use their money to do good. They should be rich in good works and generous to those in need, always being ready to share with others. (NLT)

Notice this Scripture doesn't say, "Tell those who are rich to get rid of all their money." No, Paul said these people can enjoy what God has given them, but they must be openhanded, generous, and ready to share their blessings.

The person who is in danger is the one who allows his or her wealth and possessions to crowd out a relationship with God. The thorny hearer is a person who allows the legitimate cares of this life to become illegitimate, because they draw time and attention and affection away from the things of God.

Think how quickly your perspective in life would change if your doctor called you and said you had one month to live. You would see everything a little differently, wouldn't you? Those things that might have been so important to you yesterday wouldn't even be on the radar screen today. And maybe some of those things you haven't given much thought to for a long time would suddenly become the most important things of all.

Category 4: Fruitful Hearers

"He who received seed on the good ground is he who hears the word and understands it, who indeed bears fruit and produces: some a hundredfold, some sixty, some thirty." (Matthew 13:23)

This parable is found in three of the Gospels, and each one of the accounts gives us a little bit more understanding about this final category.

Here in Matthew, the good hearer is someone who *hears the word and understands it*. In Mark 4:20, he is described as one who *accepts* the Word. That means he takes it in, and it becomes a part of him. In Luke 8:15, the good hearer is said to be the one who *keeps* the Word. In other words, he holds on to it and practices it in his life. Luke also added that the good hearers "bear fruit with patience." Don't expect a great harvest overnight! It takes time to grow spiritually, and there are no shortcuts.

My granddaughter Stella and I have a little game that we play. I call it taking her the secret way. Sometimes if we're out together and go into a restaurant, I will say, "Now, that is the normal way people go in. But then there is the *secret* way. Who wants to go the *secret* way?"

"I do, Papa."

"Okay. Let's go."

So we will go around and walk in a side door. As we are walking in, I will say, "Be really quiet. Don't let anyone see this because it's the *secret* way."

Or maybe we will be in the car, driving along, and instead of taking the regular way home, I will say, "Now, we could go the regular way home or . . . we could go the *secret* way."

"Oh Papa, I want to go the *secret* way!"

Then I will turn off on some random street and drive on it for a while. "Now," I will tell her, "we're on the *secret* way." And she gets all excited.

Sometimes we look for that in the spiritual life. What is the secret way? What is the shortcut to spirituality? I hate to break this to you, but there is no secret way. There are no Cliffs Notes on growing in Christ. It takes time, and lots of it. It means that you sink your seed into the soil and bring forth fruit with patience. Conversion may happen instantaneously, but transformation takes a lifetime.

Again, in Matthew's version of this parable, the good hearer understands the Word. He hears it, follows it through from beginning to end, and thinks about it. It's like chewing your food rather than swallowing it whole.

A person is better off reading ten verses every day and thinking about those verses than flying through ten chapters and not remembering a thing afterward. The idea is that we are to think about the Word, ponder the Word, and meditate on the Word day and night.

Psalm 1 speaks of the blessed individual whose "delight is in the law of the LORD, and in His law he meditates day and night. He shall be like a tree planted by the rivers of water, that brings forth its fruit in its season, whose leaf also shall not wither; and whatever he does shall prosper" (verses 2-3).

That's exactly the picture Jesus is giving us here in the final category of the Parable of the Sower. The idea is that we let the Word sink in. As Charles Spurgeon once said, "Nobody ever outgrows Scripture; the book widens and deepens with our years." And the result is that you will bring forth spiritual fruit.

BUT WHAT IS SPIRITUAL FRUIT?

That's a good question. Here are a few thoughts to consider.

1. Spiritual fruit is what we say in our lives.

Hebrews 13:15 says, "Therefore by [Jesus] let us continually offer the sacrifice of praise to God, that is, the fruit of our lips, giving thanks to His name."

When we offer praises to God, we are using our tongues, our mouths, and our vocal chords for the primary purpose they were created for. God loves to hear you sing His praise out loud, no matter what kind of voice you have, and He loves to hear you proclaim His name.

Sometimes we'll say, "I feel it in my heart, but I feel uncomfortable saying it." That is like a husband saying, "I love my wife, but I feel awkward saying the words 'I love you' out loud."

Really? Get over it! Husbands need to say "I love you" to their wives, and wives need to say the same to their husbands.

And God says, "I want to hear the fruit of your lips, glorifying My name."

2. Spiritual fruit is winning others to Christ and helping them grow.

Paul wrote in Romans 1:13, "I often planned to come to you . . . that I might have some fruit among you also, just as among the other Gentiles."

When you have the privilege of leading someone to Christ, that is fruit. When you have the opportunity to help a person who has already come to faith grow spiritually, that, too, is fruit.

3. Spiritual fruit is demonstrating the change in our conduct and character.

Galatians 5:22-23 tells us, "The fruit of the Spirit is love, joy, peace, longsuffering, kindness, goodness, faithfulness, gentleness, self-control."

Notice the Scripture speaks of the *fruit* of the Spirit, not the *fruits*. The fruit (singular) of the Spirit is love. It's the Greek word *agape*, the word used for love more than any other in the New Testament. And how do you define love? You define it by the words that follow: joy, peace, longsuffering (patience), kindness, goodness, faithfulness, gentleness, and self-control.

That's the kind of fruit Jesus is looking for in our lives. And how do I produce this fruit? The answer is that I don't produce it; Jesus produces it through me.

In John 15:4-5 Jesus said, "Remain in me, and I will remain in you. For a branch cannot produce fruit if it is severed from the vine, and you cannot be fruitful unless you remain in me. Yes, I am the vine; you are the branches. Those who remain in me, and I in them, will produce much fruit. For apart from me you can do nothing" (NLT).

If you're looking for the secret to spiritual growth, it's right here. Remain, or abide, in Jesus. The word *remain* means "to stay in a given place," thus producing lasting fruit. It is to maintain unbroken fellowship with God. It is regularity, and it is consistency.

Imagine that I planted a tree in my front yard, saying, "That looks just perfect. I love it."

But the next day I said, "No, I think it might be better in the side yard."

So I dig the tree up, roots and all, and plant it in a new place. Then the next day, I do it again, moving it to the backyard. If I were to keep doing that over and over again, the tree would become traumatized and die.

Some people are like that in their walk with God. They go to church for a few weeks, and then they stop for a few weeks. They start reading the Bible for a few days, and then they set it aside for a week. They try to start their day in prayer, talking to God, and then they stop doing that. Or maybe they keep going back and forth between their old life and their old ways and the new life in Christ.

You'll never grow that way. If you want to produce lasting fruit, you need to have the daily discipline of walking with God. Walking speaks of consistent, regular motion.

In Psalm 51:10, David prayed, "Create in me a clean heart, O God; and renew a right spirit within me" (KJV). The *right spirit* could be better translated "steadfast spirit" or "constant spirit."

This means that every day, you get up in the morning and make time to read the Word of God and pray. Yes, life is busy. But you do whatever you have to do to connect with the God who loves you and take advantage of the wonderful spiritual resources He has provided for you.

If you do, you will begin to bear fruit in your life.

And it will be fruit that lasts forever.

8

WHAT EVERY LAST-DAYS BELIEVER NEEDS TO KNOW

These are certainly days to watch the headlines.

Yes, it's informative to read the articles too. But even just scanning the headlines in your newspaper or on your favorite news website can give you a good idea of the way our world is drifting. You can almost hear our planet's groans and sighs as it awaits the King who will redeem it.

An article I read recently claimed that the terrorist group Al Qaeda is now on the brink of acquiring nuclear devices. Quoting certain leaked diplomatic cables, the article said that Al Qaeda was on the verge of producing radioactive weapons — after sourcing nuclear material and recruiting rogue scientists to build dirty bombs.

This is news that makes you pause, shake your

head a little, and maybe whisper, "Wow. What's next?"

What are we supposed to do, and how are we supposed to respond when we hear things like this? Panic? Give in to anxiety? Fill our garages up to the rafters with emergency supplies?

No, that is not what Jesus said. In Luke 21:28, He declared, "When these things begin to happen, look up and lift up your heads, because your redemption draws near."

Don't you like that? We're not to look from side to side, like people who are anxious or nervous, and we're not to look down, like people who are discouraged. We are to look up, like people who know where their help and salvation are coming from.

So now that we've established that we are very likely living in the last days, how are we supposed to live as believers? What sort of qualities should characterize our attitudes and our lives?

In this chapter, we will check out some of the highlights of Matthew 13 and the Lord's parables concerning the kingdom of God. As Jesus related some word pictures about the kingdom of God on earth, it helps us to consider how to order our lives in increasingly difficult and anxious times.

BIRDS, SEEDS, AND TREES

> Another parable He put forth to them, saying: "The kingdom of heaven is like a mustard seed, which a man took and sowed in his field, which indeed is the least of all the seeds; but when it is grown it is greater than the herbs and becomes a tree, so that the birds of the air come and nest in its branches."
> (Matthew 13:31-32)

Jesus said, *"The kingdom of heaven is like . . ."*

He didn't say, "The kingdom of heaven *is*."

He said, "It's *like* this," or maybe, "Compare it to this."

And the comparison He made was to a mustard seed (of all things). Frankly, that doesn't mean a lot to us today. We have Dijon mustard, deli mustard, hot Chinese mustard—all kinds of mustard. But what in the world is the significance of a mustard seed?

When Jesus walked the earth, however, people would have immediately understood this. A mustard seed is regarded as one of the smallest of all seeds. Jesus Himself called it "the least of all the seeds." On another occasion He said, "If you had faith even as small as a mustard seed, you could say to this mulberry tree, 'May you be uprooted and thrown into the sea,' and it would obey you!" (Luke 17:6, NLT).

So the idea here is that a mustard seed is about the smallest thing you could imagine.

Mustard seeds, however, don't grow into trees, as in the parable; they grow into bushes or shrubs. So what Jesus was talking about here wasn't normal growth at all; it was remarkable, supernatural growth. He was saying, "The kingdom of God is like something very, very small that grows into something incredibly, even freakishly, big."

It would be like saying, "The kingdom of heaven is like a Chihuahua that grew to be the size of an elephant." You see, a Chihuahua the size of a bus or an elephant would be something way beyond any normal expectation, and that's the idea being conveyed here.

So here is this little bush that grows into a giant tree. What does that mean? One interpretation paints this in a very positive light, reminding us that big trees in Scripture almost always portray something of power and great influence. King Nebuchadnezzar was compared to a tree, as was a pharaoh. So the bottom line, according to this view, is that the church is powerful and influential, impacting the world, and all of the birds come and nest in its branches.

That's one interpretation, but to me, it doesn't line up with other New Testament passages.

In Luke 18:8, Jesus asked, "When the Son of Man comes, will He really find faith on the earth?" As I understand it, I don't believe the Bible teaches that we will create some kind of super church on Planet Earth before the Lord's return.

And what about those birds in the parable?

Earlier in Matthew 13, in the Parable of the Sower, birds are portrayed as a symbol of evil—of the "wicked one" who comes and snatches away the good seed of the Word of God. (Did you ever see Alfred Hitchcock's horror classic *The Birds*? You'll never look at birds exactly the same way again after seeing that film.)

I believe this is a picture of the church being invaded by imposters in the last days. That certainly fits with what we see in the contemporary church scene today. As the Bible predicts, there are many who hold to "a form of godliness but [deny] its power" (2 Timothy 3:5).

It's somewhat easy to talk about "the church," because that seems big and vague and not very personal. The true church of Jesus Christ, however, is made up of people, and you are one of those people. And we are all—every one of us—in danger of compromising our faith and our walk with God. Compromise remains one of the most effective weapons in Satan's arsenal.

The devil realizes he probably can't take you down all at once, so he is contented with destroying you one bite at a time. That's his approach, and that's been his strategy ever since the first man and woman walked this earth.

Satan doesn't walk up to you and say, "Hey, you, I have a plan for your life, and I want you to consider it for a moment. I am thinking you ought to . . . well, let's see . . . be unfaithful to your wife. Or how about multiple affairs? Eventually, after trying to make the marriage work, your wife will give up and leave you. That's when you'll start drinking and become a full-blown alcoholic or maybe a drug addict—whatever you prefer. And then you can be estranged from her, from your children, ruin your life, slip into despair, and then maybe one day commit suicide. So that's my plan. What do you say?"

What fool would agree to terms like those?

The devil is much more clever than that. He comes with just a little bit of compromise, all wrapped up in shiny paper and ribbon.

"Hey, you happily married man," he says. "You've done so well! Congratulations are in order. What a good father and loyal husband you've been! But you've been pushing yourself a little too hard, haven't you? You deserve a little break today. You need to loosen up and have a little fun. Go ahead and flirt a little with that attractive woman at the office. It's just a game, isn't it? Or maybe just check out a little pornography on the Internet. Just take a quick peek. What would it hurt? And what's wrong with wandering down to the hotel bar on your business trip for a drink or two? Or why not try this drug, just once? You never have to do it again."

Little things, you see, lead to big things. Small compromises lead to devastating falls.

I'm reminded of the story of the hunter and the bear. The hunter was out in the woods, looking for a bear to kill. As he tromped along through the forest, he saw a large black bear with its back to him. So he raised his rifle to fire.

Suddenly the bear turned around and said to the hunter, "Excuse me. Isn't it better to talk than to shoot?"

"Well," said the hunter, lowering his rifle a little. "Maybe you have a point."

"Tell me," said the bear, "exactly what it is that you want."

"I want a fur coat," the hunter replied, lowering his rifle even more.

"Very good," said the bear. "And I want a full stomach. So let's be sensible and try to work out a little compromise."

So the bear and the hunter disappeared into the forest. A little bit later, the bear emerged alone, with the negotiations apparently successful. Everyone got what they wanted. The bear got a full stomach, and the hunter got a fur coat.

That's how compromise works, and that's how deals with the devil work. You will always find yourself on the losing side.

"A LITTLE LEAVEN"

> Another parable He spoke to them: "The kingdom of heaven is like leaven, which a woman took and hid in three measures of meal till it was all leavened." (Matthew 13:33)

Again, at first reading, that story may not mean a lot to us today, but it would have been immediately understood by the people of that day.

Leaven is yeast—and yeast always has negative connotations in Scripture. When Moses was giving instructions to the Israelites about the very first Passover, right before they left Egypt, he told them to get rid of all the leaven in their houses before they celebrated that sacred meal (see Exodus 12:14-20).

Picking up on that picture, Paul wrote to the believers in Corinth, who actually had been boasting about welcoming an immoral and compromising believer into their church. They had been saying, in effect, "Look how tolerant and open-minded we are. We've encouraged this guy to come and join us, even though he's involved in a twisted relationship."

Paul said, in effect, "No! You've messed up with this. That's not the way you should be living." And he told them in 1 Corinthians 5:6-7, "Your boasting is not good. Don't you know that a little yeast works through the whole batch of dough? Get rid of the old yeast that you may be a new batch without yeast—as you really are." (NIV).

Another translation puts it like this: "What a terrible thing it is that you are boasting about your purity, and yet you let this sort of thing go on. Don't you realize that if even one person is allowed to go on sinning, soon all will be affected?" (TLB).

Yeast, or leaven, represents corruption, infiltration, and compromise. In the pages of Scripture, it invariably represents negative things. Jesus said, "Beware of the leaven of the Pharisees. Beware of the leaven of the Herodians. Beware of leaven."

So you say, "Okay, great. I'll get rid of all the yeast in the house."

No, you probably don't have to worry about the yeast in your pantry or throwing out that bread machine you got for Christmas. But there may be other things in your house that you *should* rid yourself of. This is a picture of compromise in your life—a situation where little things morph into big things. And it happens more quickly than you might imagine.

Have you ever seen a baby rattlesnake? I used to really like snakes, and when I was a boy, I kept them as pets. A junior-sized rattlesnake, however, is every bit as deadly as the full-grown version. In fact, its venom is more potent than that of an adult rattler. Yes, it's almost cute with its little rattle and sharp, tiny fangs, but it will kill you if it gets the chance.

In the same way, we may coddle what we think of as "little sins" in our lives—small compromises that really don't seem to matter very much. We think, *Oh, it's just a little sin . . . kinda cute. It's really nothing. They're just small indulgences. They're just little white lies.*

But wait until those baby rattlers suddenly turn around and bite you.

That's the way compromise seeks to work its way into your life, permeating every corner.

In Psalm 66:18, the psalmist said, "If I regard iniquity in my heart, the Lord will not hear me" (KJV). What does that mean? It means that if I hang on to sin in my life, God won't hear my prayers.

And now I ask you, is there sin in your life right now that you have never dealt with? Do you imagine that it's secret and no one will see or know? Do you think you've covered your steps? Listen to this: Secret sin on earth is open scandal in heaven. There are no secrets with God. He is aware of it—not only of the act, but also of all the rationalizing thoughts leading up to it.

What is the secret sin in your life? I don't know what it is. But I know that *you* know, because right now as you read my words, you're thinking about it. And the Lord sees it, just as though it were written over your head in neon lights.

That act, attitude, or thought could represent compromise in your life. And it could very well be the thing that brings you down. Get rid of that leaven in your life before it spreads and eats away your spiritual life and your walk with God.

RADICAL MEASURES

In April 2003, while doing some solo exploring of the Utah backcountry, twenty-eight-year-old Aron Ralston was rock climbing when an 800-pound boulder suddenly shifted, crushing his right hand and pinning it against the canyon wall. Nothing he tried could dislodge his arm. Days went by, and Ralston was cold, hungry, dehydrated, and beginning to become delirious. He had no cell phone with him, no one knew where he was, and he eventually had to admit to himself that no one would be coming to his aid. Finally, he realized he would die in that place unless he undertook one last, desperate measure.

He would have to cut off his own arm, just below the elbow, with a cheap, dull knife. And that's just what he did.

It took a long time, and it was very painful. He had to hack his way through skin, muscle, blood vessels, and bone. Amazingly, after he had done the deed, Ralston was able to rappel down a 65-foot sheer cliff, walk out, and live to tell the story.

It was a terrible thing to have to do. But Aron Ralston realized that it would be better to have one arm and be alive than to have two arms and be dead. A drastic measure? Yes, it was. But that's what it took for this young man to stay alive. He is now married, and the couple has a son.[1]

Is there a drastic measure you need to take in your life? Is there an area in your life that you need to deal with?

Maybe it's a relationship, a certain individual who always drags you down spiritually whenever you're around him or her. Or maybe it's a certain place where you used to go, certain practices you used to enjoy, or certain habits you used to indulge in. But now the Holy Spirit is whispering to you, *Come away from that person. Come away from that place. Turn away from those movies or books or games or music. Cut that thing out of your life. Don't drive down the street near the bar where you used to sit every night, drinking your life away.*

Make a clear choice to turn away from the friendships or habits that drag you down and cast a shadow over your walk with Jesus Christ.

I was a fairly new Christian when Cathe and I first started dating, and at one point, I apparently told her, "If you ever get in the way of my relationship with God, I'm out of here!"

I don't remember saying anything like that, but she says that I did.

"Are you sure?" I asked her recently. "I said that?"

"Yes," she affirmed.

"Boy, I was quite the romantic, wasn't I?"

"Oh," she replied, "but I liked it."

"Really?"

"Yes. Because other guys I dated always did what I wanted them to do, and I could manipulate them. But you had convictions, and I thought that was a great thing."

Let me just offer these words if you're not yet married. As you look for a mate, make sure you find someone who builds up your faith rather than tears it down. Don't even consider a person who isn't a believer as a romantic possibility or a potential mate. More than that, you should be looking for a godly man or woman — someone with whom you can grow in the Lord and serve Him together for the rest of your lives.

TREASURE AND PEARLS

"Again, the kingdom of heaven is like treasure hidden in a field, which a man found and hid; and for joy over it he goes and sells all that he has and buys that field.

"Again, the kingdom of heaven is like a merchant seeking beautiful pearls, who, when he had found one pearl of great price, went and sold all that he had and bought it." (Matthew 13:44-46)

There are two different ways you could interpret these parables.

One way of looking at them is to say that we are like the person who finds the treasure in the field, or the pearl of great price. And as a result of what we've found, we sell all we have to obtain it. In other words, one day we hear the gospel of Jesus Christ, and we realize it's the most profound, important thing we've ever heard. As a result, we give up everything to follow Christ. He is the treasure hidden in the field; He is the pearl of great price.

That's a valid interpretation. But as I read these parables, I find myself leaning in another direction. Instead of our finding that great treasure and giving all we have to purchase it, the other interpretation says that Christ is the person who finds it . . . and *we* are the treasure.

In verse 44, we read, "For joy over it he goes and sells all that he has and buys that field." That reminds me of the story Jesus told in Luke 15 about the shepherd who had a hundred sheep, and one went astray. Jesus said,

"When he has found it, he will joyfully carry it home on his shoulders. When he arrives, he will call together his friends and neighbors, saying, 'Rejoice with me because I have found my lost sheep.' In the same way, there is more joy in heaven over one lost sinner who repents and returns to God than over ninety-nine others who are righteous and haven't strayed away!" (verses 5-7, NLT)

Do you see the theme of joy? Jesus gave up all the privileges of deity, walked among us as a man, and went to the cross and suffered and died and rose again from the dead. He bought the treasure—He bought the pearl with His own blood. He gave up all that He had. And He did it for the joy of rescuing us and bringing us Home.

CASTING OUT THE NET

"Once again, the kingdom of heaven is like a net that was let down into the lake and caught all kinds of fish. When it was full, the fishermen pulled it up on the shore. Then they sat down and collected the good fish in baskets, but threw the bad away. This is how it will be at the end of the age. The angels will come and separate the wicked from the righteous and throw them into the fiery furnace, where there will be weeping and gnashing of teeth." (Matthew 13:47-50, NIV)

This is the idea of dragging a net through the water and then sorting out what that net pulls up.

Have you ever seen something like that on TV? The commercial fishermen reel these massive nets out of the sea into their ship, and the nets are full of all kinds of things. Yes, there are fish, but there may also be a squid, an octopus, a shark—or maybe an old refrigerator or something. They never know what they're going to pull in until they empty the nets into the big bins and start sorting out their catch.

That's what we're doing in the church—and even in our Harvest Crusades around the world. We're fishing for people, and believe me, we get all kinds.

Will we bring in some bad ones along with the good? Some that won't last?

Of course.

Will we find ourselves with false believers alongside true believers?

There's no question about it.

But God knows the secrets of every heart. And He will sort it all out, in His time and His way.

Jesus said, "Follow Me, and I will make you fishers of men" (Matthew 4:19, KJV). That's our purpose and goal! And that sentence could better be translated, "Follow Me, and you will catch men alive." That particular wording is used in only one other New Testament passage, where Paul wrote, "Then they will come to their senses and escape from the devil's trap. For they have been held captive by him to do whatever he wants" (2 Timothy 2:26, NLT).

Caught alive by Satan! What a terrible picture.

So one of two things will happen to our family members, friends, neighbors, and acquaintances: Either God will catch them alive, give them a full and significant life on earth, and take them to heaven when they die, or Satan will catch them alive and keep them in darkness as POWs.

Jesus was saying, "Let's go fishing for men and women. Let's go catch some people for God's glory." Our job, with the Lord's help, is to keep throwing out that net and pulling it in. You may come up with some junk from the bottom of the sea or some strange-looking critters, but you'll also bring in some prize catches as well.

IN THE MEANTIME . . . PRESS INTO PURITY

If you're driving down the freeway and a state patrol officer pulls up behind you, what's the first thing you usually do? Most often, your eyes go to your speedometer, and you probably find yourself slowing down. Even if you have your cruise control set exactly at the correct speed limit, you probably still brake a little. Why? Because the presence of a law enforcement officer changes your conduct.

That is how we should view the return of Christ. If we really believe Jesus is coming, it should affect our conduct. Here's how the apostle John put it:

> Yes, dear friends, we are already God's children, right now, and we can't even imagine what it is going to be like later on. But we do know this, that when he comes we will be like him, as a result of seeing him as he really is. And everyone who really believes this will try to stay pure because Christ is pure. (1 John 3:2-3, TLB)

We should be seeking to live godly lives as we await the coming of Jesus.

Thinking back to those verses in the book of Exodus, Moses told the people to get rid of the old leaven in their homes—every bit of it—in preparation for Passover and in preparation for a journey. The people were about to set out for new lives in the Promised Land, and they needed to clean out their cupboards before they left.

We, too, have a journey up ahead. In just a few blinks of the eye, we will be stepping into eternity, either through death or through the coming of the Lord. With that in mind, it's time to get rid of some old things—old habits, old attitudes, old prejudices, old patterns of life—so that we'll be ready for the journey.

Scripture says that Jesus will come in a moment, in the "twinkling of an eye" (1 Corinthians 15:52). And those who believe will be caught up to meet the Lord in the air. But not everyone will go in the Rapture. Jesus said,

> "Two men will be working together in the field; one will be taken, the other left. Two women will be grinding flour at the mill; one will be taken, the other left. So you, too, must keep watch! For you don't know what day your Lord is coming " (Matthew 24:40 42, NLT)

So here is my question to you: Will you be caught up, or will you be left behind?

That's the choice, isn't it? Get right, or get left. Get right with God or be left behind.

I hope you are ready.

9

DINNER WITH JESUS

I heard the story of a lonely woman who walked into a pet store, looking for a little companionship to fill the long, empty hours.

The pet shop owner said, "You know, ma'am, you might consider buying this parrot here. I'm tellin' ya, he talks nonstop—a real chatterbox. I think if you bought this guy and took him home, he would keep you company."

Well, why not?

She bought the bird and took him home. After a week and a half, she brought the parrot back to the pet store and accosted the store owner.

"Sir," she said, frustrated, "this parrot hasn't said a word! You said he'd talk to me."

The store owner said, "Did you buy him a mirror?"

"Well, no," she replied.

He smiled. "Every parrot needs a mirror."

"All right," she said, a little dubiously. So she bought a very expensive little parrot mirror in the store and took it home. Another week and a half went by, and she came back again.

"That parrot *still* isn't talking," she complained.

"Hmmm," the store owner said. "Did you buy a ladder? You see, every parrot needs a ladder."

She replied, "Why didn't you say so before?" So she bought the little ladder.

After another week and a half, she came back yet again. Standing in front of the counter with her arms folded, she said, "That bird you sold me still refuses to talk. He hasn't said a single word! I might as well have bought a hamster."

"Did you buy him a swing?" the storekeeper asked. "Every parrot needs a swing, you know."

"Okay," she said. "*Fine.* But this had better work!" So she dug into her purse, shelled out some more money, bought the little swing, and took it home. Right on schedule, however, a week and a half later, she burst into the store, just furious.

"What's wrong now?" the store owner asked.

"That parrot *died.*"

The owner was taken aback. "That's terrible! Did he ever talk?"

"Well . . . yes," she said. "He made one statement."

"What was it?"

He said, "Do they have any food down at that store?"

Poor little parrot.

I can relate to that starving bird because I'm the kind of guy who gets hungry on schedule! I would like to be able to tell you that the first thing I think about in the morning when I get out of bed is the Word of God or the will of God. That's what I would *like* to tell you. The truth is, the first thing I think about is breakfast.

One of the things I so love about Jesus as I read the Gospels is the priority He gave to meals. Even though His time on earth was brief, the biblical record gives us a number of examples of His enjoying meals with His disciples. After He rose from the dead, to prove that He was a real flesh-and-blood person and not a ghost, He asked them to bring Him a piece of fish, which He ate in their presence. (An excellent menu choice, by the way.)

In another encounter, the risen Lord met His disciples on the shore of the Sea of Galilee early one morning. He had some coals burning on the shore with some fresh fish sizzling away on the fire. Remember this beautiful verse in the gospel of John? "Jesus said to them, 'Come and eat breakfast'" (John 21:12).

Do you even have any doubt about how good those fish must have tasted? Grilled fish from the inventor of fish! In the book of Revelation, Jesus even used the analogy of eating to illustrate what it means to have fellowship with Him. In Revelation 3:20, He said, "Behold, I stand at the door and knock. If anyone hears My voice and opens the door, I will come in to him and dine with him, and he with Me."

When Jesus issued this invitation, He wasn't talking about a microwave dinner.

It's pretty typical in our culture today for people to eat *quickly*. This is especially true when we're eating lunch at work. We maybe have an hour, and often less than that. So we'll go to a take-out restaurant and grab a bag of something to take back to work.

But they didn't have take-out food in the first century. You couldn't just hop into your chariot and hit the drive-through at the local McDavid's. No, in that day and time, meals were leisurely, drawn-out affairs, where people would take time to really enjoy each other's company.

In Matthew 14, we come to the miracle of the feeding of the five thousand—which is the only miracle found in all four of the Gospels. I find that interesting. You would have thought that the Gospel writers might have picked the resurrection of Lazarus from the dead or the healing of blind Bartimaeus. But no, it is this miracle, the feeding of five thousand with a few loaves and a few fish. I think we can conclude, then, that God really wants us to understand the implications of this event. We have four camera angles on it to help us gain maximum insight into what happened on that particular day.

When Jesus went out He saw a great multitude; and He was moved with compassion for them, and healed their sick. When it was evening, His disciples came to Him, saying, "This is a deserted place, and the hour is already late. Send the multitudes away, that they may go into the villages and buy themselves food."

But Jesus said to them, "They do not need to go away. You give them something to eat."

And they said to Him, "We have here only five loaves and two fish."

He said, "Bring them here to Me." Then He commanded the multitudes to sit down on the grass. And He took the five loaves and the two fish, and looking up to heaven, He blessed and broke and gave the loaves to the disciples; and the disciples gave to the multitudes. So they all ate and were filled, and

they took up twelve baskets full of the fragments
that remained. Now those who had eaten were about
five thousand men, besides women and children.
(verses 14-21)

In total, there were likely many more than five thousand
fed. If you factor in women and children, it could have
been as high as ten thousand, perhaps even more.

In the timeline of His ministry, Jesus was in the peak of
His popularity and renown. He was the talk of the town, and
multitudes of people were anxiously following Him. In this
account, we have an exceptionally large crowd that had
gathered to hear Him, but there were no food vendors within
miles of the place, and the people were hungry. We read in
verse 14 that Jesus "was moved with compassion for them."

I find that fact fascinating.

It became quickly obvious that these people were not
following Jesus because they believed He was the long-
awaited Messiah of Israel. The reason they were following
Him was because of the miracles He was performing.
John 6:2 says, "A huge crowd kept following him wherever
he went, because they saw his miraculous signs as he
healed the sick" (NLT).

These people were effectively thrill seekers. They
were in it to be dazzled and entertained. But even though
they were fickle and maybe had mixed motives, Jesus had
compassion on them. The word translated *compassion* here
means "to have your inner being stirred." Have you ever
had that happen to you, where you found yourself being
deeply moved or stirred by something you saw?

And by the way, compassion is not just caring; it is
caring enough to do something. It is not just pity.
Compassion is pity *plus* action. Jesus had compassion on

these multitudes, and He saw they were hungry.

If I had been in the Lord's sandals (scary thought), I don't think I would have responded in quite the way that He did. If I had been in that circumstance, knowing what Jesus knew in that moment, I would have never fed those ungrateful hangers-on (even if I could have). I would have said, "I know why you guys are following Me, and I'm not going to give you lunch. In fact, I'm going to eat lunch right in front of you! How do you like that?" (Aren't you glad I'm not the Messiah?)

Jesus, however, had compassion on these people and wanted to feed them and meet their needs. But He also used the miracle as an unforgettable teaching moment for His own followers.

In John's account of this miracle, three primary individuals emerge from the story, and you might find yourself relating to one of them. The Bible records the Lord's encounters with Philip, then Andrew, and finally with a nameless little boy with his lunch bag.

PHILIP'S BIG TEST

Surrounded by the massive crowds and seeing they were hungry, Jesus turned to His disciple Philip and gave His first test. And by the way, this is the only recorded time in the Gospels where Jesus ever asked anyone for advice:

> When Jesus looked out and saw that a large crowd had arrived, he said to Philip, "Where can we buy bread to feed these people?" He said this to stretch Philip's faith. He already knew what he was going to do. (John 6:5-6, MSG)

In the course of His ministry, Jesus asked people some deep and searching questions. This wasn't one of them! *"Hey, Philip, how are we going to deal with this problem?"* It shouldn't have been a difficult question at all. For Philip, it was like standing in front of Niagara Falls and wondering where you're going to get a drink of water.

Philip *could* have said, "Well, let's see. . . . Considering the fact that You are God in human form, and . . . considering that You created the heavens and the earth, I'm sure You could come up with a solution to feed all of these people."

But that is not how Philip replied. In fact, if he had been graded on this little pop quiz, he would have received a failing grade. Philip effectively said, "It would take a small fortune to feed them all, Lord. There's just no way."

How could Philip have responded this way after walking with Jesus for over two years, hearing His teaching, seeing Him perform miracle after miracle? The fact is, Philip may have had the awesome privilege of walking with Jesus, but he was still spiritually dull to the obvious. He was looking at this situation through human eyes and evaluating it on the basis of human resources.

How pathetic is this?

Let me restate that. *How like us is this? How like* me *is this?*

I can think of times when I have come up to what seemed like impossible situations and thought to myself, *How in the world are we going to handle this? What are we going to do? What's the answer for this?*

And I actually have come to my senses and said, "Wait a minute. The Lord knows exactly what I'm facing here, and He has the answer! I need to commit this to Him in prayer right now."

But we forget that sometimes, don't we? And we find ourselves overwhelmed by our situations and circumstances.

Do you ever find yourself (like me) having to relearn the same life lessons, again and again? Maybe when you were younger, the Lord taught you to trust Him for His provision, and you did. But now, as you've gotten older and have enjoyed a stable income for a number of years, maybe it's time to relearn that lesson.

Or maybe there was a time in your life when you didn't know the will of God, and you sought after Him with all your heart and waited on Him for direction. But some time has passed since those days, and you find that you're not relying on Him as you once did. Days slip by, and you realize that you haven't been opening the Word or seeking Him in prayer as you once did. And God has to reteach you — perhaps through some trying circumstances — what it means to be completely dependent on Him once again.

I'm reminded of the words of Hebrews 5:

> You have been believers so long now that you ought to be teaching others. Instead, you need someone to teach you again the basic things about God's word. You are like babies who need milk and cannot eat solid food. For someone who lives on milk is still an infant and doesn't know how to do what is right. (verses 12-13, NLT)

I know people like this and, most likely, so do you. They have known the Lord for years and years, yet they're still like little spiritual babies who have never learned to fend for themselves or feed themselves spiritually. They need everything simplified for them, given to them in prechewed, bite-sized portions. They don't know how to open up the Bible and read it, letting God speak to their own hearts.

We need to learn how to feed ourselves!

One of my great privileges is to take my granddaughter Stella out for lunch. I've done that since she was about fourteen months old! Even at that age, she could feed herself. No, not with a fork or chopsticks, of course. She just picked the food up off her little plate or tray and popped it into her mouth. Since that time, of course, she's learned how to eat with utensils, and she's doing a great job.

You and I need to do the same thing with the Word of God.

On the other hand . . . it's easy to tell someone else to trust the Lord for provision until *you* have to. It's easy to tell someone else to trust the Lord for healing until *you* find yourself needing to trust Him as well.

Philip didn't do so well on this particular test. *"Well, Lord, we really don't have enough money to handle it."*

So then it was Andrew's turn.

ANDREW COMES CLOSE

Andrew, of course, had been listening to this whole exchange with Philip. And even though Jesus hadn't asked him for advice, he was ready to offer an opinion.

We don't know a lot about Andrew, overshadowed as he was by his brother, Simon Peter. He didn't write any books of the Bible, and—as far as we know—he performed no miracles. But what little we do know is quite impressive.

Andrew was originally one of the followers of John the Baptizer. And it was John who pointed to Jesus and said to Andrew and some others, "Behold the Lamb of God!" (John 1:36).

So Andrew became a follower of Jesus, and the first thing he did was bring his brother Simon Peter to the Lord. In fact, every time we read about Andrew, he is always bringing someone to Jesus! If that is all we ever learned about Andrew, what a great pedigree that would be.

In this particular story in John 6, Andrew brings a little boy to Jesus — a boy with a sack lunch.

> There's a young boy here with five barley loaves and two fish. But what good is that with this huge crowd? (verse 9, NLT)

Give Andrew credit. He at least came close! He knew enough to bring this small provision to Jesus but then seems to second-guess himself, saying, "But what am I thinking? What good will this do when the need is so great?"

If only he had followed his first instinct! Right out of the box, the first thing Andrew did was bring this boy and his small supply of food to Jesus. That was the best and wisest course he could have taken, and Andrew came close to taking a step in faith, but not close enough.

Neither Philip nor Andrew is the hero of this story. The real hero is a little boy, and we don't even know his name.

THE LITTLE BOY WITH THE LUNCH

We may not know this boy's name, but we do know this much: He was poor. How do we know that? Because he brought barley bread with him — the cheapest of all breads at that time. Actually, this bread was held in contempt by many people of that day — the kind of food you'd feed to an animal, not to a person.

And then he had a couple of small fish — no doubt little, dried-up things. It's almost as though he was bringing his stale crackers and sardines to Jesus, or his thin sandwich bread and cold lunchmeat. Whatever it was, it wasn't much. It wasn't a gourmet feast, and it certainly wasn't impressive. *But he brought it to the Lord.*

The lunch was as insignificant as it could be. The boy was as insignificant as he could be. But here's the point of the whole story: *What was insufficient from the hands of the insignificant became sufficient and significant when placed in the hands of Jesus.*

Don't make the mistake of thinking you have so little to offer that you might as well not even bring it to the Lord.

God can do a lot—more than you could envision in your wildest dreams—with a little.

And that has to be the understatement of the century.

So I can take my life—my talents, my time, my resources, my abilities, such as they are—and lay it down as an offering before God. Then just watch what He does! I'm no longer the one doing these things; it is almighty God, working in and through me.

TOO BIG . . . OR TOO SMALL?

Getting back to our story, why was it that no one seemed to get the idea that Jesus could feed these people? Was it because it seemed like too big of a task for Him? Yes, that might have been part of it.

But maybe some of them didn't think it was too big of a task, but too *small* of a task for the Lord. In other words, what does God care about something as insignificant as lunch? God cares about great, dramatic, and newsworthy things like raising the dead, restoring sight to the blind, casting out demons, and healing leprosy.

But lunch? Does He really concern Himself with what we eat?

Actually, He does.

In His Sermon on the Mount, Jesus spoke of some basic human needs and said, "Your heavenly Father knows that you need all these things" (Matthew 6:32). He is concerned about what concerns you. And the fact of the matter is, we do think about what we're going to eat. And we do think about what we're going to wear, or where we're going to live. We do think about the necessities of life.

That's not evil. That's not even carnal or fleshly. It's just *human*.

In Psalm 103:14, the Bible reminds us, "He knows our frame; He remembers that we are dust."

Jesus said, "Seek first the kingdom of God and His righteousness, and all these things shall be added to you" (Matthew 6:33).

He knows, and cares, about little details—things you might not imagine God would concern Himself with. He knows your name, your address, your phone number, your fondest dreams that you've never shared with anyone. He knows everything about you. In fact, the Bible tells us that the very hairs of our head are numbered. Now, experts tell us the average person has 100,000 to 200,000 hairs on his or her head. (I have about a hundred, give or take.) But the point is, God knows about every one of those hairs. He knows about every sparrow that falls to the ground.

The psalmist said that God knows about every tear that falls from your eyes. In Psalm 56:8 we read, "You have collected all my tears and preserved them in your bottle! You have recorded every one in your book" (TLB). Jesus shows that nothing is too big for Him to handle, and nothing is too small for Him to care about.

The story goes on:

> Then Jesus said, "Make the people sit down." Now there was much grass in the place. So the men sat down, in number about five thousand. And Jesus took the loaves, and when He had given thanks He distributed them to the disciples, and the disciples to those sitting down; and likewise of the fish, as much as they wanted. (John 6:10-11)

Did you catch that phrase? *"As much as they wanted."*

This wasn't a limited-portion arrangement. No one had to order off the light-eater or senior menu. As the disciples were passing around the food, they weren't required to say, "Please, just take one piece of bread and one piece of fish. Let's make sure there's enough for everyone."

No, there *was* enough for everyone. Jesus made sure of that.

Have you ever been to one of those restaurants that serve so-called "gourmet portions"? You know what I mean. A little pile of half-cooked food in the middle of a plate, with some decorative sauce drizzled around the edges. Two bites, and you're done.

No, thank you! I like food that fills a plate. I like to eat until I'm full.

So here were the people on the shore of the Sea of Galilee. They had been hungry, Jesus was feeding them, and they kept on putting it away until they were full.

"Oh, could I have another piece of that bread? It's so fresh! Tastes like it just came out of the oven. And what is it about that fish? Best I've ever tasted. Just a little more, please."

Where was it all coming from? How was this miracle accomplished? Have you ever tried to visualize how it took place? Maybe you picture Jesus standing with His hands outstretched over these little loaves and fishes and saying, "Be multiplied!" And then, in the blink of an eye, there's this mountain of food.

No, I don't think it was anything as dramatic as that. I think the disciples would go out, distribute a basketful, come back, and there would be more. Then they would hand that out, and there would be more . . . and more and more and more, until everyone was satisfied.

God gives us what we need when we need it, not necessarily before — and never after — but when it is needed.

You might find yourself struggling with some anxious situations in your life right now. And you say, "What would I do if *this* happens?" "How would I ever handle it if *that* happens?" Or maybe, "What would I do if this situation came or this opportunity arose?"

The lesson is simply this: The Lord will give you what you need when the need is there. For right now, He will give you what you need for the moment. Your responsibility is to simply bring your loaves and fishes to Jesus.

"FAN INTO FLAME"

God gives to each one of us certain gifts and abilities, and the simple fact is that gifts don't come from God fully developed. You have to *use* them. You have to apply them. You have to practice and gain experience. Sometimes discovering your abilities and gifts is as simple as discovering what you're *not* good at.

It may be a humbling experience, but a lot of times we simply have to go out there, get our hands dirty in the work of the Lord, and find out what we're not particularly good at. You roll up your sleeves and try things. And after a while, with the help of the Holy Spirit and the counsel of others, you can determine how effective you are at what you do.

Then, after you've worked in several different capacities, you find out, "Hey, this is really working. I enjoy it. People are being blessed. God has made me good at this!" Then take that gift, develop it, and cultivate it.

That is what Paul was talking about when he wrote to young Pastor Timothy, "For this reason I remind you to fan into flame the gift of God, which is in you through the laying on of my hands. For God did not give us a spirit of timidity, but a spirit of power, of love and of self-discipline" (2 Timothy 1:6-7, NIV).

In other words, "Take that ability, take that spiritual gifting, and pursue ministry with all your heart!" God has given to each of us the ability to do certain things well. So get after it! I like the way the J. B. Phillips translation speaks to this in Romans 12:

> Through the grace of God we have different gifts. If our gift is preaching, let us preach to the limit of our vision. If it is serving others let us concentrate on our service; if it is teaching let us give all we have to our teaching; and if our gift be the stimulating of the faith of others let us set ourselves to it. Let the man who is called to give, give freely; let the man who wields authority think of his responsibility; and let the man who feels sympathy for his fellows act cheerfully. (verses 6-8)

The idea is to take the gift God has given you and use it for His glory.

The young boy in John 6 brought what he had to Jesus, and the Lord multiplied it in a way that has had people talking about it for two thousand years. How did the people react? I love the way it's worded in verses 14-15: "Then those men, when they had seen the sign that Jesus did, said, 'This is truly the Prophet who is to come into the world.' Therefore when Jesus perceived that they were about to come and take Him by force to make Him king, He departed again to the mountain by Himself alone."

To me, the whole idea is laughable. Take Him by force? *"Hey, You're going to be our king, whether You want to be or not. We just decided it!"* Why were they doing this? Because these people wanted to use God instead of be used by God.

At this time, of course, they were under Roman occupation—and most loyal Jews wanted their freedom back. They seemed to be reasoning here that if they had Jesus on their side—this miracle worker—they could drive out the Romans.

It wasn't because they recognized Him as the Messiah or because they wanted to submit to His rule and reign. No, they were excited about a leader who could feed them! They were energized by the idea of someone who could work miracles and impress people.

People do this all the time, don't they? They use God for their own purposes. When we enter into an election cycle, we tend to see more and more religious rhetoric from our politicians. We'll hear some politicians talk about their faith in God, and we'll think to ourselves, *Really? I didn't even know they went to church.* You'll see photo ops where they'll be standing in front of a church with a Bible in hand, because they're going after that coveted evangelical vote.

I would simply say, don't be misled.

Just because someone says, "Yes, I'm a Christian. And, oh yes, I believe in God," doesn't mean he's saved. It's more important to look at their lives, to look at their actual voting records, than it is to hear nice Christian words coming out of their mouths.

Salespeople will do this, too. They'll be cussing and using crude language, trying to sell you something. And then if they happen to find out that you're a believer, it's "Hey, praise the Lord, brother!"

A young man might use God in an attempt to soft-talk an attractive Christian girl. He'll claim to have "seen the light," when all he really sees is her. And if she's not wise and careful, she will be deceived.

The fact is, people will use God in an attempt to get what they want. And that's what these people in John 6 were doing. They wanted to take Jesus by force and make Him king. Why? So they could use Him against the Romans. In other words, they wanted Jesus on their terms, not His terms.

His response?

He withdrew from them. He simply walked away from them and all their schemes. God is no genie in a bottle. Jesus will not be used by us. *But He will use us* if we will come to Him and submit our lives to Him.

So what do we learn from this story?

WE NEED TO SHOW COMPASSION TO THOSE WHO ARE IN NEED

Knowing these people were false at heart and would eventually reject Him, Jesus served them anyway. He showed compassion anyway. The miracle in John 6, however, was also a demonstration for the sake of His disciples (and us). In meeting people's physical needs, we're also to minister to their spiritual needs. Jesus showed this very clearly by immediately transitioning from the topic of physical bread to that of heavenly bread, from satisfying a hunger of the stomach to satisfying a hunger of the soul.

Many churches and ministries do wonderful things for people who are in need—feeding them, clothing them, giving them medical treatment, and even building homes for them. There is no doubt that this is Christlike behavior. Come to think of it, I have never seen an atheist relief ministry. Have you? I've never witnessed an agnostic feeding program. On the contrary, these are usually the people who seek to mock, attack, and undermine such efforts. All over the world there are followers of Jesus Christ who have responded to deep physical needs of men, women, and children. It doesn't even matter whether they're from our country or whether they share our faith. We reach out in the name of Jesus to them and say that we care and that we want to help.

But let me add something to that. Any church or ministry that provides relief to people in need but fails to give them the gospel is failing in their mission. This is very important, and it's why I support organizations like Samaritan's Purse with Franklin Graham. It's a relief organization that always brings the saving message of Jesus Christ wherever they go, whomever they serve.

It's a praiseworthy thing to pick people up out of the gutter to feed and clothe them. It does them little good if you simply hand them a gospel tract, say "Jesus loves you," and then walk away.

On the other hand, to simply help people out of the gutter without ever telling them how their lives can permanently change and be transformed by Jesus Christ, and how they can have the hope of heaven in His name, misses the point! Every one of those people that I feed and clothe will have to stand one day before the throne of God and give an account for their lives. Apart from the salvation of Christ, they will be separated from God for all eternity. That is why we can never separate our giving of physical bread to the hungry from our priority of giving them the Bread of Life, who will sustain them forever.

OVERWHELMING NEED POINTS US TO AN ALL-POWERFUL GOD

There always will be situations in life in which you and I will not have the resources or ability to respond. There will be times when we are in over our heads, out of our depth, and beyond our capacity. Such times as these will serve as tests in our lives. Have we really learned anything about walking with a faithful, powerful, loving God? Have we learned to trust Him? Have we learned to walk by faith when the way seems dark before us?

The way to pass such a test is to see your utter inability to do anything on your own.

That's all Philip needed to do. All he had to say was, "Lord, I have no idea how to handle this situation, but You do. And You're here right now. I'm looking to You. What do You want to do about this, Lord?"

Sometimes you and I find ourselves in a set of circumstances that seem absolutely overwhelming, and we'll say to ourselves, *There's no way out of this one!*

Those times will come to all of us: When that unexpected bill or expense pops up and you wonder, *How am I ever going to pay this?* When you have that crisis with your spouse and you wonder, *How will we ever get through this?* When that so-called perfect child of yours gets himself or herself into serious trouble, and you wonder, *How will we ever survive this?* Or maybe you're facing a problem at work that seems so far beyond your capacity to deal with it that you say, *How am I going to make it through the day?*

Can you trust God? You must. God will allow us to enter into situations where the only way out is Him. And then, after He enables us to escape the inescapable and accomplish the impossible, He will get the glory.

NOTHING IS TOO BIG — OR SMALL — FOR GOD TO RESPOND TO

The Bible tells us, "Cast all your anxiety on him because he cares for you" (1 Peter 5:7, NIV).

Which anxieties do we cast on Him? Our anxieties for the mountain-sized problems or the gigantic dilemmas in our lives? Yes, but we're also to cast on Him our anxieties over those little worries, nagging fears, and nettlesome problems that buzz around our heads like a swarm of bees. It's been said that a person can bleed to death from a thousand paper cuts. In other words, the little worries and burdens in our lives, as more and more of them weigh on our shoulders, can bring us down as effectively as the big issues.

He wants all our anxiety. Why? Because He cares for us.

BRING ALL OF YOUR ABILITIES AND RESOURCES TO JESUS

Your talents may seem insignificant to you. Your resources may seem ridiculously small in your own eyes. But God can do so very much with so very little!

Just ask the little boy with the sack lunch, whose meager little snack, in the hands of Jesus, fed a multitude.

10

A SPECTACULAR FAILURE

All of us know what it means to fail.

Some of us have failed quietly, and others of us have failed rather spectacularly.

Sometimes you and I will even fail when we're trying to do something for the Lord. Maybe you tried to share the gospel with someone, and it didn't go so well. They didn't want to hear what you had to say, or it ended up in an argument. Maybe you started a Bible study, only to have no one show up, except your dog. (And he was sleeping.) Or maybe you prayed that someone who was sick would be healed, and they actually got worse.

That has happened to me. A friend of mine who was feeling nauseated said, "Would you pray for me?"

I said, "Of course," and I prayed a wonderful prayer for his healing. Before I could even say

"Amen," however, he ran into the bathroom and threw up.

"Never pray for me again!" he said.

Nevertheless, if you have ever attempted something for the Lord, for His kingdom, and for His glory, only to meet with failure, I question whether you have really failed at all.

I would far rather try and fail than never attempt anything at all. In the greater scheme of things, failure isn't always such a bad thing. Failure usually precedes success because we can learn from our mistakes.

You've probably heard the old expression, "If at first you don't succeed . . ." We all know how that one ends: *Try, try again.* For the purposes of this chapter, however, I'd like to state that in a new way: "If at first you don't succeed, *relax.* You're just like the rest of us."

The fact is, most of us tend to beat ourselves up if we don't hit the ball out of the park every time we're up to bat. What we forget is that by failing or falling short, we learn what not to do so that we can achieve more and more success in the future.

Matthew 14 presents us with a story of a failure. It may be one of the most well-known and spectacular failures of all time. But it also happens to be a story of courage and faith.

And it all begins on a dark and stormy night . . .

Immediately Jesus made His disciples get into the boat and go before Him to the other side, while He sent the multitudes away. And when He had sent the multitudes away, He went up on the mountain by Himself to pray. Now when evening came, He was alone there. But the boat was now in the middle of the sea, tossed by the waves, for the wind was contrary.

Now in the fourth watch of the night Jesus went

to them, walking on the sea. And when the disciples saw Him walking on the sea, they were troubled, saying, "It is a ghost!" And they cried out for fear.

But immediately Jesus spoke to them, saying, "Be of good cheer! It is I; do not be afraid."

And Peter answered Him and said, "Lord, if it is You, command me to come to You on the water."

So He said, "Come." And when Peter had come down out of the boat, he walked on the water to go to Jesus. But when he saw that the wind was boisterous, he was afraid; and beginning to sink he cried out, saying, "Lord, save me!"

And immediately Jesus stretched out His hand and caught him, and said to him, "O you of little faith, why did you doubt?" And when they got into the boat, the wind ceased.

Then those who were in the boat came and worshiped Him, saying, "Truly You are the Son of God." (verses 22-33)

Matthew, the one who captured this exciting account in his gospel, was an eyewitness to it all!

Earlier in this book, we made the point that storms will come into every life. There will be literal, physical storms that hit different areas of the country in different ways — whether blizzards, hurricanes, tornadoes, dust storms, firestorms, or torrential rainstorms.

But storms will come in life as well: hardships, disappointments, crises, and even tragedies. There's no getting around either kind of storm.

In the Matthew 14 account, did Jesus know a storm was coming — that a crisis was in His disciples' immediate future? Yes, He did. And He also knew that He would go to them, walking through the middle of the storm, and that He would be with them to rescue them.

What can we learn from this account?

WHEN YOU FIND YOURSELF IN A STORM, JESUS IS WATCHING

Matthew 14:23 tells us that "when He had sent the multitudes away, He went up on the mountain by Himself to pray." The gospel of Mark, however, adds an important detail: "Then He saw them straining at rowing, for the wind was against them" (6:48).

Jesus was watching them.

I don't know how that hits you. Tell some people that Jesus is watching them, and they'll think, *Oh man I'm in big trouble now!* The reality is that having Jesus watch you in the storms of your life is one of the best things that could ever happen to you. Jesus was watching His guys on that wild, stormy night, and He is watching you as well. They may have lost sight of Him, but He never lost sight of them. He saw them out there on the sea, pitching back and forth. He saw them pulling hard on the oars, fighting that contrary wind. And all the while, up there on that mountain, He was praying for them.

He prays for us, too. In Romans 8:34, we read, "Who then will condemn us? Will Christ? No! For he is the one who died for us and came back to life again for us and is sitting at the place of highest honor next to God, pleading for us there in heaven" (TLB).

Jesus had not forgotten about His friends out there on the crashing sea. And in addition to watching them and praying for them, He climbed down the mountain and walked right through the teeth of the storm to come to them.

JESUS HELPS US IN OUR STORMS

After watching and praying, Jesus came to them. But *when* did He come? At almost the last moment, evidently.

In Matthew 14:25 we read, "Now in the fourth watch of the night Jesus went to them, walking on the sea." When is the fourth watch of the night? That is the last part of the night, just before the breaking of day. That means the disciples had been at sea, struggling in this killer-of-a-storm, for at least nine hours.

Why did He wait so long to come to them? We don't know the answer to that question. To the disciples, He may have seemed late. But God is never late. Was He testing them? Was He waiting for them to completely exhaust their own resources?

That seems likely to me.

Someone has said that when you get to the end of your self, you get to the beginning of God. Many times when you and I face a hardship, we will dust off one of our own plans and try that first. If that doesn't work, we'll go to Plan B, and then maybe Plans C, D, E, F, and G. And then you find yourself in one of those places where you say, "If God doesn't come through for me, it's all over."

Moments like that seem terrible to us, but they may end up being some of the greatest moments of revelation we will ever experience. Why? Because when we come to the end of all our resources, clever plans, and multiple options, God has the opportunity to show His glory in our lives and in our situation.

It wasn't an easy night for those twelve disciples, and they may have longed with all their hearts for Jesus to come sooner. But He came to them when the time was right.

The lifeguard knows only too well the danger in attempting to save a drowning person. More than one lifeguard has lost his life being drowned by the panicked, flailing swimmer he was trying to save. That is one of the reasons lifeguards use flotation devices. They will say, "Here, you hang on to this, and I'll swim ahead of you and pull you back in again."

The Lord knows the right time to step in and help us—and that time may not be when we are in full panic mode, thrashing around, yelling, and fighting anyone who comes near. Jesus came to His men at the last moment, but it was the right moment. And that's what He may do for us as well.

How did He go to them? Verse 25 says, "Jesus went to them, walking on the sea." Now, if I were Jesus, I would have *flown* in. In fact, if I were Jesus, I would flown everywhere. Why walk when you can fly?

But Jesus didn't fly in the course of His earthly ministry. He walked the dusty roads like everyone else, facing weariness, hunger, heat, and cold. But on that particular night, Jesus went to them, walking across the waves. Why did He do that? Perhaps it was to show His disciples that the very things they feared the most in that moment, the wind and the sea, offered only a staircase for Him to come to them.

How did they react when they saw Him? Do we read, "They lifted their hands in praise and adoration"? No, the truth is, they screamed like little girls.

"*Aaiiieee!* It's a ghost!"

Where did they get that idea? Had they been telling ghost stories to each other out on the lake? And why didn't they know it was Jesus?

Because they weren't looking for Him.

If they had been walking by faith and waiting by faith, they would have recognized Him immediately. Instead they jumped to the false conclusion that He was a phantom or some disembodied spirit.

In our own life crises, I think there are times when the Lord comes to us and is speaking to us, but we don't see Him or hear Him because we aren't looking for Him. We don't really expect Him to be there for us.

We have so much chaos, turbulence, and heartbreak in our world today. Instability. Terrorism. War. Threat of nuclear conflict. Earthquakes. Tsunamis. And what did Jesus say we should do in such times? "When these things begin to happen, look up and lift up your heads, because your redemption draws near" (Luke 21:28). In other words, look for Jesus! Don't be overwhelmed by a world in turmoil. Look for God's hand in all these things, and listen for His voice as you read His Word and carve time out of your day to pray and converse with Him.

It's the same in our personal lives. When the winds blow and darkness descends, look for Jesus. Watch for Him. Wait for Him. Cry out to Him. As the Lord told the prophet, "You will seek Me and find Me, when you search for Me with all your heart. I will be found by you, says the LORD" (Jeremiah 29:13-14).

Look for Him! If you are in a crisis right now, look for Jesus, because He is there.

In more than forty years of preaching, I have preached certain truths over and over again (and probably told certain jokes way too many times). I have declared things to people that I know are true, but they haven't all been things I have experienced firsthand. You can only experience so many things in the course of so many years. As time has gone on, however, I find that I am experiencing—literally *living*—the truths that I preached to others for so many years. It's been so glorious for me to realize that all these things I have declared from God's Word are true. As Job once said to the Lord, "My ears had heard of you but now my eyes have seen you" (Job 42:5, NIV).

I have been through many storms, especially over the last four years, and I have seen the Lord in ways I have never seen Him before and known Him in ways I have never known Him before. I have spoken these truths in front of people, but now I have seen them. Now I am experiencing them.

It happened to those disciples out in the middle of that violent sea, just before dawn. The Lord came to them in a way He had never come to them before, and they came to know Him in a mighty way they had never known Him before. That's what will often happen in the midst of a terrible storm. And when it's over, you will say, "Lord, I always knew this was true, but now I know Your help and provision by experience. With my own eyes, I have seen You accomplish what You promised You would do."

It's easy to say to someone who has lost his job, "Just trust the Lord, and He will provide." It's easy to say to someone who is sick, "Just keep praying and trusting, and the Lord will heal you (or help you through this crisis)." It's easy to say to someone who has lost a loved one, "Remember, you will see him or her again in heaven."

That is fine. But what about when these things happen to you? Will you be just as confident? Will your experience match your words? It's been a wonderful realization for me to see that all of those biblical truths I have declared for forty-plus years actually work in real life.

So Jesus suddenly showed up where His men never expected to see Him, and what did He say? "Be of good cheer! It is I; do not be afraid" (Matthew 14:27). The expression *be of good cheer* could better be translated "be courageous."

He was saying, "Come on, guys, man up! You'll be okay. I'm here with you. Take courage!"

Peter was so moved by that statement that he impulsively wanted to prove his courage to Jesus then and there. In verse 28, he said, "Lord, if it is You, command me to come to You on the water."

And the Lord said, "Come."

PUTTING IT ALL ON THE LINE

Give Peter this much: He was willing to put it all on the line.

At this point, the sea was still raging, and the wind was still screaming in the boat's rigging. Yet Peter was willing to literally step over the side of the boat into that wild storm because he was looking at Jesus. And that gave him confidence and courage.

Notice that Peter didn't take this action presumptuously. He didn't say, "Hang on, Lord, I'm coming! Here goes nothing!"

No, he asked Jesus for permission to come. I think Jesus had to smile. How could He not?

"Come on, Peter. Come on over here to Me."

Peter took several steps, and then . . . he sank. Yes, it was a failure, but what a failure! If you're going to fail, this is the way to do it. It was a spectacular, amazing failure, and we're still talking about it after two thousand years.

When you look at all of Peter's *faux pas*, stumbles, and shortcomings in the Gospels, most of them seem to come from a heart that was in the right place. His actions weren't always good, and he didn't always go about things in the right way. But he loved Jesus and wanted to serve Him.

In verse 29, we read, "When Peter had come down out of the boat, he walked on the water to go to Jesus."

What a great moment. He walked on the water. One step? Two steps? Three steps? Who cares? He actually placed his full weight on H_2O and started making tracks across the sea. Whatever follows cannot undo what he actually did. We might find fault with Peter for a number of things, but how many of those other disciples climbed out of the boat? No one but Peter.

It's easy to sit back like proverbial armchair quarterbacks and critique people who step out and try things for God. Many of us are more than ready to criticize people who are out there leading, getting beat up and bruised in the battle, and trying to make a difference for God. We say things like, "I don't really like the way he goes about it." Or, "I don't like the way she leads the Bible study. I think so-and-so would do a better job."

I'm reminded of the story about the famous evangelist Dwight L. Moody, who was once confronted by an irate lady in church. "Mr. Moody," she huffed, "I don't like the way you do your evangelism."

Moody replied, "I don't necessarily like all of it either, but it's the best way I know how. Tell me, how do *you* do it?"

"Oh," she replied, a bit taken aback. "I don't."

"Well," said Moody, "I like the way I'm doing it better than the way you're not doing it."

It's easy to critique, but what have you done lately? What have you risked for the kingdom of God? Have you taken a step of faith? Have you done anything besides critiquing or pouring cold water on other people who have stepped over the side of the boat and tried to walk on water? Again, I would rather see someone try and fail than someone who just sits in their safe, comfortable place and does nothing.

Peter stepped out, and that was a good thing.

Actually, it went well for him for a while . . . until he suddenly began to sink.

WHY DID PETER SINK?

A couple reasons come to mind.

1. Peter sank because he took his eyes off Jesus.

Verse 30 says, "But when he saw the wind, he was afraid" (NIV).

Obviously, you can't see the wind. But you can see what a wild, rushing wind does out in the open sea, and it can make you afraid. In the same way, circumstances in our lives can be very frightening.

Maybe your boss calls you in and says, "I'm sorry, but with the economy the way it is, we have to downsize. You've been a good employee, but I'm going to have to let you go." Or maybe your doctor asks you to meet him in his office. When you're both sitting down, he says, "I don't like what I see on these tests. I'm afraid it's not good news. You may not live very long." You might even have an enemy—someone who has threatened to sue you, harm you, or even kill you.

Those are frightening, devastating things, aren't they? And if you aren't careful, you can start looking around at those scary circumstances and take your eyes off the Lord.

2. Peter sank because he was afraid.

Faith gives way to fear, and trust gives way to worry. Where faith reigns, however, fear has no place. Faith and fear don't get along—not at all!

Do you have people in your extended family who simply can't get along? Maybe you've been at a family reunion and you were careful not to get Uncle Joe and Cousin Clyde in the same room because they argue and fight every time. They're like oil and water and just don't mix.

That is a picture of faith and fear. If you bring in faith, fear walks out the back door. Or if you invite fear in as a resident, faith starts packing its bags.

Peter started out his little walk over the waves with faith—and his eyes locked like glue on Jesus. If he had kept it up, all would have been well. Instead, he started thinking about it. *Hey, this is impossible. Nobody walks on water. This is crazy. Wow, that was a strong gust of wind. Oh no, here comes a big wave!* Turning his attention to the weather, he momentarily turned his attention away from Jesus and immediately began to sink.

It happens in our lives, too, and not necessarily because of the weather. There are any number of life circumstances that can draw our attention away from Jesus. But the result is still the same: We sink just like Peter did.

Could that be happening to you right now? Do you feel yourself sinking? What should you do?

Do what Peter did.

WHEN YOU ARE SINKING, CALL OUT TO JESUS

This is becoming a major theme in this book, isn't it? Cry out to God!

In verse 30, we read, "And beginning to sink he cried out, saying, 'Lord, save me!'"

I love the fact that it says he was *beginning* to sink. He didn't wait until he was four feet under. No, when he felt that water beginning to lap against his knees, he yelled to Jesus. *"Lord, help! Give me Your hand! Give me a snorkel! Anything! Lord, save me!"*

There is no shame in that. Sometimes we might be embarrassed to admit to God that we need help. I've heard people say, "Well, I feel like I ought to work this out myself." How would that have worked out for Peter? No, when you are sinking, you need to immediately cry out to Jesus. And then watch what He can do for you.

Do you think that this failure of Peter's came as a surprise to Jesus? Of course not. The Lord knew all about Peter. He had his number, and He had his number on the day He called him and gave him his new name: Peter, or Rock. But Jesus also knew what Peter would *become*. He didn't just see him for what he was; He saw him for what he would one day be.

That is how God sees you. You and I get obsessed sometimes with our shortcomings and flaws. When we walk in front of a mirror, most of us immediately notice all the things wrong with us. God looks at you and says, "I see what you will become. You just see a blank canvas, but I see a finished piece of art. A masterpiece! You just see a lump of coal, but I see a multifaceted diamond."

Jesus knew very well that Peter would fail — not only out there on the waves, but later, in a moment of great crisis, when he would deny his Master three times.

In fact, Jesus brought this future failure to Peter's attention on one occasion. Jesus turned to Peter and said, "Simon, Simon! Indeed, Satan has asked for you, that he may sift you as wheat. But I have prayed for you, that your faith should not fail" (Luke 22:31-32). A literal translation of verse 31 says, "Satan has been asking excessively that you would be taken out of the care and protection of God."

Can you imagine how frightening that would be? What if Jesus said that to you or me? "Greg, Greg, the devil has been asking for you by name lately, that you would come out of My protection." Oh man, may it never be!

Jesus went on to say to Peter, "When you have returned to Me, strengthen your brethren." Paraphrasing Peter's reply, he said, "When I *return*? I'm not going anywhere! I will go to prison for You, Lord. In fact, I'll take it a step further. I'm ready to die for You, Jesus."

But the Lord devastated Peter with His next words: "I tell you, Peter, the rooster shall not crow this day before you will deny three times that you know Me" (Luke 22:34).

Peter's failure out on the waves that stormy night was no shock to Jesus, and neither is yours. Just as Peter was sinking, immediately Jesus stretched out His hand and caught him, and said to him, 'O you of little faith, why did you doubt?'" (Matthew 14:31).

In the original Greek, those two words translated "little faith" in our Bibles are one word: *littlefaith*. There is almost a tenderness to it, like a nickname. *"All right, Littlefaith, hold on to My hand. You were doing so well! Why did you doubt?"*

Jesus reached down, lifted him up, they got into the boat, and the wind ceased. It doesn't say that Jesus picked up Peter and carried him back. That means Peter walked . . . at Jesus' side, holding His hand.

Not a bad way to move through life!

Sometimes we miss the fact that, yes, Peter had a failure in faith and sank a little, but he also got back up on that water and walked on it with Jesus back to the boat.

Most of us will have our miraculous moments in life—our spiritual highs and our mountaintop experiences. And if we had our way, that's the way life always would be. We would be like Peter, up on top of the Mount of Transfiguration with Jesus, Moses, and Elijah: We would want to build a tabernacle right there on the summit and never come back down again.

But that isn't the way it works. Mountaintops are usually followed by valleys. In fact, it is the mountaintops that *prepare* us for the valleys of life, just as calm waters prepare us for the storms.

So where did Jesus take them? Back to the land again. It wasn't long before they had wonderful terra firma beneath their feet again, and they could rest for a while from their traumatic experience out on the waves.

Are you starting to sink right now? Is your life being flooded with fear, worry, and defeat? Maybe your marriage is in trouble, or perhaps you find yourself in the grip of some relentless addiction. You ask yourself, *What should I do? Struggle through this on my own? Pull myself up by my own bootstraps?*

No. No. No.

Follow the example of "Littlefaith," Simon Peter, and simply cry out, "Lord, save me!" He will never rebuke anyone who is seeking to come to Him by faith.

DON'T LET HIM WALK ON BY

In Mark's version of this story, we're given one very interesting detail: "He came to them, walking on the sea, and would have passed them by" (Mark 6:48).

So let's go back to the story. Here is the storm, raging, with the wind screaming in the rigging, the waves crashing over the boat, and the disciples crying out in fear. And along comes Jesus, walking on the water. But He doesn't walk right up to them as you might imagine. No, it's as though He was walking *by* them, going on His way. He would have walked right past them, but they cried out to Him.

Here's my point: Jesus will not force His way into your life. The simple fact is that not everyone who is in trouble *wants* His help. Not every alcoholic wants to stop drinking. Not every immoral person wants to stop sleeping around. Not every malicious gossiper wants to stop spreading dirt. Some of these people want to keep right on doing what they've been doing.

That is why Jesus said to one man, "Do you want to be made well?"

Maybe he did, and maybe he didn't. Maybe he'd grown accustomed to his way of life and didn't want to rock the boat. The fact is that we can't help anyone who doesn't want help. You can't help a drowning person if he is going to thrash his way right back into deep water again.

Do you really want to be made well? Do you really want to be saved?

If you say, "Yes! Yes! I really want Jesus to help me!" then reach out, and He will take hold of you and help you. He will step into your life, into your world, into your circumstances, and make an immediate difference.

All He's waiting for is an invitation.

11

THE POWER OF PERSISTENT FAITH

What is faith?

Sometimes we make it a little bit too mystical. In reality, faith is something we use every day and apply wherever we go.

When we go into a restaurant, we apply faith when we make that order. We have faith that the kitchen staff (totally invisible to our eyes) will prepare our food properly, use healthy ingredients, and follow normal hygiene standards.

When we board a flight at the airport, we have faith that the plane will get off the ground (despite the fact that it weighs thousands of pounds), there will be adequate fuel in the tanks, and the pilot and copilot have been trained well and know what they're doing.

How much faith do we place in these things?

A very great deal of faith.

We actually place our very lives in their hands!

What about submitting to a surgeon's knife on some procedure we have been told we need? We have faith the surgeon has been adequately trained and knows what he or she is doing. We have faith that our problem was diagnosed correctly and that afterward, the pharmacy will supply us with the right medications in the right dosages.

That's a lot of faith!

The truth is, we apply that faith each and every day. Then Jesus comes along and says, "Have faith in God," and some people balk at that.

"Faith in God? Why, that is outrageous."

But why is it outrageous? People put faith in objects and in other people every day. Why should it be difficult to put faith in our Creator and Savior?

There is no safer place in the universe to put your faith than in God.

BUT WHAT IS FAITH?

In Hebrews 11:1, the Bible defines faith like this: "Now faith is the substance of things hoped for, the evidence of things not seen."

The New Living Translation puts it this way: "Faith is the confidence that what we hope for will actually happen; it gives us assurance about things we cannot see."

I like those words. Faith is a *confident assurance.* It's our title deed to everything God has done for us and provided for us. Sometimes we treat faith as though it were something fragile, like a museum piece or an egg. "Don't jostle my faith! Don't breathe on it! Don't touch it! You might break it!"

No, faith isn't like an egg. Faith is like a muscle that gets stronger through use. As any weightlifter knows, muscles actually build up when you break them down by using them. If you don't use your muscles, they will atrophy. In the same way, faith is something you need to *apply*—put to work—not something decorative you put on top of your bookshelf and dust off every few weeks.

Faith implies movement. It's something that you need to *use*. It is a living, restless thing, always moving toward its object. Faith can't remain inoperative or it will shrivel. We must *use* it.

This is the faith that saves us.

We are told in Ephesians 2:8-9, "For by grace you have been saved through faith, and that not of yourselves; it is the gift of God, not of works, lest anyone should boast."

What saves is faith alone, but the faith that saves is never alone.

In other words, if you have real faith, there will be *evidence* of that faith in your life. I can't determine that you have faith because you say so; I can't see your heart! The only way I can tell that you have faith is because I see the works of faith in your life. I can see your actions. I can see the things that you do. But it is through this faith that we put our trust in Christ.

This is the faith we must live by.

Galatians 3:11 says, "The just shall live by faith." It doesn't say they will live by feelings, nor does it say they will live by circumstances. No, the just will live *by faith*. Faith can make the difference between something happening and not happening.

Yes, God is the one who does the work, but He chooses to accomplish that work primarily through human means. For instance, the Lord could have sovereignly caused the

Red Sea to part for the Israelites without the help of Moses. He didn't really need Moses to stretch out his staff over the water. Nevertheless, God chose to make Moses an integral part of it all. He told Moses, "Raise your staff and stretch out your hand over the sea to divide the water so that the Israelites can go through the sea on dry ground" (Exodus 14:16, NIV).

Could God have brought fire down on the altar at Mount Carmel without the prayer of Elijah? Of course He could have done that. But He called Elijah to take a step of faith and to pray. In front of a great crowd of Israelites, Elijah cried out and said, "Answer me, O LORD, answer me, so these people will know that you, O LORD, are God" (1 Kings 18:37, NIV).

Could Jesus have instantly healed every person who was alive and walked this earth two thousand years ago? Absolutely. In a heartbeat. He could have simply said, "Be healed," and everyone everywhere in the world would have been healed instantaneously. But what we find happening is that it was primarily those who reached out to Him by faith who received His healing touch.

Remember Jairus, whose little girl was dying?

Remember the woman who touched the edge of Jesus' garment?

We also read that Jesus could do no mighty works in His own hometown of Nazareth because of the people's unbelief (see Matthew 13:58). Faith, then, can make all the difference between something happening and not happening.

Without faith it is impossible to please God.

Hebrews 11:6 tells us, "But without faith it is impossible to please Him, for he who comes to God must believe that He is, and that He is a rewarder of those who diligently seek Him."

So the Bible has a lot to say about faith. The Scriptures speak of weak faith, strong faith, bold faith, rich faith, abiding faith, steadfast faith, precious faith, common faith, working faith, obedient faith, and even dead faith. The bottom line is that we want to make sure we are using the faith that God has given us.

In the previous chapter, we spoke about Peter, who had possessed enough faith to climb out of the boat during a storm and walk on the water toward Jesus. But then, as you'll remember, he became afraid of the wind and the waves, took his eyes off Jesus, and quickly began to sink. And Jesus said to him, "O you of little faith, why did you doubt?" (Matthew 14:31).

In the Greek language, as we pointed out, the two words "little faith" are actually one word. So effectively Christ said, "Oh Littlefaith." It was almost like a nickname. "Oh *Littlefaith*, you were doing so well. Why did you doubt?"

In this chapter, we'll look at a woman whom Jesus might have nicknamed "Greatfaith."

"GREAT IS YOUR FAITH!"

She had not been raised as a Jew, growing up knowing the true and living God and the Scriptures, as Peter would have known them. She certainly never had the privilege of walking and talking and sharing meals with Jesus, as Peter had. In fact, the woman in this story was a pagan, raised in a godless home filled with idols.

Nevertheless, she knew a little about Jesus. And with the little she knew, she applied dramatic faith.

In Matthew 15:28 Jesus said, "O woman, great is your faith!"

The Greek word He used for *great* in this verse could also have been translated "exceedingly," "greatest," "high," "large," "loud," or "mighty." I find that interesting. Jesus was clearly an expert on the subject of faith. And He was saying to this pagan woman, "Your faith is amazing to Me. It is a *great* faith." As a result, her faith was enshrined in the pages of Scripture that will last forever. He wanted His disciples—including you and me—to always remember her example.

This woman's exercise of faith began where so much of faith begins: in a time of great trouble and heartache. She had a daughter who had been afflicted by demons. But somehow this troubled, worried mother had heard of the rabbi from Nazareth and that He healed people. It was being whispered that He was the Messiah, the very Son of God, and she believed those reports. So she made her way to Him to seek healing for her girl.

Here is how Matthew records this remarkable story:

Then Jesus went out from there and departed to the region of Tyre and Sidon. And behold, a woman of Canaan came from that region and cried out to Him, saying, "Have mercy on me, O Lord, Son of David! My daughter is severely demon-possessed."

But He answered her not a word.

And His disciples came and urged Him, saying, "Send her away, for she cries out after us."

But He answered and said, "I was not sent except to the lost sheep of the house of Israel."

Then she came and worshiped Him, saying, "Lord, help me!"

But He answered and said, "It is not good to take the children's bread and throw it to the little dogs."

And she said, "Yes, Lord, yet even the little dogs eat the crumbs which fall from their masters' table."

Then Jesus answered and said to her, "O woman, great is your faith! Let it be to you as you desire." And her daughter was healed from that very hour. (Matthew 15:21-28)

Let's consider who this woman was and where she was from.

WHO SHE WAS

Verse 22 says she was "a woman of Canaan." What do you think about when you hear the word *Canaan*? You probably think about the land of Canaan, as it was when Israel first entered the land under General Joshua. The people who lived in Canaan, the Canaanites, were bitter enemies of Israel. So right out of the gate we discover that this woman was a Canaanite, which means she was an enemy of Israel. She was a Gentile, a non-Jew.

Matthew's account said that she lived in the area of Tyre and Sidon, an area of land outside of Israel where the enemies of the Jews lived. Tyre is about twenty-five miles north of Galilee, and Sidon is another twenty-five miles beyond that. This was a long journey and would have taken a considerable amount of time. We think nothing of hopping in our car and driving twenty-five miles away. In Southern California, that's like driving around the block. But this was a journey done on foot. And when you're walking, twenty-five miles is an intimidating distance.

So picture the scene: Here is Jesus, with the momentum building in His ministry. His popularity is soaring, and He has just performed His most stunning, wildly popular miracle to date, the feeding of the five thousand.

And suddenly, He leaves the country.

Jesus leads His men to the area of Tyre and Sidon, twenty-five to fifty miles away. Why? Apparently because He had an appointment to meet a Canaanite woman with a demon-possessed daughter.

Most likely, the woman worshipped Ashtoreth, the goddess of fertility, and other pagan deities as well. No doubt she had known these "gods" all her life. But how much help had they been to her? No doubt she was disillusioned with these false gods, and that's what prompted her to seek out Jesus Christ, the one true God. Somehow, she had heard about Him. She had a basic understanding of who He was and knew that He—and He alone—could touch her poor daughter.

A DEMON-POSSESSED DAUGHTER

How had this woman's daughter become demon-possessed? The Bible doesn't say, but I'm sure it had something to do with all the pagan idols in her home and all of her false worship.

Sometimes parents don't stop to think about the impact of their choices on their children. You have heard the expression "The apple doesn't fall far from the tree." There is truth in that because your children *will* emulate your behavior. Little eyes are watching. Little ears are listening. Adults who drink in front of their kids wonder why their little ones end up with alcohol problems one day. Parents who watch questionable programs on television wonder why their kids end up watching worse on the Web. Or maybe a dad and mom will fight in front of their kids, screaming at one another and using profanity. And then it comes as a shock to them when they see their kids doing the same thing.

It shouldn't surprise us that our kids are watching what we say and do. I heard the story of a father and his young son who were climbing a mountain and came to a difficult and dangerous place on the trail. When the dad stopped to consider which way he should go, he heard his little boy say from behind, "Choose the right path, Dad. I'm coming right behind you!"

That's a good word, isn't it? Make the right choice, Dad. Choose the best way, Mom. There are little ones who are following right behind you.

The fact is that it's easier to build a child than it is to repair an adult. Start early with the training of your children. It is not the job of the public school system to teach your children about spiritual things, and it is not even the job of the Sunday school teacher. It is the parents' job to bring their children up "in the nurture and admonition of the Lord" (Ephesians 6:4, KJV).

Nurture and admonition? That speaks of both sides of parenting: providing limitations, restraint, and discipline as well as love and encouragement. The idea is to give parameters to your children, teach them right from wrong and show them there are penalties for wrong choices, and also provide motivation for them. Stimulate in them a thirst and a hunger for the things of the Lord. The cure for crime is not in the electric chair, it is in the high chair. Start now in training your children in the ways of the Lord.

The mom in this story had raised her child in a pagan home where there had been no teaching about the true and living God. But then she heard about Jesus and learned that He was actually in her area. So she hurried to find Him and seek His help . . . and she wasn't ready to take no for an answer.

Did she have the child with her? Matthew doesn't tell us. All we know is that she brought her biggest fear, her greatest worry, her most profound heartache to the feet of Jesus Christ. And she cried out for mercy.

"Have mercy on me, O Lord, Son of David! My daughter is severely demon-possessed."

And how does the Lord answer this desperate woman? With silence.

Verse 23 says, "But He answered her not a word."

What a curious response. He had made a long, hot journey from Galilee to the Tyre and Sidon area, evidently for no other reason than to meet with this needy woman. And then when she approached Him and asked Him for help, He treated her like she wasn't even there!

Have you ever had that happen to you? Maybe you're in a grocery store and ask for some help finding something, and the employee ignores you. Or maybe you're in a restaurant, needing a fork to eat your food and trying to catch the attention of a waitress. But she walks by you with averted eyes, as if you aren't even there.

Jesus ignored the woman's heartfelt pleas, looking for all the world as though He didn't care at all. Nevertheless, that wasn't the case. He already knew the faith of this woman and knew she would stay with it and not give up easily. Why was He delaying in giving her an answer? It may have been to provide an example for His own disciples. *Littlefaith Peter, are you paying attention? Watch what this woman does! Watch how nothing discourages or deters her!*

The disciples, however, misinterpreted what He was doing. In verse 23 they said to Jesus, "Tell her to go away. . . . She is bothering us with all her begging" (NLT).

How far they were from the heart of Jesus at this point! He wasn't about to send her away. The disciples may have been annoyed or perhaps embarrassed by the way the woman followed them around, crying out for help. But they didn't have a clue what Jesus actually had in mind.

WHY DOESN'T HE ANSWER?

Have you ever had a time when you prayed about something and there was no answer from heaven? Maybe you find yourself in that situation right now. You've been praying, perhaps even with tears, about a certain troubling situation in your life, but it seems as though God isn't even listening to your prayer.

But that is not true. He is listening.

Why, then, hasn't He answered you as quickly as you hoped He would? There might be a number of reasons.

1. A spiritual battle may be raging that you know nothing about.

The Bible teaches there is a supernatural realm functioning right alongside the natural realm that we perceive with our five senses. The wall that separates us from that supernatural world is very thin. And in this unseen spiritual realm, there are events and activities and warfare that we often know very little about.

In the book of Daniel, we read a fascinating story in chapter 10, where we find that the prophet has been praying. Finally, an angel arrives and gives Daniel the scoop on what has been going on behind the scenes.

Listen to this amazing account:

> I heard his voice. At the sound of it I fainted, fell flat on the ground, face in the dirt. A hand touched me and pulled me to my hands and knees.
>
> "Daniel," he said, "man of quality, listen carefully to my message. . . . Don't be afraid. From the moment you decided to humble yourself to receive understanding, your prayer was heard, and I set out to come to you. But I was waylaid by the angel-prince of the kingdom of Persia and was delayed for a good three weeks. But then Michael, one of the chief angel-princes, intervened to help me. I left him there with the prince of the kingdom of Persia. And now I'm here to help you." (verses 9-11,12-14, MSG)

Doesn't it make you wonder what might be going on behind the scenes in your life and your situation? You haven't received the answer to your prayer as quickly as you had hoped. It might be that some spiritual battle has been raging all around you that has delayed God's answer to you. Just remember this: God's delays are not necessarily His denials. Just because the answer to your prayer hasn't come as quickly as you would like doesn't mean it won't come at all. So keep praying.

2. Your prayer may not be answered because there is unconfessed sin in your life.

Nothing will bring a prayer life to a halt faster than unconfessed sin. Psalm 66:18-19 says, "If I had not confessed the sin in my heart, the Lord would not have listened. But God did listen! He paid attention to my prayer" (NLT). Then in Isaiah 59:1-2, we read, "Listen! The LORD's arm is not too weak to save you, nor is his ear too deaf to hear you call. It's your sins that have cut you off from God. Because of your sins, he has turned away and will not listen anymore" (NLT).

If there is sin in your life that you have neglected to deal with, it can put the brakes on answers to your prayers. One of our problems is that we don't want to call sin "sin" anymore. We will call it something else. "Well," we will say, "I have this weakness." Or maybe, "I have my shortcomings." Or perhaps, "I have this sickness in my life." (Everything is a sickness or a disease these days.)

Why don't you call it what it is — a sin?

Why don't you admit it, turn from it, and ask God to forgive you for it?

3. There may be an idol in your life you need to deal with.

If we have idols in our hearts, God may refuse to listen to our prayers. What is an idol? An idol is any person, place, thing, or activity in your life that you have placed before your relationship with God. In Ezekiel 14:3, we read, "Son of man, these leaders have set up idols in their hearts. They have embraced things that will make them fall into sin. Why should I listen to their requests?" (NLT).

Is there someone or something that is more important to you right now — an idea, philosophy, habit, occupation, sport, whatever — than God Himself? Anything that decreases your trust in God and your loyalty to Him could potentially become an idol in your life and keep your prayers from being answered.

This could be something sinful, but it also could be something good. You could make an idol out of your career, your house, your money, your hobbies, your husband, your wife, your children, your boyfriend, or your girlfriend. Of course, there is nothing wrong with any of these things in their proper place. But if that relationship, thing, or activity keeps you from close, daily, intimate fellowship and friendship with Jesus Christ, then it can become an idol.

You can't have another god before the true and living God. Idols can hinder your prayers.

JESUS DREW HER OUT

Why wasn't this woman's prayer answered immediately?

Jesus wanted to draw her out and keep her praying. He didn't put up barriers to keep her away, but to draw her closer. He erected barriers that only genuine, persistent faith could hurdle, and He knew she would rise to the occasion.

Listen to Jesus' puzzling reply to this woman's plea for help: "It is not good to take the children's bread and throw it to the little dogs" (Matthew 15:26).

What? What kind of thing is that to say to someone? It helps to note here that two words are used for *dogs* in Scripture. One refers to the mangy, dirty, roaming packs of dogs that would live off garbage and dead animals — almost like wolves or coyotes.

Years ago I remember being in a developing nation and going out for a run one morning. Almost immediately, I encountered these crazy, psycho dogs. I don't know if they were people's pets, but these dogs weren't playing; they fully intended to bite me. I ran very fast that day!

But that is not the dog Jesus was referring to.

Another word for *dog* referred to a little family pet. That is the word Jesus used. He was saying to her, "It isn't right to take the food from the table and give it to the family pet." (It may not be right, but we do it all the time, don't we?) So Jesus used the word for family pet, but even that wasn't much of a compliment.

I'm pretty sure this woman knew what was up and that Jesus eventually would give her what she needed. I think she could see the love in His eyes rather than hatred or rejection. I think she could hear the compassion in His voice. Perhaps she even detected a little smile.

I love her response in verse 27: "Yes, Lord, yet even the little dogs eat the crumbs which fall from their masters' table."

I think she was playing along, thinking to herself, *I know what You are doing, and I am rising to the occasion. I am not backing down.*

The disciples, I think, were in another zone and completely missed what was going on. This Gentile lady had been annoying them, following them around and crying for mercy. Jesus ignored her, which they interpreted as a rejection. In fact, they were ready to tell her to beat it. Then He started talking to her about little dogs eating the children's bread, and she replied, telling the Lord that at least the dogs get the few crumbs that fall to the floor.

And then . . . their Master turned to this woman, His eyes shining, and said, "Woman . . . your faith is large, and your request is granted" (verse 28, TLB).

What? I can just imagine the disciples staring at each other. *Did I just hear what I thought I heard?* In the blink of an eye, Jesus had gone from effectively blowing her off to giving her carte blanche.

This Gentile woman pressed on and would not be discouraged. When the door was shut in her face, she just knocked at it. When Christ compared her to a dog, she accepted the comparison and asked Him to spare her a few crumbs from His table. She loved her child, and she would not take no for an answer.

What, then, do we learn from this story?

FAITH IS OFTEN FOUND IN UNLIKELY PLACES

It is grace and not place that makes people believers. One would have thought the strongest faith—the kind of faith that amazed the Lord Jesus—would have come from one of Jesus' disciples like Peter, James, or John. But no. It came from this pagan woman.

In fact, the only other time Jesus called out someone's faith as an example was the story of the Roman centurion, another Gentile.

Here's my thought on this: A child can be raised in a Christian home by Christian parents and only allowed to listen to Christian music and have Christian friends and watch Christian TV, and he or she can still end up as a rebel. Sometimes the worst kids around are preachers' kids. Why is that? Because sometimes when we are raised in a Christian environment, we take it for granted. And in the very place where our heart should be transformed, it can become hardened.

It all comes down to the way you listen. Jesus Himself said, "Consider carefully how you listen. Whoever has will be given more; whoever does not have, even what he thinks he has will be taken from him" (Luke 8:18, NIV). You, and no one else, must decide how you will react or respond to what you hear.

The woman in this story was a complete pagan, but when she heard about Jesus, her heart leaped in response and no one, not even Jesus Himself, could turn her aside.

She made the most of what little knowledge she had, and she rose to the occasion.

NO MATTER WHAT, BRING YOUR PROBLEM TO JESUS

Whatever you might be struggling with comes as no shock or surprise to Him. He already knows about it—and in infinitely more detail than you do.

Don't ever get caught up in the false humility that says, "I'm just not worthy to approach God." I hate to break this to you, but you never were worthy. And in your own efforts, you never will be. Just accept it and then get over it. *It is not about worthiness; it is about the grace of God.* Did you think you were *more* worthy when you were reading your Bible every day or praying regularly than you are right now, because you have messed up and entertained an impure thought or said an unkind thing?

Here's the bottom line: I don't approach God on the basis of my worthiness; I approach God on the basis of His grace. So whatever your problem might be, no matter how complicated, twisted, or impossible it may seem to you, bring it to Jesus.

In verse 22 this woman said, "Have mercy on me, O Lord."

She didn't say, "Have justice on me." Don't ever pray that way! If God dealt with you justly, He would send you to hell, because that is what you and I deserve.

So don't ask for what you deserve. Ask for His grace and mercy.

Jesus said in John 6:37, "Whoever comes to me I will never drive away" (NIV).

WHEN YOU ARE SEEKING THE WILL OF GOD, PRAY WITH PERSISTENCE

The reason Jesus gave this woman everything she asked for was because she got her will in alignment with His. Sometimes we want to know the will of God in a certain situation, but we don't know how to pray. The answer is to read the Word of God so that you will understand the heart, the mind, and the purpose of God.

My objective in prayer is not to persuade God to do what I want Him to do. My objective is to get me to do what *He* wants me to do. My job is not to get my will in heaven, it is to get God's will on earth.

Lord, I want Your will in this situation.

So what is His will? Find it, pray accordingly, and don't give up. Sometimes it may seem as though He isn't listening, but that may only be a barrier that He wants you to hurdle.

Rise up in faith, and don't back down.

12

CHILDLIKE FAITH

"Greg Laurie, will you just grow up?"

It was a statement I heard more than once as a child.

Adults usually would say that to me because I was goofing off or pulling a prank or acting crazy.

The truth is, "growing up" is something we all want to do.

When you're a kid, you look forward to growing up. And then after you grow up, you wish you were a kid again! It's funny how that works. When you're a child, you can hardly wait until you're old enough to hang out with the big kids and do the things they do. And then as you get older, you find yourself looking back wistfully on those days of childhood as "the good old days."

Jesus, however, tells us that we are to have the

faith of a child. So how does that work? How can you grow up and still maintain a childlike faith?

That's what we'll think about in this chapter.

JESUS AND CHILDREN

Jesus loved kids during His time on earth — and loves them still.

Some people get irritated when children are being children and start making a lot of noise. But Jesus got irritated when people tried to keep the kids away. Remember how the moms wanted to bring their little ones to Jesus so He could bless them? The disciples shooed them away, saying, "Don't bother Him right now." That's when Jesus made that famous statement: "Let the little children come to Me, and do not forbid them; for of such is the kingdom of heaven" (Matthew 19:14).

He always had time for kids. When He fed the five thousand, He found a little boy and used his small lunch of bread and fish to bless the multitudes. And when He went to the bedside of Jairus's daughter, He said to her, "Little girl, arise" (Luke 8:54), calling her back from the dead.

In Matthew 18, He used a child as an example of what faith ought to look like:

> At that time the disciples came to Jesus, saying, "Who then is greatest in the kingdom of heaven?"
>
> Then Jesus called a little child to Him, set him in the midst of them, and said, "Assuredly, I say to you, unless you are converted and become as little children, you will by no means enter the kingdom of heaven. Therefore whoever humbles himself as this little child is the greatest in the kingdom of heaven.

Whoever receives one little child like this in My name receives Me.

"Whoever causes one of these little ones who believe in Me to sin, it would be better for him if a millstone were hung around his neck, and he were drowned in the depth of the sea." (verses 1-6)

At a place called Caesarea Philippi, Jesus had revealed to His disciples that He, the Son of Man, would soon be betrayed, tortured, and crucified and would rise from the dead on the third day.

Yet even though the disciples had heard those sobering words and had a chance to think about them for a while, they fell back into their old argument of "Who is going to be top dog in the new kingdom?"

Does that strike you as just a little bit insensitive?

Jesus tells them He will soon have to die, and they start arguing about who is the number one disciple.

That would be like telling your friend, "I just came from the doctor's office and found out I'm going to die in one month."

And your friend replies, "Seriously? Could I have your car?"

On more than one occasion, the disciples tuned out what they ought to have been thinking about and became preoccupied with who was the best, who was the brightest, and who was the most successful among them.

It's happening to this day. People still want to know how to be number one, how to climb the ladder of success, or how to come out on top, even at the expense of everyone else.

That was the discussion among the disciples. And when they couldn't come to any firm conclusion, they decided to take the question to Jesus to let Him settle it. So they asked

Him, "Who is greatest in the Kingdom of Heaven?" (Matthew 18:1, NLT).

Jesus, however, bypassed their question and did something completely unexpected. Seeing a small child nearby, He called the little one over to Him and put him in their midst.

Can't you just see it? There was that little one, staring around wide-eyed at all those serious-looking men with beards. I imagine that Jesus gave the child a hug and then said these words: "I tell you the truth, unless you turn from your sins and become like little children, you will never get into the Kingdom of Heaven. So anyone who becomes as humble as this little child is the greatest in the Kingdom of Heaven" (Matthew 18:3-4, NLT).

Jesus was saying, "You need to be childlike."

But what does that mean?

AWE AND WONDER

Children, especially when they are small and before they have learned to look bored, have a sense of awe and wonder. That's why I recommend that you always go to Disneyland with a child rather than with adults. Adults are cynical, gripe about the cost of everything, complain about the food, comment on how things look fake, and remark that it was better in the old days.

Little children, however, take it all in. To borrow the title of a Disney song, it's a whole new world to them. And when they see Mickey Mouse or Donald Duck, they think they are the genuine articles.

It's really fun to see Disneyland through the eyes of a child.

For that matter, it's fun to be around a child who tastes

ice cream for the first time . . . or plays in the snow . . . or wades in the ocean. It gives you the opportunity to rediscover the wonder in some really wonderful things that you've possibly taken for granted for years.

I think that's part of what Jesus was communicating here when He said we should become like little children. He's not saying we should be childish, but *childlike* . . . and there is a big difference between the two.

Being childlike doesn't mean we should be immature. The fact of the matter is, we need to grow up spiritually. In Ephesians 4:14 we are told, "Then we will no longer be immature like children. We won't be tossed and blown about by every wind of new teaching. We will not be influenced when people try to trick us with lies so clever they sound like the truth" (NLT).

So we have to grow up, yet at the same time we still want to be childlike. How does that work?

THE HUMILITY OF A CHILD

"Therefore whoever humbles himself as this little child is the greatest in the kingdom of heaven." (Matthew 18:4)

The twelve disciples were arguing about greatness and who would be the best. So Jesus brought a little child into their midst to illustrate humility. He was saying, "You need to have the humility of a child."

A little child knows he or she needs help. They know they need you to pick them up when they get tired of walking on those little legs. They know that you will be the one who takes them out of the car seat and puts them back in the car seat. They know they need you to change their diaper, cut up their food, help them get into their clothes, or comfort them when they're scared in the middle of the night. They depend on you. They understand that, and they're fine with that.

So Jesus was saying, "Just as a little child is happily dependent on his parent, so you should be dependent upon Me." Referring to their argument, He tells the disciples that the way to be strong is to recognize their innate weakness, and the way to greatness is along the path of humility.

So which would you rather have happen? Would you rather humble yourself or have God humble you? I don't know about you, but I definitely prefer option A. The apostle Peter wrote, "Therefore humble yourselves under the mighty hand of God, that He may exalt you in due time" (1 Peter 5:6).

Jesus said, "Whoever exalts himself will be humbled, and he who humbles himself will be exalted" (Matthew 23:12).

That sounds like a really good plan to me.

I would much rather get down on my knees before the Lord in real humility than, in my pride, have the Lord force me to my knees (or flat on my face). In other words, don't wait for God to humiliate you, perhaps allowing circumstances in your life that will reveal to you and everyone else how weak you really are.

Jesus summed it up clearly when He said, in essence, "Fall on the Rock and be broken, or the Rock will grind you to powder" (see Matthew 21:44).

The first, best step on the road to greatness is to humble yourself like a little child before the Lord.

DON'T EVER CAUSE A CHILD TO STUMBLE

"Whoever causes one of these little ones who believe in Me to sin, it would be better for him if a millstone were hung around his neck, and he were drowned in the depth of the sea." (Matthew 18:6)

The people in our world who have set out to undermine the faith of Christians, especially young ones, will be in for a terrible day of reckoning. God takes these matters very, very seriously. People who would go out of their way to try to challenge, damage, or destroy someone's spiritual life will come into severe judgment. Jesus said it would be better for them if a millstone were tied around their neck and they were thrown into the sea.

What we all need to remember is that we are being watched by young believers every day. Paul told Timothy, "Be an example to all believers in what you say, in the way you live, in your love, your faith, and your purity" (1 Timothy 4:12, NLT). In another passage he says, in essence, "Follow me as I follow Christ" (see 1 Corinthians 11:1).

This is what every Christian should be able to say: *Follow me as I follow Christ.* You might say, "Oh no, Greg, I would never say that. Follow me? No way. I've messed up too many times and made too many mistakes."

I understand that response because I'm flawed too. And I would never say to anyone, "I am a perfect example, and you need to do everything I do." No, I couldn't say that. But I think I could say, "Follow me as I follow the Lord." You and I should be living in such a way that a younger believer could look to our example and find something in us they would want to emulate. Why? Because we are living as examples of what it means to be a genuine follower of Christ in this day and age.

Is your life a stepping stone or a stumbling block? Are you helping people to come to Jesus through your example, or are you driving them away? The truth is that everyone is an example. The only question is, are you a good one or a bad one?

Jesus said, "If your hand or foot causes you to sin, cut it off and cast it from you. It is better for you to enter into life lame or maimed, rather than having two hands or two feet, to be cast into the everlasting fire" (Matthew 18:8). In other words, if there is anything in your life that causes you to stumble, then deal with it. Because if it can cause you to stumble, it can cause someone else to stumble as well.

How do we cause others to stumble? By not caring about them. In Matthew 18:10 we read, "Take heed that you do not despise one of these little ones, for I say to you that in heaven their angels always see the face of My Father who is in heaven." Don't cause these little ones to stumble! Be a good example for your children.

I think of couples who have children and decide to divorce. They will say, "Oh, don't worry about the kids. They're resilient."

Yes, we've heard that before, haven't we?

People can say that all they want, but it *does* hurt the children. It hurts them profoundly. I know from personal experience what it's like, as I saw my own mom married and divorced seven times. Jesus is definitely saying, "Think about the young ones before you make life-changing decisions. Don't put stumbling stones in their path just as they're learning how to navigate life."

It's true with younger believers too. Sometimes we will take our so-called liberties and flaunt them in the face of young Christians, causing them to stumble in their faith.

Paul told us in Romans 14:21, "It is better not to eat meat or drink wine or to do anything else that will cause your brother to fall" (NIV).

You might say, "Well, that's *their* problem."

No, it is *your* problem and *our* problem. Because the Bible teaches that we don't live and die to ourselves. What we do affects other people.

After wrapping up His discussion about being humble like little children in Matthew 18:10, Jesus switched the metaphor and began to talk to them about something even more humble and lowly than a child: a sheep. And a lost one at that.

THE SHEPHERD CALLS A SEARCH PARTY

"For the Son of Man has come to save that which was lost.

"What do you think? If a man has a hundred sheep, and one of them goes astray, does he not leave the ninety-nine and go to the mountains to seek the one that is straying? And if he should find it, assuredly, I say to you, he rejoices more over that sheep than over the ninety-nine that did not go astray. Even so it is not the will of your Father who is in heaven that one of these little ones should perish." (Matthew 18:11-14)

What do we learn from these words?

1. God cares for us as individuals.
Jesus used the picture of a shepherd looking for a wayward sheep, a familiar metaphor found throughout the Bible.

Isaiah 40 says of God, "He will feed His flock like a shepherd; He will gather the lambs with His arm, and carry them in His bosom, and gently lead those who are with young" (verse 11). In 1 Peter 2:25 we read, "For you were like sheep going astray, but have now returned to the Shepherd and Overseer of your souls."

We love that image of God as a shepherd and we as His sheep. But we need to understand that the picture is as revealing as it is beautiful. If you know anything about caring for sheep, then you know they are among the dumbest animals on the face of the earth.

2. As sheep, we have a natural tendency to go astray.

Isaiah 53:6 says, "All we like sheep have gone astray; we have turned, every one, to his own way."

Why do we go astray?

Simple answer: We're stupid, just like sheep.

Do you know how sheep are slaughtered? They follow a goat, known as a Judas goat, that will lead them up a ramp to where they're slaughtering sheep. They'll just get in line and follow the goat to their deaths.

We say, "Man, that is one stupid animal."

But don't we do the same thing? Don't we go astray? Don't we do things that are outright foolish? Don't we try, at times, to run from God, disobey the Word of God, and resist His will in our lives? Of course we do. We go astray and turn to our own way, even though it hurts us and eventually will destroy us. That's just the way we are.

And, by the way, there are plenty of Judas goats out there, ready to lead us to destruction.

What we need to do is follow the Good Shepherd. In John 10:27-28, Jesus said, "My sheep hear My voice, and I know them, and they follow Me. And I give them eternal life, and they shall never perish; neither shall anyone snatch them out of My hand." The word Jesus used in this verse for *follow* means "one who deliberately decides to comply with instructions."

We come to realize that God's plan for us is better than our plan for ourselves and that when He leads us to a different place, it is for our ultimate good. It might not be for our *temporary* good, and it might not make much sense to us at the time. But He has a plan, and if we follow Him and comply with His directions, we always will be the better for it.

Psalm 23 is the classic passage that deals with us as sheep and God as the Shepherd:

> The LORD is my shepherd;
> I shall not want
> He makes me to lie down in green pastures;
> He leads me beside the still waters.
> He restores my soul;
> He leads me in the paths of righteousness
> For His name's sake.
>
> Yea, though I walk through the valley of the shadow
>   of death,
> I will fear no evil;
> For You are with me;
> Your rod and Your staff, they comfort me.
>   (verses 1-4)

He *makes* me to lie down in green pastures. Sheep are so dumb sometimes that they have to be made to do things that will keep them alive. A shepherd will lead them to a green pasture, but if he doesn't guide them on, they'll stay in that one place forever. Even after the grass is long gone, they will huddle in the dirt, continuing to nose around for one last blade of grass. The shepherd has to lead them on to new pastures, whether they want to go or not. He also has to take them to still waters, and *then* they will drink.

3. Despite our wandering, God never gives up on us.

Even though God loves us and has our best interests in mind, we sometimes will go astray anyway. What does the Lord do in those circumstances? Does He say something like this? "Oh well, you win a few and lose a few. That's life." No, that is not what He does. He sends out a search party! He looks for you, longs for you, and waits and waits for you.

In Luke 15:1-7 (a parallel passage to Matthew 18:10-14), Jesus described how a shepherd would leave the ninety-nine sheep in the fold and go searching for the one that went astray. And he keeps looking for it until he has found it and brought it home to safety. That is something you need to know about God. If you wander away from Him, He will keep seeking you, trying to bring you back.

Have you ever lost something of value? I don't know why it is, but I always lose valuable things. I hardly ever lose things I don't care about. If I have a pair of junky sunglasses that are all scratched up, I can't seem to lose them even if I *try*. But if I get a really nice pair that I want to take care of, I'll lose them within three days.

Maybe you have lost a pet and put up posters for it, or you have driven up and down the street looking for it. It is one thing to lose a pet, but it's something else entirely to lose a child.

In one of our out-of-town crusades years ago, our family was staying in a hotel. Jonathan was about five years old at the time. I was walking with him when he spied the elevator and ran ahead of me because he loved to push the buttons. "Wait for me!" I called to him. "Don't get in the elevator until Dad gets there."

But just as I came around the corner, I saw Jonathan standing in the elevator as the doors slid shut. I thought I would have a heart attack on the spot! I pushed every button I could see and waited for the elevator to come back.

Have you ever noticed that constantly pushing the button on an elevator doesn't get it to you any faster? Finally the elevator arrived, but when the door opened, there was no Jonathan.

I took the elevator down to the lobby and ran up to the front desk, where the employee was on the phone. "Excuse me, ma'am," I said. "My little son just got off the elevator—somewhere. Can you call security?" I wanted security, the police, a SWAT team, the Navy SEALs—whoever could help me find our little boy.

But she wouldn't even get off the phone! In fact, she turned her back on me.

I kept saying, "Ma'am, excuse me, excuse me," but I was being ignored. I thought, *Okay, I've got to find him myself.* So I went back to the elevator and pushed every button for every floor, and each time the door opened up, I yelled his name as loud as I could.

I would have torn that hotel apart, room by room, to find him. Losing him was not an option. Well, I did find him. I don't know what floor it was on, but he was just standing there, and I swept him into my arms.

That is the picture—with all its emotional intensity—that we have here in Matthew 18. God will not give up on you. He will seek you out, no matter how far you run. You will never escape His presence.

It's a thought that really gripped David in Psalm 139:

I can never escape from your Spirit!
　　I can never get away from your presence!
If I go up to heaven, you are there;
　　if I go down to the grave, you are there.
If I ride the wings of the morning,
　　if I dwell by the farthest oceans,
even there your hand will guide me,
　　and your strength will support me.
I could ask the darkness to hide me
　　and the light around me to become night—
　　but even in darkness I cannot hide from you.
To you the night shines as bright as day.
　　Darkness and light are the same to you.
　　　　(verses 7-12, NLT)

I have a friend who has some military hardware, including a pair of night vision goggles. Have you ever looked through those? You can go into a pitch-black place, slip on those goggles, and literally see in the dark.

God, however, doesn't need night goggles. He sees you wherever you go. Closing a door won't keep Him out, turning off the lights won't remove you from view, and speaking in hushed tones under your breath won't keep Him from hearing you. He sees everything, He hears everything, He knows everything, and He will never stop searching for you because He loves you.

I love the picture God gives us in the book of Isaiah, when He says, "I have stretched out My hands all day long to a rebellious people, who walk in a way that is not good, according to their own thoughts" (Isaiah 65:2). That's quite an image, isn't it? The Father stands with His arms open,

His hands outstretched, waiting for His people to come home to Him.

4. As our Shepherd seeks us, so we should seek others.

"And if he should find it . . . he rejoices more over that sheep than over the ninety-nine that did not go astray." (Matthew 18:13)

In Luke's version of this teaching, we read, "When he has found it, he lays it on his shoulders, rejoicing. And when he comes home, he calls together his friends and neighbors, saying to them, 'Rejoice with me, for I have found my sheep which was lost!'" (Luke 15:5-6).

This is a beautiful picture of God's carrying us when we have wandered away or fallen. The shepherd wraps the wandering sheep around his neck and brings it back home again.

We read in Isaiah 46:4, "Even to your old age, I am He, and even to gray hairs I will carry you! I have made, and I will bear; even I will carry, and will deliver you."

My grandkids like for me to carry them. They will say to me, "Uppy, Papa," which means, "Pick me up so I don't have to walk anymore." Sometimes, I have to switch them back and forth in my arms because they get a little bit heavy. But they want to be carried, and I love carrying them.

This is the idea: God carries you right through life, even to your gray hairs — or when there is no hair to turn gray!

I have been preaching for forty years and have pastored a church for thirty-eight years. And God has carried me right through it all — the good times and hard times, the setbacks and the victories. I can say with Jacob, "God . . . has been my shepherd all my life to this day" (Genesis 48:15, NIV).

In Luke 15:7, Jesus declared, "There will be more joy in heaven over one sinner who repents than over ninety-nine just persons who need no repentance." Don't ever doubt it! Whenever there is a conversion on earth, there is a party in heaven. As C. S. Lewis once said, joy is the serious business of heaven.

By the way, I do believe people in heaven are aware of what happens on earth. No, I don't think our loved ones are sitting up there in grandstands with binoculars, watching everything we do. But I do believe there is a measure of awareness. This much I know clearly: When someone comes to faith in Christ and repents of his or her sins, the Bible tells us that the news somehow gets all over heaven, and there is joy.

5. God gets excited when lost people come to repentance, and so should we.

If the residents of heaven want to party over the conversion of one person on earth, then we should reflect that same excitement when we hear that someone has come to the Lord.

Sometimes I think we become so absorbed in ourselves and in our own thoughts and plans that we are nonchalant about men and women who find salvation in Christ. We shrug our shoulders and say, "That's great, but I'm already saved. I'm already going to heaven."

I think Jesus is taking on that attitude in this passage. He is saying, in effect, "Quit being so preoccupied with yourselves. Think about all of those lost sheep out there. Think about the little children that I care for."

Sometimes, because I preach in a large Southern California church, some people will slip out of the service early, trying to get to their cars and get a head start on the traffic. Most people know that I always give an invitation for people to receive Christ at the end of my messages, so when they hear me begin to speak of that, they head for the back door.

But that is not a good time to slip out of church. That is a time to be praying with all your heart that people outside of Christ will have their eyes opened, yield to the voice of the Holy Spirit, and give their hearts to Jesus.

Again, in Luke 15:5 we read, "And when he has found it, he lays it on his shoulders, rejoicing."

I believe that is what kept Jesus going, even to the cross. Because He was God, He knew what was ahead: the suffering, the rejection, the agonizing death, and the sins of the world falling on His shoulders. But He refused to turn back. He set His face like a flint (see Isaiah 50:7) and kept going.

How could He do it? How could He press on, in spite of what waited for Him? What was it that motivated Him to keep going? Pause just for a moment to consider these amazing words in Hebrews 12:1-2:

> Therefore we also, since we are surrounded by so great a cloud of witnesses, let us lay aside every weight, and the sin which so easily ensnares us, and let us run with endurance the race that is set before us, looking unto Jesus, the author and finisher of our faith, *who for the joy that was set before Him endured the cross, despising the shame, and has sat down at the right hand of the throne of God.* (emphasis added)

It was joy that drove Him on—the joy that was set before Him. What was that joy? It was you. It was me. It was all those who would receive His forgiveness and the promise of heaven through the ages to come. We were the joy. We were the prize. We were the treasure.

And He gave up all He had to obtain it.

HOW TO STAY CHILDLIKE

One of the things I love most about being a grandfather is the chance to get down on the floor, play games with my grandkids, and just be silly for a while. They laugh, I laugh, and people watching us probably laugh, too.

Being around children is a great way to stay young at heart.

In the same way, it's a good thing to be around young believers, too. They need you, and you need them. The young believer needs your stability, your experience of walking with Christ through the years, and (hopefully) your knowledge of the Word of God. But you need them, too. You need to share that sense of excitement and freshness they experience as they discover the truths of God for the first time.

We need each other. In His Great Commission, Jesus commanded us to go into all the world and make disciples of all nations, teaching them to observe all things that He has commanded us (see Matthew 28:19-20). Our job description as followers of Jesus is to go after lost sheep, try to win them to Christ, take them under our wing, help them get up on their feet spiritually, and then go out and repeat the process again and again and again.

Yes, we all have our shortcomings, and no mature believer wants to be a stumbling block to younger Christians. *So don't be!*

Live your life alongside young Christians, and if you mess up, tell them so and apologize. Then keep going.

You really can say, "Follow me as I follow Christ."

Just make sure that you are really following Him.

13

HOW TO PRAY (AND HOW NOT TO PRAY)

I love praying with kids.

They haven't quite got it figured out yet, so the results can be touching—or outright hilarious. Sometimes their prayers are as heartfelt and sincere as can be. At other times you'll see them cheating or not praying at all.

I was praying with my granddaughter Stella the other day before our meal. I said, "Let's pray." As we were praying, I glanced at her. She had her eyes closed, but she was stuffing food in her mouth like there was no tomorrow. I guess she figured that as long as her eyes were closed, it was okay.

What a wonderful privilege we have to come before the Lord in prayer. We can pray anytime, anywhere, under any circumstances. We might think the most spiritual place to pray is in a church, and yes, church is as good a place as any. But the fact is, you can pray anywhere at all. Paul prayed when he was in a dungeon in chains. Daniel prayed in a cave filled with hungry lions. Peter prayed on the surface of the water. And Jonah? He prayed *under* the water. So wherever you are, you can pray.

Sometimes we might attach a lot of churchy-sounding verbiage to our prayers, hoping that our eloquence will add some weight to our words. Or we might attach length to our prayers, saying the same things over and over, hoping it might hold God's attention.

The truth is, God doesn't care about those things. He's not really interested in how eloquent you are, nor is He impressed by the length of your prayers. I personally think our prayers in private should be long, and our prayers in public should be short.

Do you know the shortest prayer in the Bible? We saw it a few chapters back, when Peter walked on water, became distracted, and started to sink. He yelled out, "Lord, save me!" (Matthew 14:30).

Notice that Peter didn't use a great amount of eloquence, praying, "Oh great, omniscient, all-powerful, all-loving Father . . ." He would have been about twenty feet down before he got to the point of his prayer.

No, sometimes "Lord, save me!" is good enough.

WHY SHOULD WE PRAY?

We might find ourselves wondering, *What's the objective of praying? Am I really telling God anything He doesn't already know? Am I actually going to convince God to do something He doesn't necessarily want to do?*

The answer to those two last questions is no. God knows all things, and God will do what He wants to do.

So why should we even pray?

Prayer should be thought of as a relationship between a father and child. Prayer's value is that it keeps us in touch with God, keeps us walking and talking with Him through the days of our lives. Have you noticed that God doesn't give us everything we need for every situation all at once? We might think that would be nice, but in reality, it would be dangerous. If God were to give us all of His glorious gifts in one lump sum, we would find ourselves in danger of enjoying the gifts and forgetting the Giver.

God gives His gifts and His provision to us as we need them—which keeps us dependent on Him, exactly as we need to be. We were created to be dependent on God, and that is what gives us the greatest joy and fulfillment in life. As Jesus put it, we're the branch attached to the Vine. If we stop drawing on His life, then we will begin to wither and die.

We need to be coming back each day for God's help, "so that we may receive mercy and find grace to help us in our time of need" (Hebrews 4:16, NIV).

Maybe you had a stingy father, and it somehow colored your view of God, your heavenly Father. I heard about a boy who had just gotten his driver's license and wanted to drive the family car.

His dad said, "I'll tell you what, son. I'll make a deal with you. If you get straight As in school for this semester, keep your room clean, do the yard work, take the trash out every week, and finally get your hair cut, I'll let you drive the family car."

So the boy came back in a few months and had done the things his dad had asked him to do. He had diligently performed all the household chores and brought his grades up to straight As.

"You've done well, son," his dad said. "But what about your hair? I notice that you didn't get your hair cut."

"But, Dad," his son protested, "Jesus had long hair."

His father replied, "That's true. And Jesus walked everywhere He went."

The boy got his hair cut.

Thankfully, we don't have a stingy dad. We have a Father in heaven who loves us and loves to bless us, lavishing gifts upon us. He is more than generous. Jesus said, "Do not fear, little flock, for it is your Father's good pleasure to give you the kingdom" (Luke 12:32). So we come to Him day after day, seeking His blessing, seeking His provision, enjoying His presence, and drawing on His life.

The principal objective of prayer is to get my will into alignment with God's will. Once that takes place, I will see my prayers answered more often in the affirmative.

Jesus summed it up like this in John 15:7: "If you abide in Me, and My words abide in you, you will ask what you desire, and it shall be done for you." What a great promise! And what is His condition for fulfilling that promise? I need to abide in Him, letting His Word abide in me. Another way to translate this verse would be, "If you maintain a living communion with Me and My Word is at home with you, you will ask at once for yourself whatever your heart desires, and it will be given."

If I am truly maintaining that living communion with Him and spending time in His Word, allowing it to change me and shape me, then it will have an impact on the things I pray for. True praying is not overcoming God's reluctance; it is taking hold of His willingness.

This brings us to Matthew 20 and two very different scenarios of prayer. Interestingly, both of these prayers begin with the Lord's saying, "What do you wish?"

HOW *NOT* TO PRAY

Imagine if God came to you and said, "I will give you whatever you want."

What would you ask for?

In Matthew 20, a mother came before Jesus with a request for her sons. This was a mother who evidently loved her sons very much and was ambitious for them. But what she asked for was completely inappropriate.

> Now Jesus, going up to Jerusalem, took the twelve disciples aside on the road and said to them, "Behold, we are going up to Jerusalem, and the Son of Man will be betrayed to the chief priests and to the scribes; and they will condemn Him to death, and deliver Him to the Gentiles to mock and to scourge and to crucify. And the third day He will rise again."
>
> Then the mother of Zebedee's sons came to Him with her sons, kneeling down and asking something from Him.
>
> And He said to her, "What do you wish?"
>
> She said to Him, "Grant that these two sons of mine may sit, one on Your right hand and the other on the left, in Your kingdom."
>
> But Jesus answered and said, "You do not know what you ask. Are you able to drink the cup that I am about to drink, and be baptized with the baptism that I am baptized with?"
>
> They said to Him, "We are able."
>
> So He said to them, "You will indeed drink My cup, and be baptized with the baptism that I am baptized with; but to sit on My right hand and on My left is not Mine to give, but it is for those for whom it is prepared by My Father." (verses 17-23)

Verses 17 to 19 in Matthew 20 contain the third prediction of Jesus' death and resurrection. Every time He spoke about it, He revealed a little bit more of what would take place. In Matthew 16, for instance, He revealed that He would be mistreated by the elders and chief priests and teachers of the law, would be killed, and would rise again on the third day. In chapter 17 He mentioned there would be a betrayer, and one of His own would be involved in this act of crucifixion. Now in chapter 20 He reveals that He will be turned over to the Gentiles, who would mock Him and flog Him, and He would die specifically by crucifixion.

This was a major revelation that Jesus was dropping on His disciples. What does this show us? It shows us that God will tell us what we need to know when we need to know it. As they say in the military, you and I are on a need-to-know basis. There may be times when we long to know more, but God says, "You don't need to know those things right now."

In this chapter, Jesus took His twelve disciples aside on the road and gave them more specific information about what He and they would be facing in the days to come.

But they weren't getting it.

At that point, the disciples didn't show much interest in floggings or crosses. In fact, they still thought Jesus intended to establish His kingdom on earth.

So along comes the mother of James and John (Salome, as we learn from other passages), who offers this prayer: "In your Kingdom, please let my two sons sit in places of honor next to you, one on your right and the other on your left" (verse 21, NLT).

Why was this such a bad prayer?

Because it was utterly selfish.

From Mark's telling of the story, we deduce this wasn't just Salome's idea, and that James and John were in on it, too. Also in Mark's version, we learn they prefaced their request with the words "Teacher, we want You to do for us whatever we ask" (Mark 10:35). In phrasing their question, they were basically asking for a blank check, with no limitations whatsoever. But God would very rarely give such an option to a believer. In fact, it would be disastrous. It would be like letting a four-year-old drive your car. He wouldn't have any idea how to go forward or backward or stop. If God gave us carte blanche, we would invariably ask for the wrong things — hurtful things.

Jesus essentially responded to this reckless request with "What do you want? Let Me hear your request first before I respond to that."

God did give that privilege to Solomon, when he was a young man just ascending to his father David's throne. He came to Solomon at night and said, "What do you want? Ask, and I will give it to you!" (1 Kings 3:5, NLT).

Solomon's wise answer to that offer showed that his heart (at that time) was in the right place — which is probably why God gave him such a privilege. In essence, he replied, "Lord, I need Your help. I feel like a little child here with a great big kingdom to run, and I really don't know what I'm doing. I need wisdom to rule Your people." God gave him what he asked for that night, and much, much more.

In the same way, we should humble ourselves before the Lord and say, "Lord, I want what You want for my life even more than what I want."

In fairness to James, John, and their mom, Salome, they at least prayed, bringing their request to Jesus. That much was commendable. Even so, their request was entirely self-centered, and their timing was terrible. How insensitive could you possibly be?

Jesus had just revealed that He would soon die by crucifixion, one of the most horrific, agonizing executions imaginable. Everybody knew what that meant. Crucifixion wasn't designed to merely end a life; it was a very slow death, designed to inflict the maximum amount of torture on a person. It was also designed to humiliate, as the crucified person would be hanging on a cross by the side of a Roman road for all to walk by, mock, and laugh at.

So this was a selfish prayer, to say the least, and offered at a very inopportune moment.

Jesus responded with a powerful question of His own in verse 22: "You don't know what you are asking! Are you able to drink from the bitter cup of suffering I am about to drink?" (NLT).

They replied, "We are able!"

You would think they might have paused for a moment before answering the Lord's question. Before saying, "Oh yes, we're able," they might well have asked, "Umm . . . what cup are You talking about here? Maybe You should define this cup before we say yes."

But they answered quickly, even though they had no idea what they were asking for.

We know, of course, that Jesus was referring to the cup filled with the wrath of God that He would have to drink as He hung on the cross, taking upon Himself the sin of the world. Jesus would recoil from this very cup in the Garden of Gethsemane, where His sweat would become like great drops of blood, as He prayed, "My Father, if it is possible, let this cup pass from Me" (Matthew 26:39).

Even Jesus didn't want to drink this cup. But He had to in order to absorb the wrath of God on our behalf.

James and John really had no idea, but they both piped up, saying, "Yes, we want that. We're all in. We're ready."

When the other disciples heard about this, they were angry. We read in verse 24, "And when the ten heard it, they were greatly displeased with the two brothers." Were they displeased because it was such a selfish, insensitive, ill-timed request? Perhaps. But the more likely reason was they wished they had thought of it first.

I was with my granddaughters the other day, and one of them had a birthday. One of the presents was a little electric Jeep, just big enough for a child to sit in and drive. Before long, however, two girls began to fight over who would drive the Jeep and where each of them would sit. So what was supposed to be fun turned into a big conflict, complete with tears.

That's human nature, isn't it? When we're little, we fight over toys. When we get a little bit older, we fight over a spot on the team, or we fight over a certain guy or certain girl. Before long, we're fighting over a position in the company or a seat on a plane. As the book of James says, "You want what you don't have, so you kill to get it. You long for what others have, and can't afford it, so you start a fight to take it away from them" (James 4:2, TLB).

That's exactly what the disciples were doing. They were fighting about place and status and privilege, and their hearts were in the wrong place.

Thankfully, Jesus did not answer the prayer of Salome. As she would soon see, the right spot and the left spot in Jesus' immediate future were not thrones, but crosses. In fact, to her credit, the Bible says that Salome did stand at the foot of Jesus' cross, along with Mary, the mother of our Lord, and Mary Magdalene. And when she looked up, it wasn't her sons on the right and the left of Jesus; it was two criminals, dying on their own crosses.

I'm reminded of the Garth Brooks song that says,

"Sometimes I thank God for unanswered prayers."

Amen to that! We can thank the Lord again and again for not giving us what we asked for at various points in our lives, because we really didn't know or understand what we were asking for or what damage and destruction it would cause in our lives.

God is good, and so very much more loving than we could begin to understand.

If, then, Salome's request was the wrong way to pray, what is the right way? Matthew 20 has the answer to that question as well.

THE RIGHT WAY TO PRAY

Now as they went out of Jericho, a great multitude followed Him. And behold, two blind men sitting by the road, when they heard that Jesus was passing by, cried out, saying, "Have mercy on us, O Lord, Son of David!"

Then the multitude warned them that they should be quiet; but they cried out all the more, saying, "Have mercy on us, O Lord, Son of David!"

So Jesus stood still and called them, and said, "What do you want Me to do for you?"

They said to Him, "Lord, that our eyes may be opened." So Jesus had compassion and touched their eyes. And immediately their eyes received sight, and they followed Him. (Matthew 20:29-34)

Jesus was on His way to Jerusalem to die on a cross. His heart was heavy. He had just dropped the bombshell that He would be crucified, and He knew the end was near.

Yet think of it. He took time for these two men alongside the road who had a great need. In fact, when He heard their cries, the Bible says that He stood still, listening. It reminds me of a mother who hears the particular sound of her child's cry and stands still to listen. This is just another reminder that God is never too busy for you. You might think the Lord has so much going on in the universe and here on earth with the billions of people. And yes, it's true, He does have a great deal to do, but you are His child and He always has time to hear your prayer.

David was the author of many psalms, including Psalm 8. He was probably sitting out in the pastures one night, just taking in all the glory of God's creation, staring up at the Milky Way, gazing at the moon. And he wrote this down in his journal: "When I look at the night sky and see the work of your fingers — the moon and the stars you set in place — what are mere mortals that you should think about them, human beings that you should care for them?" (verses 3-4, NLT).

It's a good question. Why would God care about me? Why would God care about you? I have no idea . . . but I know that He does because He says so. If something concerns you, it concerns Him, too. If it is a burden to you, then (in effect) it's a burden to Him, too, that He wants to deal with and resolve.

These were two men in need, Jesus was walking by, and their opportunity was at hand.

So what do we learn about right praying in this account?

1. They prayed.

That's where everything starts. They didn't think about praying or talk about praying or have a Bible study on praying. They just prayed, crying aloud to Jesus. They didn't miss the opportunity to bring their need to His feet. It has been said that if your knees are knocking, kneel on them. That is what you need to do when conflict comes your way. Philippians 4:6-7 says, "Don't worry about anything; instead, pray about everything. Tell God what you need, and thank him for all he has done. Then you will experience God's peace, which exceeds anything we can understand" (NLT).

That is the objective of prayer: to get my will in alignment with God's will and to put me in touch with the Father who loves me.

In his excellent book *How to Pray*, R. A. Torrey wrote, "Prayer is God's appointed way for obtaining things, and the great secret of all lack in our experience, in our life and in our work, is the neglect of prayer."[1]

Now, that is not all that prayer is for. But it's certainly one of the things prayer is for. James 4:2 is very clear about that: "You do not have, because you do not ask God" (NIV).

So what are you facing in your life right now? A conflict? A physical need? A spiritual struggle? A need for wisdom? Financial problems? Relationship issues?

Have you prayed about it?

Have you laid out your situation in detail before the Lord and said, "Lord, here is my problem. Here is my need. And I am bringing it before You right now."

Ephesians 6:18 speaks of "praying always with all prayer and supplication in the Spirit, being watchful to this end with all perseverance and supplication for all the saints." Look how many times the apostle Paul used the word *all* in this verse: "with *all* prayer . . . with *all* perseverance . . . for *all* the saints."

The southern translation would be "Y'all ought to be praying all the time, y'all." This is really what Paul was saying. Pray all the time. Never get discouraged. Never give up. Never back off.

2. They prayed with passion and persistence.

Acts 12 tells the story of a crisis situation in the young church. James, the brother of John, was put to death by King Herod. That act scored so many favorability points with the Jewish leadership that the king went out and arrested Peter. Clearly, he intended to execute Peter as well.

So what did the church do? Yes, they prayed. But they didn't just pray any old prayer. They prayed with great passion.

Acts 12:5 tells us, "But while Peter was in prison, the church prayed very earnestly for him" (NLT). The phrase *prayed very earnestly* carries with it the idea of being stretched outwardly, as though reaching for something.

Have you ever dropped something in your car while you were driving, tried to reach for it, but found it was just out of reach? That is how they were praying. They were stretching themselves out before God, praying with all their hearts. There was nothing casual or routine about it. This was a storm-the-gates-of-heaven entreaty for their apostle and friend, and they weren't backing down.

This is the same word that is used of Jesus in Luke 22:44, where it says that "being in anguish, he prayed more earnestly, and his sweat was like drops of blood falling to the ground" (NIV).

This is the kind of prayer that prevails with God—prayer in which we pour out our soul, reaching out toward God in agonizing desire. Much of our praying has no power in it simply because we put so little heart in it.

So you say, "I prayed about something."

Did you? How many times?

"Well, umm, maybe twice. I kind of figured that would cover it."

That is not the way the church prayed for Peter, and that is not the way these two blind men called out to Jesus for help. They put everything they had into their prayers.

Sometimes we will pray about something, and when the answer doesn't come right away, we conclude that God is saying no. That may be the case. But then again, maybe He wants us to keep on praying—to pray with passion and persistence.

Coming back to the two blind men in Matthew 20:31, we read, "The multitude warned them that they should be quiet; but they cried out all the more, saying, 'Have mercy on us, O Lord, Son of David!'"

I love that.

The crowd told them to shut up, so they yelled all the louder. They stayed with it and refused to be muzzled or shut down. They knew that Jesus was coming by, and nothing was going to keep them from screaming out their appeal as loud as they could.

And guess what? Jesus heard their prayer. In fact, as I mentioned earlier, their prayer stopped Jesus in His tracks:

> Jesus stood still and called them, and said, "What do you want Me to do for you?"
>
> They said to Him, "Lord, that our eyes may be opened." (verses 32-33)

This story reminds us that when we passionately cry out to God by faith, He will hear us. In Psalm 50:15, God says, "Call upon Me in the day of trouble; I will deliver you, and you shall glorify Me."

In one modern translation of Jeremiah 29:13, the Lord says, "When you come looking for me, you'll find me. Yes, when you get serious about finding me and want it more than anything else, I'll make sure you won't be disappointed" (MSG).

3. Jesus answered their prayer in the affirmative.

Sometimes when we say that God hasn't answered our prayers, we're not being truthful. It may be that He did answer, but we just didn't like the answer!

God answers prayer in one of three ways: yes, no, and wait.

The fact is, He may have a very good reason for the trial or hardship that has come into your life, and He wants you to go through the challenge of facing it with His help. In the book of 2 Corinthians, we read that the apostle Paul came to the Lord with a very troubling physical problem. We don't know what it was, but most commentators believe it was either a disability or an injury that he had incurred in his preaching. Through his years as an apostle and missionary, the apostle Paul absorbed more vicious hits than an NFL running back with a twenty-year career. He had been imprisoned, shipwrecked, scourged, beaten with rods, and even stoned and left for dead.

No doubt he had some lingering injuries and one in particular that really bothered him and cramped his style. He prayed about it and basically said, "Lord, please take this away from me." Paul brought this to the Lord on several occasions.

But the Lord said, "My grace is sufficient for you" (2 Corinthians 12:9).

Sometimes, then, God chooses not to take away our adversity because He wants us to grow through it. He may answer our prayer, not with yes or no but with *grow*.

In the case of the two blind men in this chapter, however, God didn't say no or grow; He said *go*: "Jesus had compassion on them and touched their eyes. Immediately they received their sight and followed him" (Matthew 20:34, NIV).

THE BARRIER OF UNBELIEF

These two blind men had no doubt whatsoever about Jesus' ability to heal them. They cried out to Jesus with absolute confidence that He *could* heal them if He *would* heal them.

Faith sees what could be, even if those things happen to be invisible at the moment. It's not just passive intellectual assent; it is action. It is stepping out and acting on the basis of what we believe. Another way to say that? Faith is a consent of the will to the assent of the understanding.

Can you see what could be right now? Then start praying about it and use a little faith.

Think about this: Would these two blind men have been healed if they hadn't called out to Jesus? If they had just sat there in silence along the Jericho road, would the Lord have stopped and turned toward them and touched them? Perhaps. But then again, there must have been scores of blind people, deaf people, and men and women with all kinds of physical problems who crossed paths with Jesus during His earthly ministry.

But He didn't heal them all, did He?

In fact, we usually find that *He responded to the person who called out to Him*. So in this case, the two blind men refused to let Jesus just walk on by without crying out to Him in their need. The people told them to shut up, but they wouldn't shut up. They believed, and they were persistent. And they went home that night with twenty-twenty vision.

What is your need? Do you need a touch in your body like the two blind men? Call out to Jesus. Do you have a child who needs help, like the Canaanite woman did? Cry out to Him, and don't give up or become discouraged if the answer doesn't come right away.

Jesus said, "Keep on asking, and you will receive what you ask for. Keep on seeking, and you will find. Keep on knocking, and the door will be opened to you" (Matthew 7:7, NLT).

14

WHAT'S YOUR EXCUSE?

Deception starts very early in life.

Before a six-month-old child can even say one word, he learns how to engage in fake crying. Even though there's nothing really wrong with him, he understands that Mommy will come running if he cranks up the volume and starts screaming.

It's all downhill from there. In our natural state, all of us are well-versed in deceit. In Jeremiah 17:9, the Lord set it down in plain language when He said, "The heart is deceitful above all things, and desperately wicked; who can know it?"

One of the most subtle outgrowths of that tendency to deceive is the fine art of excuse making.

What's the difference between a lie and an excuse?

Frankly, not all that much.

An excuse has been defined as the skin of a reason stuffed with a lie. Or put another way, an excuse is a lie all dressed up for dinner. But it's still a lie. A fancy lie, if you will, but a lie nonetheless.

WHY DO WE OFFER EXCUSES?

Why do we do it? Why do we rely on excuses rather than reasons?

A reason is what we offer when we are unable to do something. An excuse is what we offer when we don't *want* to do something and hope to get out of it. It has been said that he who excuses himself accuses himself.

We all know an excuse when we hear one, don't we?

We may smile and nod our head at the person making the excuse or even try to look sympathetic. But inside we're thinking, *I'm not really buying this. This is just an excuse.*

There is one person in my life who is always late to our appointments and meetings. Every time he shows up, it's always with the same excuse: "There was a lot of traffic."

This is L.A., and he's right: There *is* a lot of traffic. But why does everyone else always make it to the meetings on time?

Or someone might say, "I'm sorry I didn't turn the assignment in. My dog ate my homework." I would like to know if a dog anywhere on earth, ever in human history, literally ate someone's homework. It sounds pretty sketchy to me.

Or how about this one? "Sorry I'm late. My alarm didn't go off." I never used to believe that one until it happened to me last Easter Sunday. We had a very, very early sunrise service, and the pastor was just a little bit late. I didn't even have the heart to tell everyone the reason because it's the oldest excuse in the book!

Lying, deception, and phony excuses have become far too common in our culture. Studies show that most résumés are full of misrepresentations. Seventy-one percent of applicants will increase the tenure of their previous job. Sixty-four percent will exaggerate their accomplishments. Sixty percent will overstate the size of the department they managed. Fifty-three percent will cite partial degrees as full. And 48 percent will inflate their salary history. Studies also show that one-quarter to one-third of all workers tell lies to explain their tardiness or absence.

Do you see how easy it is to stretch the truth a little?

When it comes to lame, deceptive excuses, we have all heard them — and probably used them. George Washington (the same guy who supposedly said, "I cannot tell a lie") once said, "It is better to offer no excuse than a bad one."

One of my all-time favorite excuses in the pages of the Bible is what Aaron said once to his brother, Moses. God had called Moses to climb up Mount Sinai to receive the Ten Commandments, and Aaron was left in charge of the Israelites. When Moses was gone a long time, the people became restless and frustrated. They told Aaron, in essence, "We don't know where Moses is. We want gods to worship." Instead of standing strong and discouraging this, Aaron immediately caved, saying, "Bring all of your gold earrings to me." He melted those thousands of gold earrings into the shape of a calf, put it up on a pedestal, and told everyone that this was a feast to the Lord.

Meanwhile, up on Mount Sinai, Moses had been bathing in the glory of God and watching the finger of the Lord write His commandments on tablets of stone. On his way back down, he heard a noise in the camp. Was it a battle? Had a war started? No, it was an *orgy* — the biggest party of all time.

When Moses, accompanied by Joshua, came in view of the camp, they saw the Israelites dancing naked before a golden calf.

When Moses demanded an explanation from his brother, Aaron's story went like this:

> Don't get upset. . . . You yourself know how evil these people are. They said to me, "Make us gods who will lead us. We don't know what happened to this fellow Moses, who brought us here from the land of Egypt." So I told them, "Whoever has gold jewelry, take it off." When they brought it to me, I simply threw it into the fire — and out came this calf! (Exodus 32:22-24, NLT)

It's as though he was saying, "So what else could we do but strip off our clothes and worship it?"

Apparently animals can offer excuses, too. I read recently about Coco, a gorilla that uses sign language to communicate. Coco must have had a bad morning not long ago, because she tore the sink off the wall in her pen. When the trainers came to see what happened, Coco used sign language to indicate that her pet kitten had done the damage. "Cat did it," she signed. (I like that story so much that I almost titled this chapter "Cat Did It.")

In Matthew 22, Jesus told a parable that featured the great generosity of a king and the flimsy excuses of those who rejected and misused his kindness.

THE GREAT BANQUET

> Jesus answered and spoke to them again by parables and said: "The kingdom of heaven is like a certain king who arranged a marriage for his son, and sent out his servants to call those who were invited to the wedding; and they were not willing to come. Again, he sent out other servants, saying, 'Tell those who are invited, "See, I have prepared my dinner; my oxen and fatted cattle are killed, and all things are ready. Come to the wedding."' But they made light of it and went their ways, one to his own farm, another to his business. And the rest seized his servants, treated them spitefully, and killed them. But when the king heard about it, he was furious. And he sent out his armies, destroyed those murderers, and burned up their city. Then he said to his servants, 'The wedding is ready, but those who were invited were not worthy. Therefore go into the highways, and as many as you find, invite to the wedding.' So those servants went out into the highways and gathered together all whom they found, both bad and good. And the wedding hall was filled with guests." (Matthew 22:1-10)

The parable begins with a king who wants to throw a great banquet in honor of his son's wedding. This wasn't just any wedding; it was a royal wedding and a magnificent feast of feasts. To be a preinvited guest to a wedding of this importance and magnitude would have been the greatest of honors.

In those days, the banquet would have been more than just a meal; it was a celebration that went on for weeks, with people actually invited to stay in the king's palace. No expense would be spared, the tables would be elaborately decorated, the finest chefs would work overtime, and the musicians and entertainers would all be top-notch and well-rehearsed. It was just an amazing thing to be invited to.

Now the protocol at this time was to extend two invitations, one following another. In the first invitation, you would be asked to RSVP, just as people do with weddings today. If you received the invitation and couldn't come, this would be the time to decline so the host could know how many places to set at the table, how much food to buy, and so forth. If you accepted the first invitation, it was a really big deal to accept the second invitation as well, which essentially said, "Everything is ready. Please come now."

As Jesus unfolded the story, we see people—one after another—rejecting the second invitation after they had already indicated they would come.

It would have been far, far better for those invitees to have never accepted the king's invitation than to accept it and then, at the last minute, impulsively decide not to show up.

But that is exactly what these people in Jesus' parable were doing. In fact, the whole thing was a joke to them. They made light of it and went on their way. In the original language, the phrase *made light of it* in verse 5 is linked to the idea of being careless or neglectful. These people the king had so extraordinarily honored couldn't have cared less about showing up at his son's wedding. They were laughing it off and tossing out lame excuses.

In Luke's account of the same story, we get more details on what those actual excuses were:

The first said to him, "I have bought a piece of ground, and I must go and see it. I ask you to have me excused." And another said, "I have bought five yoke of oxen, and I am going to test them. I ask you to have me excused." Still another said, "I have married a wife, and therefore I cannot come." (Luke 14:18-20)

These aren't even good lies. A man bought a field without even looking at it. Really? I don't think so! Another man bought ten oxen without testing them first. I doubt it! The third excuse-maker was classic: "Hey, count me out. I got married."

These guys would have known how much money had already been spent, and they had already accepted the king's gracious invitation and sent back their RSVP. To turn the king down at that point was downright insulting. They were deliberately dishonoring this king, and they didn't really care. Why? Because they were thinking of themselves. Matthew 22:5 words their conduct like this: "But they made light of it and went their ways, one to his own farm, another to his business."

The first two excuses, checking out a piece of property and testing oxen, have to do with material possessions. The third excuse, a recent marriage, has to do with affections. The fact is, possessions and affections cover virtually every reason people say no to God. Every excuse you have ever heard as to why people won't follow Christ probably will fit under one of these two headings.

EXCUSES FOR NOT FOLLOWING CHRIST
Excuse 1: Possessions are more important than God.

"I have bought a piece of ground, and I must go and see it. I ask you to have me excused." (Luke 14:18)

Was this guy a complete idiot? He bought a field without looking at it. Have you ever bought something without seeing it first?

I remember when I was a kid, I would sometimes order things from the ad pages of my favorite comic books. I remember one ad that promised 200 World War II soldiers for $1.98. Now, that was impressive. They would send you 100 American army guys and 100 German soldiers. I remember thinking, *That's a lot of soldiers. I could have fun with those.* So I scraped together $1.98 and ordered them.

When they finally arrived, however, what a disappointment! They were smaller than ants! Yes, there were 200 of them, but they were microscopic.

Have you ever read the descriptions of homes that real estate agents give? They're very creative in their wording, aren't they?

Retirement haven. (A thirty-year-old Sunbeam trailer.)

Ocean view. (Never mind that you have to get up on the roof with a high-powered telescope to catch a glimpse of the ocean.)

Steps from the beach. (Yes, that's right. About 250,000 of them.)

Cute fixer-upper. (This is a house with no roof, but with excellent ventilation.)

Great starter home. (That's a pile of lumber, with plans thrown in for good measure.)

The reality is that in Jesus' day, a buyer would have had many opportunities to examine the piece of land he was purchasing before putting his money on the line. So to say, "I bought a piece of land and have to go see it" was an outright lie. The man simply didn't want to go to the wedding and threw up a threadbare excuse.

It is not that he was particularly nasty about it. In the original language, there was a surface politeness about the excuse. The man was saying, in effect, "Oh, please excuse me. I'm so sorry about this, but I bought a piece of land, and I simply must go see it. I hope you understand."

But a no is still a no. And he was rejecting the second invitation after he had already accepted the first.

He had an "excuse," but it was really no excuse at all.

Excuse 2: Career is more important than God.

In Luke 14:19, the second excuse-maker said, "I have bought five yoke of oxen, and I am going to test them. I ask you to have me excused."

This man was either a complete fool or a blatant liar. Who would buy ten oxen without looking at them or trying them out? What if they were diseased or maimed?

Would you purchase a car without test-driving it? Imagine you are looking at a used car and say to the salesman, "I'm interested in this car. Can I take this out for a spin?"

What would you think if he said, "No, I'm afraid I can't let you do that"?

"Is the car in good working order?" you ask.

"Yes, it is."

"Well then, let me drive it."

"Sorry, I can't allow that."

Wouldn't that make you just a little suspicious? Of course it would. Yet this man was claiming to have made this significant purchase of ten oxen without even looking at them or testing them. Jesus' audience would have immediately recognized how ridiculous that was—and what a feeble excuse he was throwing out there.

Why would you need ten oxen? To plow your field and make a living by farming. So you might say that this man's career kept him back from God. Of course, there's nothing wrong with a career. I think believers should be the most diligent, trustworthy, hardest-working men and women of all, no matter what the profession. It doesn't matter if you are heading up a corporation, flipping burgers, typing letters, or closing big sales deals. Whatever you do, you should do it for the glory of God, do it well, and work hard at it.

But that is not the issue here.

The issue is when your job or your career becomes more important to you than your relationship with God. If advancing my career assumes greater priority in my life than advancing my walk with the Lord, something is out of its proper order.

Excuse 3: Relationships are more important than God.

In Luke 14:20 the third man says, "I have married a wife, and therefore I cannot come."

In contrast to the first two men who offered excuses, this guy wasn't even polite about it. In the original language, there is a raw edge and a bluntness in his reply. In contrast to the first man who said, "I'm so sorry, but I can't come," this third guy says, in effect, "Nope, not coming. Get lost. Can't you see I'm married?"

What? Don't you think your wife might enjoy a break from cooking to attend a royal feast? It would be like getting an invitation to go to a White House dinner or a banquet with the queen in Buckingham Palace. What woman wouldn't love that? The whole excuse about being married was nothing more than a thinly veiled excuse — and would have been highly offensive to the generous king who had issued the invitation.

The first man to make an excuse was possessed by his possessions. The second man was preoccupied with his career. This third individual allowed human affection to keep him away from God's best for his life.

On one hand, there is nothing more virtuous or commendable than the love of a husband for his wife and a wife for her husband. Certainly Jesus isn't putting down the marriage relationship. After all, He is the One who created man and woman, brings us together in marriage, and blesses us in that union. But the reality is, this man was using his marriage as an excuse to keep him from God.

PHONY EXCUSES TO THIS DAY

We still do this, even as Christians. We will offer excuses as to why we can't go to church or why we can't make it to our small group or Bible study.

"Oh, we can't go to church today. We were up too late last night."

"I'm going to skip Bible study this time. It's just too hot out there. (Or too cold.)"

"I think it might rain. We don't want to be out there on those slick roads."

We have plenty of excuses, and very few of them are actual *reasons*.

Look at the commitment sports fans demonstrate, and how they will support their team no matter what the weather conditions or circumstances. They will dress in team colors, paint their faces, and maybe even camp overnight outside the ticket window in subfreezing weather to get a good seat at the big game. When their team scores a touchdown, a goal, or a homerun, they go wild with excitement, yelling and screaming and pounding on both friends and complete strangers. What's more, they can remember all the sports scores and major players going back twenty years.

What if people were like that about church, never missing a service, never losing an opportunity to worship the Lord?

I've tried to imagine what it would be like if people offered the same excuses for not going to football games that they offer for not going to church.

"Hey, I heard you quit going to the games. I can't believe it! You were such a fan!"

"Yeah, I don't go to games anymore."

"But why?"

"Well, to tell you the truth, the people who sit around me don't seem all that friendly. Besides that, there are just too many people, the games last too long, the seats are kind of hard, and it isn't all that easy to find a parking place."

"Really?"

"Yes, and what's more, the coach never personally came and visited me. Not once."

"What?"

"And besides that, I read a book on football, and I think I know more than the coach. Anyway, my parents took me to a lot of football games when I was growing up, so now that I'm old enough to decide for myself, I just don't want to go anymore."

Those are the kinds of things people will say about church, but you would never see the same excuses applied to a sporting event.

And then we will offer up excuses as to why we can't read the Bible.

"I'm just so busy these days. Life is so full. I just can't find the time."

"The Bible is so big . . . I just don't know where to start."

"I tried to read it, but there are some parts I don't understand."

"We read the Bible in church on Sunday. Doesn't that count?"

Those are excuses. Not reasons.

Let's imagine you got a call this week from your doctor, who said, "You need to make an appointment with me. I've reviewed those tests we did on you, and we need to talk."

Then further imagine that you learned you only had mere weeks to live. If you found yourself looking eternity in the face like that, do you think your schedule might flex a little, allowing you time to open the Bible? Of course it would! You would realize that the afterlife was almost upon you, and you would need God's perspective, God's comfort, and God's peace to face the days ahead.

It all depends on your perspective, because *we will make time for what is important to us.* You find time to read the newspaper, watch your favorite TV program, or go online and spend hours looking at virtually nothing. And yet you don't have time to open up God's Word and let Him speak to you?

We need to be honest — with others and with ourselves. Instead of offering excuses, we need to make time for the things that matter most in life.

So what's the antidote for offering up weak, self-serving excuses?

PUTTING IT IN STARK TERMS

In Luke's version of this story, Jesus made a strong challenge to the crowds who had been listening to Him and following Him. Immediately on the heels of this parable, Jesus turned to the people and said, "If anyone comes to Me and does not hate his father and mother, wife and children, brothers and sisters, yes, and his own life also, he cannot be My disciple. And whoever does not bear his cross and come after Me cannot be My disciple" (Luke 14:26-27).

This is what you might call a hard-core statement. Many feel these are some of the most controversial words Jesus ever spoke. *Hate* your father and mother? Really? Hate your brother, sister, and kids? What's that all about? Was Jesus actually telling us to hate our loved ones?

This is a passage that cries out to be put in context.

After all, God Himself tells us to honor our fathers and mothers, that it may go well with us. And in Ephesians 5, husbands are commanded to love their wives as Christ loves the church. In Titus 2:4, young women are instructed to love their husbands and children. We're even told to love our enemies. So what does Jesus mean when He uses the word *hate*?

A better translation might read like this: "You must love God more than your husband, more than your wife, more than your children, more than your mom or dad. In fact, compared to your love for God, all of these other loves should seem like hatred by comparison."

The fact is, if you really love God as you ought to, you will have *more* love for your spouse and family and *more* love for your children and parents. Let's get our priorities in order: The love of God is the most important love of all. That's the idea being communicated here.

The word *disciple* comes from the root word *discipline*, which certainly includes the idea of making time for what is truly important. In contrast to the people in this story who offered up see-through excuses for not attending the king's banquet, true disciples prioritize God in their lives. They make time for God's Word, time for prayer, and time for being with God's people.

The answer to weak, deceptive excuses is to keep Jesus at the very center of our lives.

THE WEDDING GARMENT

There is a final, fascinating movement in the Lord's parable in Matthew 22:

> "When the king came in to see the guests, he saw a man there who did not have on a wedding garment. So he said to him, 'Friend, how did you come in here without a wedding garment?' And he was speechless." (verses 11-12)

It seems to me that one of the biggest challenges of being invited to a royal event would be choosing what to wear. What's the right apparel? What's the dress code? It could be very important.

Have you ever dressed inappropriately for some event because you didn't know what to wear? Maybe it was more formal than you thought, and you felt really out of place in a T-shirt, shorts, and flip-flops.

I have a "friend" (I use the word loosely) who had a party for one of his daughters and invited me to come. "It's kind of a costume party with a theme," he explained. "We're all dressing up like cowboys and cowgirls."

I don't own a cowboy hat, but I did put on my western shirt, jeans, big cowboy belt buckle, and cowboy boots.

Then, when I walked through the door, I knew I'd been had. Everyone else was dressed normally, and I came in looking like John Wayne. My friend's one desire had been to make me look stupid, and he completely succeeded.

At the wedding feast in Jesus' story, the appropriate

garments were apparently handed out at the door, at no cost. People arriving for the celebration didn't have to worry about what to wear because it was provided by the king. Everyone had appropriate attire—except one.

Was he a gate-crasher or just a man who refused to play by the rules? Apparently, when offered the wedding garment at the door, he blew it off and said, "I don't want that."

The answer might have been, "Sir, you are required to wear it."

"I don't care if I am."

"But sir, you need to do this. It's very important. Just slip it on, and everything will be fine."

"Get out of my way. I wear what I want to wear, when I want to wear it. I don't need your provision. Let me through."

So he pushed the gatekeeper aside and strolled into the party . . . on his own terms. Of course, he stuck out like the proverbial sore thumb and was an offense to the king. The man had ignored all protocol, rejected the free gift the king had offered him, and broken all the rules. By doing so, he had gravely insulted and offended the king.

This is a picture of what happens to people who say they will get to God or enter heaven on their own terms or through their own good works, without receiving God's provision of grace in Christ. When you claim that your good life or your good works or your sincerity will get you to heaven, you are effectively saying that the death of Jesus was a waste.

If living a good life could get you to heaven, why did Jesus have to suffer, shed His blood, and die? When you reject Christ, you are in effect saying no to the wedding garment and that you'll elbow your way into God's presence without accepting His free provision for salvation.

When we become believers in Jesus, we are clothed in

the righteousness of Christ. The Bible says we are actually "hidden with Christ in God" (Colossians 3:3).

In the Lord's story, He is speaking of a person who rejects God's provision, rejects God's forgiveness, and says, "I'm betting that God will let me into heaven based on my own strength, my own ability, my own track record, and my own merit."

When the king finally confronted this would-be gatecrasher in Matthew 22:12, the man was speechless. He had no smug remarks, no clever comebacks, and no reason at all for forcing his way into the king's party without wearing the provided garment.

In other words, he had no excuse.

In the same way, the only reason anyone will be admitted into heaven will be because they received God's precious gift of grace and forgiveness and salvation in Jesus Christ.

Don't even think about approaching the door of heaven without this.

15

THE GOD OF THE LIVING

I heard a story about a man who had just died and found himself standing outside the pearly gates. Simon Peter himself greeted the recent arrival and immediately began leafing through the Book of Life to see if the man was qualified to enter heaven.

"Hmmm . . ." said Peter.

"What?" said the man, a little concerned about Peter's hesitation. "What's the matter?"

Peter looked up from the book. "You know what, buddy?" he said. "I'm looking up your records, and frankly, I'm not finding a lot on you. It's not like you've done anything really bad in your life, but then again, I don't have any record of anything good you've done. Can you tell me one good thing you ever did while you were on earth?"

"Well, yes," the man replied, "as a matter of fact I can. There was this one time when I was driving down the street and saw a motorcycle gang gathered around a woman. Her car had broken down, and they were circling, closing in on her. So I pulled my car over, jumped out, popped the trunk, grabbed a tire iron, ran right into the middle of the group, and said to them, 'If you want to get to this girl, you have to go through me first.' And then I hit one of them on the head to make my point."

"Well, well," said Peter. "That is impressive. When did that happen?"

"Ummm, like maybe three minutes ago," he replied.

Now that joke is so riddled with theological errors that it would take me the rest of the chapter to correct them. But it does make one valid point: We never know when we will suddenly find ourselves standing in the presence of God and entering into eternity.

Many older people I've known through the years find themselves thinking about that moment and are at least somewhat aware of its approach. But there are also times when there are no warnings, no indications, no hint that the end of life was even approaching. A friend of mine told me about one of his coworkers, a guy in his early forties, who had been helping another family move into an apartment. After they got the couch through the door, the man said, "I need to sit down," and he promptly slumped over, dead from a massive heart attack. No one had any clue that he wasn't in perfect health.

Death could come in a car crash, where you're heading across an intersection on a green light and get broadsided by someone running a red light. One minute you're behind the steering wheel, thinking about the next thing on your schedule, and the next instant your life is over, and you are hurtled into the presence of God.

When I'm preparing to go on a trip, I always check on

the weather at my destination. Is it cold? Is it warm? Is it raining? I want to at least try to pack the right clothes and be prepared. (Although it usually seems like I bring the wrong stuff anyway.)

I like to know the lay of the land in the place where I'm going, maybe talking to someone who has been there before and can give me a few tips. I might say, "Tell me about this place. What can I expect? Where are the good places to eat?" (That's important.)

The fact is, if we have placed our faith in Jesus Christ, we are headed to heaven, whether sooner or later. So wouldn't it be a good idea to learn what we can about our future destination so that we'll be prepared for what we find there?

Heaven is a prepared place for prepared people. Before He left for heaven, Jesus said, "There is more than enough room in my Father's home. If this were not so, would I have told you that I am going to prepare a place for you?" (John 14:2, NLT).

Many people around the world believe in the afterlife. In fact, the numbers are higher than ever. A recent global survey was conducted, asking people about their belief in God and the afterlife, polling 18,000 people across twenty-three countries. Fifty-one percent of the respondents indicated they were convinced of the existence of God and life after death. In the United States, those numbers were even stronger. The survey showed that 76 percent of Americans believe in heaven, with 71 percent saying it is an actual place.

SOLAR BOATS AND THE HAPPY HUNTING GROUND

Belief in the afterlife is certainly not unique to our time. Almost every culture through the ages has believed in life beyond the grave. In Egypt, archaeologists discovered a "solar boat" in one of the tombs of the pharaohs who died over five thousand years ago. It was intended for the pharaoh's use in sailing through the heavens into the next life.

Ancient Greeks would often place a coin in the mouth of a corpse to pay their fare across the mystic river of death into the land of immortal life. American Indians would bury a pony and a bow with arrows beside a dead warrior so that he would be well-equipped when he rode into the happy hunting ground. Similarly, Norsemen would bury a dead hero's horse with him so he could ride proudly into the afterlife. The Romans believed that the righteous would picnic in Elysium fields with their horses grazing nearby. Eskimos of Greenland who died in childhood were customarily buried with their dog, who would guide them through what they believed to be the cold wasteland of death.

I don't know where all these people got their ideas about the afterlife, but there's one thing for sure: They believed in it.

In Jesus' day, a significant group of Jews had an aberrant view of life after death because they refused to believe or consider what the Scriptures taught. This group was called the Sadducees, and in the passage we'll be considering in this chapter, they came to Jesus with a trick question, meant to trip Him up and get Him into trouble. Of course, it didn't work, because Jesus knew their game before they ever started it.

A BLEAK OUTLOOK

Sometimes when we read about the Pharisees and Sadducees in the Gospels, we think of them as one group. In reality, however, they were two bitterly divided parties within the

Jewish leadership. The Pharisees were what we might call the theological conservatives of their day. They believed in the Scriptures, in an afterlife, in angels and spirits, and in a final judgment. The Sadducees might be described as theological liberals. They did not believe what the Scriptures said about a judgment or the afterlife or an ultimate resurrection. In fact, they only accepted the first five books of Moses as being inspired by God.

Even so, the Sadducees were very powerful. They were the aristocrats of Jerusalem and were largely in control of the temple and the operation of the Jewish priesthood. They obtained a great deal of wealth from operating the temple "concessions" of money-changing and the selling of animals for sacrifices.

Needless to say, they weren't very happy with Jesus. On two different occasions, the Teacher from Nazareth went into the temple and overturned the tables of the moneychangers, saying, "You have taken My Father's house—which should be a house of prayer—and turned it into a den of thieves." As a result, they were furious with Him.

The question they posed to Him that day was intended to put Him on the spot, but He turned the tables on their attempt, putting them on the spot instead.

No life beyond the grave? No heaven? What a bleak worldview. Yet it's a belief held by many in our day as well.

Actress Natalie Portman was asked about the afterlife in a recent interview, and she said, "I don't believe in that. I believe this is it, and I believe it's the best way to live."

When actor George Clooney was asked for his views, he replied, "I don't believe in happy endings, but I do believe in happy travels. . . . It's a mean thing, life."

Like the Sadducees of old, they have a sad, empty outlook on life beyond the grave. In their view, when a person dies, he simply ceases to exist and his lamp is extinguished forever.

According to Jesus, however, there is most certainly life after this life.

Why should He be qualified to speak on this topic? Why should we accept His view over the word of another? Because Jesus came from heaven, lived on earth, and has returned to heaven. When He speaks of life beyond the grave (as when He speaks on anything else), He can address the topic with authority.

Again, if I want to know about a place—let's say a country where we are planning to hold a Harvest Crusade—I will ask an expert about it. I will say, "Tell me about this place. You were born there." Or maybe, "You've been there many times and know it so well. What's it like?"

In the New Testament, Jesus tells us what heaven is like as one who had already been there and knows it well. In John 6:38 He said, "For I have come down from heaven to do the will of God who sent me, not to do my own will" (NLT). In John 3:13 He declared, "No one has ascended to heaven but He who came down from heaven, that is, the Son of Man who is in heaven."

And heaven is where Christ is right now.

His verbal exchange with the Sadducees gives us a valuable glimpse into the unspeakably wonderful life that will one day be ours . . . and perhaps sooner than we might imagine.

A CONVERSATION ON ETERNITY

The same day the Sadducees, who say there is no resurrection, came to Him and asked Him, saying:

"Teacher, Moses said that if a man dies, having no children, his brother shall marry his wife and raise up offspring for his brother. Now there were with us seven brothers. The first died after he had married, and having no offspring, left his wife to his brother. Likewise the second also, and the third, even to the seventh. Last of all the woman died also. Therefore, in the resurrection, whose wife of the seven will she be? For they all had her."

Jesus answered and said to them, "You are mistaken, not knowing the Scriptures nor the power of God. For in the resurrection they neither marry nor are given in marriage, but are like angels of God in heaven. But concerning the resurrection of the dead, have you not read what was spoken to you by God, saying, 'I am the God of Abraham, the God of Isaac, and the God of Jacob'? God is not the God of the dead, but of the living." (Matthew 22:23-32)

Let's consider a few of the significant points Jesus made that day as He spoke about the life to come.

1. A believer never really dies.

In verse 32, Jesus said, "God is not the God of the dead, but of the living." That's another way of saying that the person who has put their faith in Jesus Christ never dies.

In fact, everyone you have ever known is immortal, whether they were a believer, an unbeliever, an agnostic, or an atheist. Every Christian, every Buddhist, every Hindu, every Muslim, every Republican, and every Democrat lives forever.

But not everyone will live forever in the same place.

The real question remains, "*Where* will I live forever?"

Let's imagine for a moment that I bought you a one-way, first-class plane ticket and told you, "I will be sending you off on a journey next week."

So you're excited, and you immediately begin to pack. But then it dawns on you to ask, "So, Greg . . . just where is it that you will be sending me?" If the destination on the ticket was Maui, Hawaii, you might like that very much. (Everyone loves Maui.) But what if the destination on the ticket was Siberia? You might not be too excited about that. No one really wants a one-way trip to Siberia, even if it's free.

It's the same with our eternal destination. The issue isn't so much, "Am I going to live forever?" but "*Where* will I live forever?"

According to the Bible, there are only two possible destinations: heaven and hell. And when you put your faith in Jesus Christ for salvation, your eternal home is heaven . . . and you won't die.

"Won't die?" you say. "What do you mean by that?"

Here is what Jesus said: "I am the resurrection and the life. He who believes in Me, though he may die, he shall live. And whoever lives and believes in Me shall never die" (John 11:25-26).

No, this doesn't mean that I'm in denial. I understand that the body breaks down over time and sometimes shuts down quickly, even unexpectedly. I understand that when we die, we are placed in a grave. When that happens, I know in that sense, we died.

But I also know that in another sense, we don't die at all.

General Douglas MacArthur famously declared, "Old soldiers never die; they just fade away." As Christians, we could have our own expression. "Old Christians never die; they just *move* away."

They move away to heaven.

2. There will be a bodily resurrection.

In Matthew 22:29, Jesus told the Sadducees, "You are mistaken, not knowing the Scriptures nor the power of God." Then in verse 30, He said, "For in the resurrection . . ."

The very essence of the word *resurrection* speaks of something that is bodily. To say, "I don't believe in a bodily resurrection" is like claiming to believe in a sunrise without a sun. Our bodies *will* be raised.

Job declared,

> But as for me, I know that my Redeemer lives, and he will stand upon the earth at last. And after my body has decayed, yet in my body I will see God! I will see him for myself. Yes, I will see him with my own eyes. I am overwhelmed at the thought! (Job 19:25-27, NLT)

When you are in heaven, it will be *you* who is in heaven. The real you. The complete you. You will have the same thoughts, feelings, and desires, but they will be perfected. After Christ rose again from the dead, He wasn't another Jesus. He was the same Jesus in His glorified state. In Luke 24, after He had been resurrected, Jesus said to His disciples: "Why are you troubled, and why do doubts rise in your minds? Look at my hands and my feet. It is I myself! Touch me and see" (verses 38-39, NIV).

He was the same, yet there were differences too. He could now appear in a room and disappear at will (which must have been a little hard to get used to).

There is a great deal of confusion about the afterlife, fostered by lack of Bible teaching and fanciful Hollywood movies and TV shows. For instance, some people believe that after we die, we become angels. People will even say this in an attempt to comfort someone who has just lost a loved one. "Well," they will say, "I guess God needed another angel up in heaven."

But that is not true. People don't become angels when they die. An angel is a completely different order of being, created by God to worship and serve Him forever. Jesus elaborated on this in Luke 20, when He was speaking on this same topic. He said,

> Marriage is for people here on earth. But in the age to come, those worthy of being raised from the dead will neither marry nor be given in marriage. And they will never die again. In this respect they will be like angels. They are children of God and children of the resurrection. (verses 34-36, NLT)

So what happens to Christians when they die? They go straight to heaven, with no layovers. When I book a flight, I always try to avoid layovers. Airports are places where you get stuck! Especially in the winter — especially in Chicago. So when I'm putting together a trip, I do my best to get direct flights.

That's what our transition to heaven will be: a direct flight with no layovers, no intermediate destinations, and no delays. The moment after you take your last breath on earth, you will take your first breath in heaven, in the presence of Jesus and our heavenly Father. As Jesus said to the thief on the cross, "Today you will be with Me in Paradise" (Luke 23:43).

In Philippians 1:23, Paul spoke of departing and being with Christ. He didn't say, "I'm about to depart and go into a state of suspended animation or soul sleep." No, he said, "I desire to depart and be with Christ, which is better by far" (NIV). In 2 Corinthians 5, he also affirmed that "as long as we are at home in the body we are away from the Lord," but that he would rather "be away from the body and at home with the Lord" (verses 6,8, NIV).

Will we have the same bodies when we get to heaven? Not exactly.

In 1 Corinthians 15, Paul explained,

> Our dying bodies must be transformed into bodies that will never die; our mortal bodies must be transformed into immortal bodies. Then, when our dying bodies have been transformed into bodies that will never die, this Scripture will be fulfilled: "Death is swallowed up in victory." (verses 53-54, NLT)

The newly minted resurrection body the Lord will give us won't be just an earthly body that has been resuscitated, but a likeness of the earthly body that has been glorified. God will recover from the dust a body with a definite relationship to your earthly body, but it will be completely transformed to suit your new environment.

When astronauts go into orbit around the earth and have to take a space walk outside their capsule, they put on a special suit, enabling them to survive in the vacuum of space. It's the same with scuba diving and all the equipment you have to wear to explore a new environment underwater. The new body that God will give you will be suited for your new home, your new environment, where you will live forever.

When do we get this new body? If I read Scripture right, it won't be in the moment you go to heaven, but at the resurrection — which takes place at the same time as the rapture of the church.

Those who are already in heaven will receive their new

bodies at that moment, and if we happen to be alive on earth when Jesus comes to call His church home, we will instantly receive our new resurrection bodies at the same time. In 1 Corinthians 15:51-52, Paul said, "Listen, I tell you a mystery: We will not all sleep, but we will all be changed—in a flash, in the twinkling of an eye, at the last trumpet. For the trumpet will sound, the dead will be raised imperishable, and we will be changed" (NIV).

All this will take place in that nanosecond when the Christians who are alive on earth will be caught up into God's presence.

3. In heaven, we will see similarities to earth, but it will be much better.

Sometimes people ask, "Will we recognize one another in heaven?"

Of course we will! In heaven we will know *more* than we do on earth, not less.

Do you recognize people now? Most of the time, we do. Sometimes if you haven't seen someone for years and run into them somewhere, you have that moment of wondering whether they're the same person. If you're at your twenty- or thirty-year high school reunion, you might have to refer to the nametag! But generally you and I recognize people we already know.

You'll be able to do that in heaven, too. Your mind will be working at full capacity, the dark shadows and stains of sin will have been finally removed, and you will have super-natural knowledge beyond anything you ever experienced on earth. So we will know one another—and much better than ever before. That's such an encouraging thought for those of us who have been separated temporarily from loved ones who have departed for heaven before us. We will be reunited with them again. Our absence from loved ones is a comma, not a period.

But what about our wife or husband? Will we still be married in heaven?

That was essentially the question posed by the Sadducees. First of all, our former earthly relationships won't be the focus of heaven; God is the focus of heaven. We will worship Him, walk with Him, serve Him, enjoy Him, and He will be sufficient to meet all our needs, forever.

Nevertheless, God created us as social beings from the very beginning, and I don't imagine that will change. We will still enjoy our loved ones and our old friends while we make new friends with the millions of people and angels who will inhabit heaven with us for eternity.

I love the quick little snapshot of heaven that we're given by the writer of the book of Hebrews:

> You have come right up into Mount Zion, to the city of the living God, the heavenly Jerusalem, and to the gathering of countless happy angels; and to the church, composed of all those registered in heaven; and to God who is Judge of all; and to the spirits of the redeemed in heaven, already made perfect; and to Jesus himself, who has brought us his wonderful new agreement. (12:22-24, TLB)

The desire for human companionship goes all the way back to the Garden of Eden, before sin had ever entered the world. Adam had perfect fellowship with his Creator, and he and God used to walk the garden paths together in the cool of the evening, talking about the day's events.

But God still knew it was not good for the man to be

alone, and He created Eve as a wonderful companion, friend, and helper for Adam.

It's not as though the Lord said, "All right, Adam. I wanted to be your all in all, but if I'm not enough, I will give you a companion."

No, this was the Lord's plan right from the start. God was saying to Adam, "You can't do this alone. You need help, buddy." So help was on the way, and her name was Eve. And then the Lord said, "This is good."

Adam desired human companionship, even when He had God Himself as a companion. That suggests to me that we will take joy in worshipping the Lord through all eternity, but we also will be able to enjoy and interact with one another—and on a deeper level than we could ever imagine here on earth. That includes our husband or wife, our family members, and the believing friends we had on earth.

Receiving a glorified body and being relocated to heaven doesn't mean a history that is erased. It means a history that *culminates*. We can't take material things with us to heaven, but we can take relationships with us.

THE TRICK QUESTION

The Sadducees had a "gotcha" question ready for Jesus and could hardly wait to spring it on Him. They were smugly sure that this question of theirs would stump this upstart Teacher from Nazareth and throw Him into confusion. They also hoped it would embarrass and frustrate their rivals, the Pharisees.

To sum it up, a woman was married, but her husband died. So she married again, and the second husband died. She went on to a third husband, and he died. (I think I would keep my distance from that person.) This went on for seven husbands, until the final one died, and then she died, too.

They must have wanted a drumroll when they got to the punch line, because they were so sure that Jesus wouldn't be able to handle it:

> Therefore, in the resurrection, whose wife of the seven will she be? For they all had her. (Matthew 22:28)

If I had been Jesus, I think I might have said, "Seriously, what's the deal with this woman? What is she cooking for all these husbands? And why would the fourth or fifth guy in line want to marry her?"

That's not what Jesus said, but He did put them in their place.

In verses 29-30, He replied, "You are mistaken, not knowing the Scriptures nor the power of God. For in the resurrection they neither marry nor are given in marriage, but are like angels of God in heaven."

So the Bible teaches there is no marriage in heaven, right?

No, there will be marriage in heaven: It will be a marriage between Jesus Christ and His bride, the church.

But what about our husband, what about our wife? What will our relationship be with one another? In his excellent book *Heaven*, Randy Alcorn said, "Earthly marriage is a shadow, a copy, an echo of the true and ultimate marriage."[1] He also said that God's plan doesn't stop in heaven and the new earth; it continues.

So no, spouses won't be married to each other like they are now. But we will still be connected to each other and related to each other. In fact, our relationships will be even stronger than they were on earth.

The hope of every follower of Jesus Christ is to one day be in heaven with Him. You don't go to heaven to find Christ; you go to Christ to find heaven *because these promises are only for the person who believes in Him.* Heaven is not the default destination of every person who departs this life. To be very blunt with you, the default destination of every man and woman on earth is hell, not heaven.

Jesus said, "Wide is the gate and broad is the way that leads to destruction, and there are many who go in by it. Because narrow is the gate and difficult is the way which leads to life, and there are few who find it" (Matthew 7:13-14).

If you want to travel to New Zealand, you can't just go to the airport, walk onto a plane bound for New Zealand, and take a seat. You wouldn't even get that far because you would be stopped by security. The TSA agents would say, "Where is your ticket? Where is your boarding pass? Let me check your ID a couple more times." You won't be seeing the wonders of New Zealand without paying the fare.

It's the same in getting to heaven. You need a ticket, and you can't pay the fare. It is more than you could ever afford in a trillion years. But the good news is that at the cross, Jesus Christ died for us and purchased our ticket (paid in full!) and now offers it to us as a gift. If we will receive that gift and put our faith in Jesus, we can be forgiven and be assured of going to heaven when we die.

The Sadducees, educated and brilliant as they may have been, were seriously mistaken about life after death. Jesus told them flat out, "You are mistaken, not knowing the Scriptures nor the power of God" (Matthew 22:29).

They had meant to leave Jesus speechless, but He went on to give them a biblical example that left *them* speechless:

> "And regarding your speculation on whether the dead are raised or not, don't you read your Bibles? The grammar is clear: God says, 'I am — not *was* — the God of Abraham, the God of Isaac, the God of Jacob.' The living God defines himself *not* as the God of dead men, but of the *living*." (verses 31-32, MSG)

Because He is the living God and we belong to Him, we, too, will live forever with Him. As C. S. Lewis wrote, "We . . . shall live to remember the galaxies as an old tale."[2]

16

LOVING GOD

Heart is one of our culture's all-time favorite words, and we use it all the time.

We will say, "I'm heartbroken."

Or maybe, "What a heartless person!"

If someone is very emotional and quick to express their feelings, we might say of them, "They wear their heart on their sleeve."

There are endless songs about the heart. The Eagles sang about "Heartache Tonight." Bruce Springsteen had his "Hungry Heart," while Neil Young sang about searching for a "Heart of Gold." And then there was Billy Ray Cyrus with his "Achy Breaky Heart." Maybe that's why Toni Braxton recorded a song called "Unbreak my Heart."

Stevie Nicks had a song called "Stop Draggin' My Heart Around," and the Bee Gees asked the world, "How Can You Mend a Broken Heart?"

So what do we mean when we say the word *heart*? I think most of us refer to the emotional center of our lives. That's why we will say, "My mind tells me to do one thing, but my heart tells me another."

When you think about it, a lot of crazy things have been done in the name of "I'm doing this from my heart."

Princess Diana once said, "Only do what your heart tells you."

I presume Woody Allen believed that when he left his live-in lover and took up with her adopted daughter. When asked why he would do such a thing, his explanation was, "Well, the heart wants what the heart wants."

Hugh Hefner, at age eighty-five, was getting ready to marry a twenty-five-year-old girl. When she abruptly broke off the relationship, she explained that she had "a change of heart." Some of Hefner's friends were concerned for him and stated that Hugh Hefner was going to die of a broken heart.

What's all this talk of the heart and following your heart?

In reality, following your heart — even though it sounds wonderful, warm, and romantic — is a very dangerous thing to do.

Why? *Because your heart can mislead you.*

The Bible also speaks of the heart. In Jeremiah 17:9, the Lord says, "The heart is deceitful above all things, and desperately wicked; who can know it?"

In Matthew 15:19-20, Jesus went on to say, "For from the heart come evil thoughts, murder, adultery, all sexual immorality, theft, lying, and slander. These are what defile you" (NLT).

Woody Allen was right that the heart wants what it wants. But sometimes what it wants can deceive you and destroy you. For that reason, we shouldn't focus on our hearts as much as we should focus our hearts on God.

A FOCUSED HEART

In the book of Matthew, Jesus tells us what to do with the human heart. Instead of endlessly talking about it, worrying about it being broken or unbroken, dragging it around, or wearing it on your sleeve, He tells you to use your heart as well as your mind and your soul for what they were created for:

> One [of the Pharisees], a lawyer, asked Him a question, testing Him, and saying, "Teacher, which is the great commandment in the law?"
>
> Jesus said to him, "'You shall love the LORD your God with all your heart, with all your soul, and with all your mind.' This is the first and great commandment. And the second is like it: 'You shall love your neighbor as yourself.' On these two commandments hang all the Law and the Prophets." (Matthew 22:35-40)

The Pharisees, who had endless arguments and debates about which commandments were greater or lesser, were trying to trap Jesus into saying something they might accuse Him with.

These ultralegalistic Jews had documented 613 commandments in the law, identifying 248 of those commandments as positive and 365 as negative. They knew that no one could keep all of the commandments, so they set out to identify some of them as "heavy" and others as "light."

In other words, they wanted to believe that some sins were worse than others. But here's the problem: God doesn't make those distinctions.

Instead of cataloging the commands in order of importance, as they wanted Him to do, Jesus jumped right to the bottom line, saying "You shall love the Lord your God with all of your heart, soul, and mind." This is known as the *Shema*, and it was a passage of Scripture every Jew would have memorized and been very familiar with.

In reminding them of this, Jesus was saying, "Instead of worrying about all of these little commands and which one might be more important than another, get back to loving God with everything in you, and all the rest of this stuff will be sorted out and fall in line."

It makes complete sense, doesn't it? If I truly love the Lord my God with all of my heart, soul, and mind, I will naturally want to do what He wants me to do. I won't want to put fake idols before Him or take His name in vain. And if I love my neighbor as I love myself, I won't want to steal from him or kill her or covet something that belongs to them. The idea, then, is that if I can get a grip on this basic truth of loving God with everything in me, all the other priorities of life will fall into place.

It was Augustine who said, "Love God, and do as you please."

At first hearing, that sounds like a radical, even dangerous, statement. But the fact is, if we really love God, we will want to do only those things that please Him.

But what did Jesus mean when He said to love the Lord with all our heart, soul, and mind? (Mark's version adds the word "strength" as well.) It means that you are to love Him with your entire self, with every part of your being.

Love God . . . with all your heart. For the Hebrew mind, the heart spoke of the center or core of one's being. Proverbs 4:23 says, "Guard your heart above all else, for it determines the course of your life" (NLT).

Love God . . . with all your soul. The Hebrew word for *soul* probably more closely correlates to our contemporary use of the word *heart*. For the Hebrew, the soul referred to the emotions. It is the word Jesus used when He cried out in the Garden of Gethsemane, "My soul is exceedingly sorrowful, even to death" (Matthew 26:38).

Love God . . . with all your mind. This is the idea of moving ahead with energy and strength.

A genuine love for the Lord is certainly a feeling, but it is also a love that is intelligent and willing to serve.

Some people love God with all of their minds, but there's no real heart in it. They love to study and have all of their theology in order, but there is no passion in their life. On the other hand, some people love God with all of their heart, passion, and emotion but haven't disciplined themselves to study God's Word and are easily led astray. The truth is, we need all of these aspects in play to love God as we ought to.

After Peter had failed the Lord so miserably and denied Him three times, the resurrected Jesus posed this question to him by the Sea of Galilee one morning: "Simon, son of Jonah, do you love Me?" (John 21:15).

He could have asked Peter, "Simon, son of Jonah, do you have faith in Me?" Or He might have said, "Simon, are you theologically correct?" Or maybe, "Simon, are you obedient to Me?"

But Jesus didn't ask Him those questions. He asked him, "Do you love Me?" Furthermore, He asked him three times in a row, perhaps corresponding to the fact that Peter had denied Him three times. Why did Jesus ask him this? Because Jesus knew that if Peter loved Him, all the other areas of life would be taken care of.

I've met some people who are sticklers for correct doctrine, and yet in their personal lives, they are miserable, mean, arrogant, and condemning. They may be "right" in their teaching, but they are more than ready to use the truth like a sledgehammer in people's lives, beating them to a pulp with their correct doctrine. I know other people who are very busy and active for God, running here and there, doing this and that, but their love for the Lord seems to be a mile wide and an inch deep.

What we learn from Jesus in Matthew 22:37-40 is that if we would love the Lord as we ought to, then everything else in our lives will find its proper balance. What we need to remember, however, is that this is no once-for-all decision; we need to refocus our hearts on the Lord every day of our lives.

We can walk away from our love for Jesus.

We can allow our love for God to fade or grow cold.

Years down the road, we might find ourselves saying, "There was a time in my walk with the Lord when my love was much stronger than it is today. It's as though I have left my first love."

This happens in marriage all the time. When two people are newly married and you see them out and about, they're so affectionate with one another. When we see some young couple holding hands, gazing into each other's eyes, or maybe kissing, we will smile and say, "They must be newlyweds." Why do we say that? Because people who have been married for a while don't do that anymore.

This can happen in our relationship with Christ as well. We lose the passion we once had, and communication breaks down somehow. In effect, the honeymoon is over.

"I HAVE THIS AGAINST YOU"

This was the situation with the church in Ephesus, to whom Jesus spoke directly in the book of Revelation.

They had been an active, busy, engaged church, but somewhere along the line, their love for Jesus had grown cold. The Lord addressed them in a personal appeal — and warning:

> I know your works, your labor, your patience, and that you cannot bear those who are evil. And you have tested those who say they are apostles and are not, and have found them liars; and you have persevered and have patience, and have labored for My name's sake and have not become weary Nevertheless I have this against you, that you have left your first love. Remember therefore from where you have fallen; repent and do the first works, or else I will come to you quickly and remove your lampstand from its place — unless you repent. (Revelation 2:2-5)

These words of Jesus were to a literal church, located in the city of Ephesus in Asia Minor. Both the apostle Paul and possibly the apostle John had pastored it. When Revelation was written, given to John the apostle on the island of Patmos, this church was in its second generation. As a result, many of those in the church would have been born to believing parents and raised in a Christian home. They had been taught the Word of God from youth.

This was an active, on-the-go congregation, busy in their service for the Lord. Jesus commended them for their perseverance and hard work. He said, "You . . . have labored for My name's sake," and that term *labored* could be translated "labored to the point of exhaustion."

These Christians were extremely hard workers, even to the point of weariness and pain. They were also discerning, intolerant of evil practices, and faithful. Anyone looking at this church from the outside might conclude that the Lord must have been very pleased with them.

But Jesus wasn't looking from the outside; He was looking at the inside. He was looking at their hearts, and what He saw there did not please Him. The Ephesians were guilty of a sin the average person could not detect: *They had left their first love.*

It doesn't say they *lost* it. Sometimes people ask the question, "Have you lost your first love?" But that is not the word Jesus used. These Christians hadn't lost their first love; they had *left* it. If you lose something, you don't know where it is. But you can also leave something or walk away from someone. And that is what Jesus said had happened to the church at Ephesus. He was effectively saying, "You no longer love Me as you first did."

These believers in Ephesus were so busy maintaining their separation, they were neglecting their adoration. They were substituting perspiration for inspiration.

Is this really a big deal?

Jesus thought it was.

If you go on reading the Lord's personal messages to the churches in Revelation 2–3, you will find the situations becoming progressively worse. It begins with the breakdown of the first love in Ephesus and culminates with the outright rejection of Christ in the church of Laodicea. In that last of the seven churches to whom Jesus wrote, you actually find Jesus on the outside, trying to get in. This is where He said, "Behold, I stand at the door and knock. If anyone hears My voice and opens the door, I will come in to him and dine with him, and he with Me" (Revelation 3:20).

We will sometimes quote that verse when we're telling unbelievers how they can accept Christ, asking Him into their lives. In its context, however, it was spoken to the church — the unbelieving church.

So yes, leaving your first love is a very big deal because it can lead to even worse things down the road.

I spoke earlier about newlyweds and their sometimes very public displays of affection. I'm not saying that after you've been married for years you will have the same emotions you had when you were dating or courting someone. Do you remember how it was? He or she walked into the room and your mouth went dry, your heart started pounding, and your head felt light. If I still felt that way with my wife after being married for almost forty years, she would probably think I was having a heart attack. The fact is, the love of an enduring marriage is a much deeper emotion than the initial feelings of attraction that brought you together.

C. S. Lewis put it this way: "'Being in love' first moved them to promise fidelity: this quieter love enables them to keep the promise. It is on this love that the engine of marriage is run: being in love was the explosion that started it."[1]

God isn't saying, "I want you to always have your heart aflutter and have an emotional experience when you think about Me." No, but He is saying, "I want a deeper, committed, lasting love, and I want it to stay strong for a lifetime."

When you first started dating your spouse, you tried to do all of the right things. Guys, you might have even opened the door for her, pulled the chair out for her at the table, and tried extra hard to communicate. Maybe you took her to a little French restaurant or bought some flowers or some little gift for her. You wanted to impress her.

Then you got married. You still open the door for her . . . you just close it before she's all the way in. You still give her little gifts . . . like your dirty laundry. And how about that French restaurant you went to last night . . . Jacque in the Box? After all, you ordered French fries. That's French, isn't it?

So things have changed since those early days when you first fell in love.

Maybe you've lost something there. And that can happen in your relationship with the Lord as well.

Remember when you first came to faith in Jesus Christ and began to catch on to the fact that you could talk to God anytime and anywhere you wanted to? It was a privilege, and you talked to Him all the time. Remember how excited you were to realize that the Bible was like an owner's manual for life, showing you how to be a good husband or wife, a good friend, and a good parent? Then there was church, and you couldn't wait to get in the door on Sunday. You would go to midweek services, prayer services, all kinds of services. Maybe you would listen to teaching tapes in your car, read Christian books, or tune into Christian radio stations.

Sharing your faith? Man, that was easy! It was the overflow of a Christ-filled life, and you were always looking for opportunities to talk to someone about Jesus.

Maybe things have changed as time has gone by. You still study the Bible, but not as much as you used to. After all, life is busier now. And prayer? Maybe you used to go for long walks in the evening, just pouring out your heart to God. But these days it's been more like a quick prayer here and quick prayer there. And yes, you still like to go to church. In fact, you still sit in the same place every Sunday—and no one had better try to take your spot! But you're unhappy if the preacher goes over his allotted time, and sometimes you'll leave a little early to beat the traffic.

Sharing your faith? Well, you'll do that now and then.

But you don't want to buttonhole people. You've convinced yourself that "setting a good example" is just as important as following the example of Jesus and actually starting a conversation with someone. (You know how awkward and uncomfortable that can be.)

So here is the question: Have you left your first love? In Revelation 2:5, Jesus said to the believers in Ephesus, "Remember therefore from where you have fallen."

Fallen? Is it falling to leave your first love? Yes, it really is. And it can lead to worse things than a loveless heart.

King David is a classic example of what can happen when we lose our focus on loving God. In the early days, he was described as "a man after [God's] own heart" (Acts 13:22) and "the sweet psalmist of Israel" (2 Samuel 23:1). He went on to become the greatest king in the history of that nation. But we also have to remember that sometime in his middle years, he became an adulterer and, in effect, a murderer as well.

How did that happen?

He left his first love.

As a young boy, watching his father's sheep, he would spend his hours of solitude writing love poems to the Lord. He was a tough young man, ready to take on wild animals that threatened the flock, but he also had a sensitive heart.

David loved the Lord—walked with Him, prayed to Him, sang to Him, thought about Him day and night. But then fast-forward into David's adulthood, and the Bible says at the time when kings would lead their troops into battle, David was back home at the palace, just kicking back and taking it easy.

Then one evening when he was bored and walking around on his rooftop patio, he caught sight of a woman bathing herself. Even though he knew she was a married woman, David lusted after her, had her brought up to his chambers, had sex with her, and got her pregnant. In the following days and years, life fell apart for David—and his family, too.

At this stage of his life, you don't read of David's writing all those beautiful worship psalms or singing to the Lord as he once did out in the wilderness—or even when he was on the run as a fugitive from the murderous jealousy of King Saul.

What happened to David's tender heart for the Lord? He moved beyond it. He left his first love, and his life was a mess as a result.

Have you left your first love? It can happen so easily. We need to get back to the "way we were" with the Lord in the early days of our salvation, and love Him with all of our heart, soul, mind, and strength.

But how can we know if our love for the Lord is cooling off? How can we gain some perspective on where we are in our love relationship with Jesus? Let's consider a few simple tests that may give us some insight.

HOW TO KNOW WHETHER YOU ARE HOLDING ON TO YOUR FIRST LOVE

1. If you really love the Lord, you will long for personal communion with Him.

When you love someone, you naturally want to spend time with them. You enjoy their company and their companionship. When you hear of husbands and wives spending less time together or maybe taking separate vacations, that is not a good sign.

My wife, Cathe, and I have been married for thirty-eight years, and I love to be with her. She's literally my best friend,

I value her opinion, and we spend a great deal of time together. The bottom line is that we are in love, and we value each other's company more than anyone else's in the world.

And if you really love the Lord, you will want to be in fellowship with Him.

2. If you really love the Lord, you will love the things He loves.

We know what He loves by what He has declared in His Word. The psalmist said, "Your word is very pure; therefore Your servant loves it" (Psalm 119:140). Do you love the Word of God? I don't mean just tolerating it or putting up with it or grinding your way through it out of duty. No, I mean, do you love the Word of God and can't get enough of it? Do you love hanging out with the people of God? Jesus loves His church, do you? Do you love lost people—men and women, boys and girls who are outside of Christ? God loves these people. God "so loved the world that He gave His only Son" (John 3:16).

If you love the Lord, you will love the things He loves.

The flip side of that is if you love the Lord, you will hate the things He hates. That's because His nature is becoming your nature. Psalm 97:10 says, "You who love the LORD, hate evil!" God hates sin, and we should do the same. In Romans 12:9, the Bible tells us to "abhor what is evil."

Sometimes we allow ourselves to be fascinated with evil. We will see something on the Internet or on TV and say to ourselves, *Whoa, what's this? I want to check this out a little.* We tell ourselves we're just doing a little research or "keeping informed," but in reality we should have nothing to do with these dark or disturbing stories and images. Turn it off. Push it way. Abhor evil. Don't allow yourself to be drawn to or fascinated by something that you know God hates.

Another thing to keep in mind is that if you love God, you will love other people in the family of God. Don't tell me you love God, whom you can't see, when you refuse to love people, whom you can see. Your love for God isn't real if you hate other Christians. The apostle John highlighted this fact in 1 John 3:14: "If we love our Christian brothers and sisters, it proves that we have passed from death to life. But a person who has no love is still dead" (NLT).

So don't talk about your love for God out of one side of your mouth while you are slandering or ripping apart another believer out of the other side of your mouth. If you love God, you'll love His kids.

3. If you really love the Lord, you will long for His return.

Near the end of his life on earth, the apostle Paul wrote, "Now there is in store for me the crown of righteousness, which the Lord, the righteous Judge, will award to me on that day — and not only to me, but also to all who have longed for his appearing" (2 Timothy 4:8, NIV).

Do you love to think about His appearing, that moment in time when He will return to earth for His own? Does the thought that He could return at any moment fill you with joyful anticipation or dread? Those who love Jesus Christ can't wait to see Him face-to-face.

4. If you really love the Lord, you will keep His commandments.

In John 14:21, Jesus said, "He who has My commandments and keeps them, it is he who loves Me. And he who loves Me will be loved by My Father, and I will love him and manifest Myself to him."

This isn't rocket science: If you love God, you will do what He says.

Let's just say that I walked up to you and said, "I love you."

"Thank you so much, Greg," you reply.

Then in the next moment, I slap you across the face.

"Hey!" you protest. "That hurt! Why did you do that?"

"I don't know," I reply. "I don't know what came over me, because I love you so much and I'm so very sorry. Will you forgive me?"

"That's a tough one, Greg. My face still stings. But okay, I will forgive you."

And then I turn around and punch you right in the stomach!

Gasping for air, you say, "Why? Why did you do that?"

Again I reply, "I don't know, I don't know. I love you so much. Why did I do that? Oh man, can you forgive me? I will never do it again."

"Wow . . . I'm just starting to breathe again. But yes . . . yes, I forgive you, Greg."

"Well, that's good. Because you have no idea how much I love you." And then I smack you right across the jaw with my fist, knocking you off your feet.

At that you get up and start to run, even as I shout after you, "I don't know why I did that. I really do love you!"

Here is the problem: My actions don't match my words.

The same strange thing happens with people who profess to love God. A woman will say, "Oh Lord, I love You. I love You more than anything else in life." And then she turns right around and sleeps with her boyfriend.

A man says he loves Jesus and even wipes some tears away during a worship service as he praises the Lord with raised hands. Then the following week, he is unfaithful to his spouse, gets drunk at some party, acts cruel to his children, or is dishonest on his job.

It doesn't follow. It doesn't add up. It isn't real.

In one of his prayers, the prophet Jeremiah said of his countrymen, "You are always on their lips but far from their hearts" (Jeremiah 12:2, NIV).

If you love God, then *keep His commandments*. And if you're not willing to keep His commandments, then stop talking about your love for God. The proof of your love is in your actions and what you do.

HOW DO YOU RETURN TO YOUR FIRST LOVE?

Let's say that you've come to realize that your love for Jesus isn't what it used to be. Somewhere along the way, you wandered away from that passionate "first love" you had for the Lord.

How do you come back?

Jesus has the answer for us, right within His letter to the church of Ephesus:

> Remember therefore from where you have fallen; repent and do the first works, or else I will come to you quickly and remove your lampstand from its place — unless you repent. (Revelation 2:5)

In this verse, Jesus gave us the three Rs of returning to our first love: *remember, repent*, and *repeat*.

1. Remember

> Remember therefore from where you have fallen. (Revelation 2:5)

This could be literally translated "keep on remembering." Remember where you were at your highest point of love for Jesus. Another translation puts it, "Remember the height from which you have fallen" (NIV). What was the high point for you in your walk with Jesus Christ? Was it a year ago? A month ago? A decade ago? Whenever that may have been, think back to those days when your faith and your joy were firing on all cylinders.

Keep that thought in mind for a few moments. That is a point of reference you want to return to.

Maybe that is what the psalmist was doing when he wrote,

> My heart is breaking
>   as I remember how it used to be:
> I walked among the crowds of worshipers,
>   leading a great procession to the house of God,
> singing for joy and giving thanks
>   amid the sound of a great celebration!
>   (Psalm 42:4, NLT)

Reflect on your best times as a Christian, and bring those things to mind.

2. Repent

First you remember. Then you repent. What does it mean to repent? It isn't a complicated concept at all. It means to change your direction, to go back to where you were before. Pull a U-turn in the middle of your life's highway and head back to where you got off course. You won't need your GPS unit to find the way, because God Himself will guide you to that place.

3. Repeat

Repent and do the first works. (Revelation 2:5)

Change your heart, change your direction, and go back quickly and do the things you used to do . . . and keep on doing them! What were you doing then that you're not doing now? Praying? Studying the Word? Listening to praise music? Hanging out with others who love the Lord? Memorizing Scripture? Do those things again. Do them whether you feel like doing them or not.

Let's go back to the marriage analogy for a moment. Let's say that your marriage isn't what it once was. In fact, it is unraveling. You're heading for divorce court, and you don't know how to fix it.

Following the Lord's counsel here, you need to go back and do what you did when your marriage was strong. What did you do *then*?

"Well, we actually talked. We communicated." *Do that again.*

"We complimented each other on things." *Do it again.*

"We had date nights and went out together." *Make it happen again. Hire a babysitter if you have to, make a reservation, and invest a little time and money in your romance.*

"We put the needs of the other before our own." *You can do that again. Just get started.*

I predict that if you would go back and do those things you used to do when your marriage was strong, your love relationship will revive again.

But don't wait for the emotion! Don't waste valuable time trying to dissect your feelings. You made a commitment before friends and family and God Himself. Are you going to keep your commitment? It doesn't matter if you don't feel like it. It doesn't matter if you don't feel sincere. Start doing those things, and you *will* feel like it again. You will feel sincere again. The feelings will come back, bit by bit! Just do what is right, and let the feelings take care of themselves.

Now . . . what did you do when your relationship with Jesus was at its highest point? Remember those things, and go back and do them again. Read Christian books. Listen to Christian radio. Pray before you go to sleep. Talk to Jesus when you wake up in the night. Carry a verse in your pocket on a card, or enter it into your iPhone and memorize it. Get with some other believers and have fellowship. Find a church that has great worship and get in on it, singing and praising the way you once did.

And do these things quickly, before you lose the moment and slip back into apathy.

The Bible says to love the Lord your God with all your heart, soul, mind, and strength. Channel everything you are into loving Him, remembering to love your neighbor as yourself.

If you do, then your life will come back into a beautiful balance.

And joy will return to your heart like a fresh sunrise.

17

NO REGRETS

If you own a television, chances are you know about wasting time.

Aren't there over a thousand channels to choose from now?

You could sit in your chair all day and just flip, flip, flip.

Sometimes I do that. I'll flop down in a chair for a few minutes, but since there's nothing worth watching, I'll never really land anywhere. I will watch two minutes of one program, switch to the next, switch to the next, and so on.

Then I will look at my watch and realize I just wasted an hour and a half watching nothing at all!

Many of us have certainly wasted time in front of our computers. (Weren't computers supposed to make our lives more productive?) The truth is, you can spend hours surfing the Net, updating your

Facebook page, answering e-mails, and on and on.

And then you walk away from your computer, saying to yourself, "I just wasted two hours I wish I could have back."

In Matthew 26, the Bible gives us the story of a woman who was harshly accused of waste . . . when there was no waste at all. In fact, Jesus Himself came to her defense.

The woman in this passage was criticized and condemned by some of the people around her, but commended by the Son of God. At the end of the day, I'm sure that what Jesus said to her meant more than all the negative criticism several others had lobbed at her.

Which is more important in your life: the approval of people or the approval of God? We may quickly reply, "The approval of God," but let's be honest about this. Most of us are very concerned about what people think of us. One of the main reasons we don't speak more about our faith in Christ is because we don't want people to think we're a fanatic or (worst of all) laugh at us. Or maybe we hold back from speaking the truth to a friend because we don't want that friend to be upset or angry with us.

That's also why we sometimes don't do the right thing, the thing we know in our hearts we ought to do, because the right thing wouldn't be popular, and people might have a bad opinion of us.

In Proverbs 29:25 we read, "Fearing people is a dangerous trap, but trusting the LORD means safety" (NLT).

In the account that follows, we will be reminded of how quick we can be sometimes to judge another person's motives when we really don't know the whole story. What we ought to be focusing on is judging our own motives and our own heart and not so much the motives and heart of another.

THE GIFT

> When Jesus was in Bethany at the house of Simon the leper, a woman came to Him having an alabaster flask of very costly fragrant oil, and she poured it on His head as He sat at the table. But when His disciples saw it, they were indignant, saying, "Why this waste? For this fragrant oil might have been sold for much and given to the poor."
>
> But when Jesus was aware of it, He said to them, "Why do you trouble the woman? For she has done a good work for Me. For you have the poor with you always, but Me you do not have always. For in pouring this fragrant oil on My body, she did it for My burial. Assuredly, I say to you, wherever this gospel is preached in the whole world, what this woman has done will also be told as a memorial to her." (Matthew 26:6-13)

Events seemed to be moving faster, and things were coming to a head in the life and ministry of Jesus. He had a number of increasingly confrontational exchanges with the religious leaders. They were angry at Him and wanted Him dead and out of the picture. But they knew they couldn't lay a hand on Him yet — not with Passover so near at hand. Thousands upon thousands of pilgrims jammed the streets of Jerusalem, and although Jesus may have been controversial, He still had many admirers. So the leaders couldn't strike yet, but they were making their plans.

Meanwhile Jesus decided to hang out with some friends at the home of Simon in Bethany.

What a conversation that must have been! Wouldn't you have loved to listen in on a little of it? Jesus had just taught what we now call the Olivet Discourse, where He spoke about the coming perilous times and the last days. It seems logical to me that His friends would have been asking Him some follow-up questions: *"Okay, Lord, going back to what You said on the Mount of Olives about the end times. Could you go over a few things with us? What was that thing about the 'abomination of desolation'? We don't quite get that. What's that all about?"*

The gospel of John tells us that Mary, Martha, and Lazarus were there, too. Jesus had just raised Lazarus from the dead, so everyone must have had questions for him as well: *"So, Lazarus, tell us about your experience. What was it like? Do you remember anything from the other side? How did it feel to be called back again?"*

John's gospel says that Martha was serving the meal, so you can imagine the room was filled with the fragrance of some of her very best recipes, drifting in from the kitchen. Nothing was too good for Jesus!

I'm sure there was a lot of energy and excitement in that home.

And a lot of love.

A woman at that dinner party (we learn from John that it was Mary, the sister of Martha and Lazarus) felt so moved by her love for Jesus that she wanted to do something extravagant—even dramatic. She wanted to demonstrate a love that went deeper than words could express.

So she came with an alabaster flask of very costly, fragrant oil and poured it on His head as He sat at the table.

It's worth noting that every time we read of Mary, she seems to be at the feet of Jesus. Maybe that is why she had the insight she did. She took advantage of every opportunity to hear what Jesus had to say.

On this occasion, she came near Jesus with a very special gift.

This is something I think women do better than men. When a guy goes to visit another guy, it never crosses his mind to bring along a gift. Are you kidding me? I wouldn't think of that in a hundred years. But it's very different with my wife, Cathe. We'll be getting ready to go to someone's house for dinner, and she will suddenly say, "Let's pick up a little gift."

"What?" I will say. "Why would we do that? We're already late. We need to get over there."

"No," she will say, "I need to get her a little gift."

"Okay, so we'll stop and pick up a plant. Something like that."

"No . . . not that. Give me a minute."

And so she will stop and think about the most appropriate gift she might give.

That is what Mary did. She may have said to herself, *I know what Jesus is going to do for us. I know He has come to die for us. It's on His mind . . . I can tell. I have to find some tangible way to tell Him I love Him. I want to show it.*

And then maybe she paused, thought about it for a moment, and said to herself, *I know what I will do! I will give Him the very best thing I have, my most precious possession. I will give Him all of it.*

So she came to Him with her alabaster bottle.

A LASTING LEGACY

What did Jesus think of Mary's gift? He was moved by it. In fact, He said in verse 13, "She will always be remembered for this deed. The story of what she has done will be told throughout the whole world, wherever the Good News is preached" (TLB).

And that is exactly what has happened in the two thousand years since Jesus spoke those words. In fact, you're reading about it right now.

It's interesting to see which miracles, teachings, and incidents are included in the Gospels. We know there were many things Jesus said and did that aren't included in any of the New Testament accounts. John 21:25 tells us that if all the things Jesus did were written down, the whole world couldn't contain the books that would have to be written. So the Holy Spirit selected certain miracles, certain teachings, and certain events in the life and ministry of Christ to be included in the four Gospels for our benefit. And this story is included in three of those accounts.

What exactly did Mary bring to Jesus? In verse 7, we read that it was an alabaster flask of very costly, fragrant oil. In his account of this event, John called it "oil of spikenard," or "pure nard" (John 12:3, NIV). We could liken this to the most exclusive, expensive perfume that one could buy. It was probably imported from India, sealed in that alabaster flask, and was no doubt a treasured family heirloom, passed from generation to generation. Just a few drops would cause a room to be filled with fragrance.

A few drops, however, wasn't what Mary had in mind.

She poured out the whole bottle on Jesus.

Why did she do it? Because she wanted to give the most precious thing she had to Jesus. It was effectively her life's savings. Pouring it out like that was an act of complete abandon, devotion, and adoration.

What is the most precious thing in your life now? Maybe it's a person, a loved one. Maybe you drive it, and it's sitting in your garage right now. Maybe it's your home, your hobby, your health, or your career. Whatever it may be, have you presented it to Jesus yet? Have you given it to

Him, with your hands wide open?

The value of a gift isn't determined by how much it costs, but by how much it cost *you*. That flask of nard cost Mary everything and was something of great sentimental and monetary value.

"WHY THIS WASTE?"

Judas Iscariot knew that value very well. With his first-century calculator close at hand, he was one of those who seemed to know the price of everything but the value of nothing. No one had to tell him that Mary's spikenard probably had a value of $25,000 to $30,000.

And she had poured it out in a few seconds. On Jesus.

"Why this waste?" he asked.

And he wasn't the only one. As we read in our Matthew account, some of the other disciples said the same thing. In short, Mary was hammered from all sides.

This is like so many people today who, instead of wondering how much they could give to God, sharpen their pencils to figure out how little they have to give. It's as though they are saying, "What is the least amount I can do and still technically be a Christian and go to heaven?" They want to give the bare minimum to God, whether it's money, time, abilities, or energy.

That's bad enough. But it's even worse to be critical of others who happen to be doing more than you—maybe even putting them down for being "too theatrical" or "too fanatical."

Mary, however, was representative of many of those first-century believers whose wholehearted abandon to Jesus turned their world upside down. When God told Philip to leave his successful ministry campaign in Samaria and head off by himself into the desert, he simply walked out the door and did what the Lord said. When God told Peter to take a crippled man by the hand and pull him to his feet, Peter immediately did so, without thinking through the implications of, *What if nothing happens?*

These men and women took risks, putting everything on the line for Jesus. As the writer of the book of Hebrews reminded his readers, "You . . . joyfully accepted the confiscation of your property, because you knew that you yourselves had better and lasting possessions" (Hebrews 10:34, NIV).

When was the last time you took a risk for the kingdom of God? Jesus was deeply moved by what Mary did. It touched Him, because He recognized it for what it really was: an act of amazing devotion.

At that warm, loving little dinner party, Mary seemed to grasp something the others either missed or refused to think about. Jesus was on His way to a cross. In mere hours, He would have to suffer and die for the sins of the world. He had told His disciples on more than one occasion, but they didn't seem to get it. It went right over their heads.

Mary got it.

Mary knew.

On that particular evening, with the intuition inherent in women, she saw the lines etching His young face and read the sorrow in His eyes. An inner sense told her the disciples were wrong in expecting Him to overthrow Rome and establish an earthly kingdom. No, Jesus was really going to die, and it was going to happen soon. Before it did, however, she had to let Him know that she understood and that she loved Him.

When you consider people who have shaped your life and whom you love deeply, who comes to mind? Have you ever told them that? Have you ever let them know how much they've meant to you? Mary didn't want to bring flowers to Jesus' funeral; she wanted to show love for Him right then, in that moment. Let me just say that if there is someone you love, and you haven't told them that for a while, you should go ahead and do that.

Why? Because you really never know when your last conversation with that person will be. Maybe it's a spiritual leader who has marked your life. Maybe it's a husband or wife, son or daughter. Maybe it's a loyal friend. Let that person know how you value him, how you love her. If you can't say it to the person's face, write a letter or card—or even an e-mail. Just get it done.

Mary was saying, "Lord, I want to show You right now what You mean to me." And she didn't pour out two drops of her precious ointment; she emptied the bottle on Him.

Judas was critical of what Mary did, although he cloaked his criticism in spiritual terms, saying, "This fragrant oil might have been sold for much and given to the poor."

Not that he really gave a fig for the poor.

The gospel of John tells us that Judas "was in charge of the disciples' funds and often dipped into them for his own use!" (John 12:6, TLB).

In other words, Judas was embezzling.

BE CAREFUL WITH YOUR CRITICISM

It's interesting that Judas accused Mary of waste, when the very word *Judas* means "son of waste." Judas complained that Mary had wasted a year's wages, but Judas had wasted much, much more than that. He had been handpicked by Jesus Himself, and he had the opportunity to spend three years with someone who was not only the greatest man who

314 • FOLLOWING JESUS IN THE MODERN WORLD

ever lived, but was the very Son of God. Yet he threw it all away for a few coins—and had the audacity to accuse a good-hearted woman of wasting her resources, simply because she gave them to Jesus.

It's often true that the most hypercritical people are involved in far worse things than the people they berate and criticize.

This is exactly what Christ was talking about when He said, "And why worry about a speck in your friend's eye when you have a log in your own?" (Matthew 7:3, NLT).

When are you and I the most critical of others? It's often when they do something we're already struggling with ourselves. After decades in the ministry, I have come to understand that those who complain the most do the least, and those who do the most complain the least.

Yes, there is a place for asking questions and offering legitimate criticism. But people who are always critical and always jumping to conclusions do a great deal more harm than good. In reality, it's a sure pathway to a lonely, unhappy life. No one wants to be around someone who is always critical and negative.

In this story, Judas appeared to be thrifty and compassionate, but in reality he was a false friend and a betrayer. He and others had painted Mary as frivolous, silly, and wasteful, when in reality she was perceptive and sacrificial.

Jesus immediately defended Mary from these unfair and shortsighted attacks. In verse 10 He said, "Why do you trouble the woman? For she has done a good work for Me." In Mark's version of this same story, Jesus said, "She has done what she could" (Mark 14:8, NLT).

Sometimes I think unbelievers look at Christians and think we're wasting our time. Last Sunday morning, I picked up a cup of coffee at the drive-through, and the girl serving me said, "Big plans for today?"

"Yes," I answered. "I'm going to church."

That remark was met by complete silence. She didn't answer a single word and didn't know what to say. It was as though I had said something off-color or embarrassing.

But who knows? Maybe she will think about it, and maybe the Lord will use that little encounter in her life to remind her that people in her town would actually invest a beautiful California Sunday morning to worship and learn about Jesus.

Jesus said of Mary, "She has done what she could," and we must also do what we can. I have heard it said, "I am only one, but I am one. I cannot do everything, but I can do something. And what I can do, I ought to do. And what I ought to do, by the grace of God, I will do."

There always will be people who think that giving up their lives for Jesus is a waste. Maybe some young person will give up a promising career to go into some developing nation as a missionary. And some will say, "She had such a great education. It seems like such a waste." Or maybe, "He had so much talent. It just seems like he's throwing it away."

Maybe you've been criticized for giving money to the church or some organization that is trying to reach people for Christ. Someone has said to you, "Why are you throwing your money away? What a waste!"

Nothing is ever wasted if it is done with the right heart for the glory of God. And in the end, the only one who can really judge our motives is God Himself.

Bottom line? Do what you can while you can, because when we stand before Jesus on that final day, we all will wish we had done more.

TESTED BY FIRE

Every believer will stand at the judgment seat of Christ. This isn't the Great White Throne Judgment, spoken of in Revelation 20. That is for unbelievers and will be terrible beyond description. Those whose names are not found in the Book of Life will be thrown into the lake of fire.

The judgment I'm speaking of won't determine whether you get into heaven; it will take place when you're already in heaven. It will be a time when rewards are meted out to God's people, where you and I will be recognized and rewarded for faithful service to the Lord.

Here is how the Bible describes that day:

> No one can lay any foundation other than the one already laid, which is Jesus Christ. If any man builds on this foundation using gold, silver, costly stones, wood, hay or straw, his work will be shown for what it is, because the Day will bring it to light. It will be revealed with fire, and the fire will test the quality of each man's work. If what he has built survives, he will receive his reward. If it is burned up, he will suffer loss; he himself will be saved, but only as one escaping through the flames. (1 Corinthians 3:11-15, NIV)

At that time, Christ will closely examine the motives of your life. It won't be a judgment about quantity as much as it will be about quality. Why did you do what you did? If you have been faithful and served the Lord with what He set before you, you will be rewarded for your faithfulness. But if you have been unfaithful or lived with wrong or self-serving motives, you will not receive that reward. The fire of the Lord will burn right through it. Yes, you will be saved, but you will be "as one escaping through the flames."

As Alan Redpath once pointed out, you can have a saved soul and a lost life.

It is not enough to just get to heaven. We want to get to heaven having done something with our lives for God's glory.

That's the story of Mary of Bethany. Jesus said, "She has done what she could," and we need to take whatever influence, opportunities, resources, relationships, and time that God has given us, and do what we can as well.

As Jesus reminds us, we need to work while it is day, for "the night is coming when no one can work" (John 9:4).

In the early 1900s, William Borden was the heir of the Borden dairy estate and was already a millionaire. When William was sixteen, his parents sent him on an around-the-world trip for a graduation present. So young Borden, a Christian, traveled through Asia, the Middle East, and Europe and found himself with a growing burden and desire to tell lost people about salvation in Christ. Finally he wrote home and told his parents he was going to give his life to prepare for the mission field. And after making that decision, William Borden wrote two words in the back of his Bible and dated them. Those two words were, *"No reserves."*

After graduating from Yale and determined to fulfill the call that God had placed on his life, Borden turned down some very high-paying job offers. His father told him that he would never work in the Borden company again. It was then he wrote two more words in the back of his Bible and dated them: *"No retreat."*

He went on to graduate from Princeton Seminary in New Jersey and decided to go to Egypt, where he would study Arabic in order to reach the Muslim people. Borden, however, contracted cerebral meningitis during his training in Egypt and died at the age of twenty-five.

Sometime later, his parents were going through his personal effects and came across his Bible. In addition to the two phrases he had written previously, William had penned two more words while he was in Egypt: *"No regrets."*

Those three statements summed up his brief life: *No reserves. No retreat. No regrets.*

Some would say, "Oh, what a waste of life!"

But the fact is, no life is ever wasted when it is invested in bringing people to Jesus and lived for the glory of God.

William Borden didn't live very long or have the opportunities to reach the Muslim world for Christ as he had so earnestly longed to do. But like Mary, he did what he could.

We can do no less.

18

FALLEN BUT FORGIVEN

I don't know where your heart might be as you begin this chapter.

Maybe you feel "beaten up" spiritually or have failed in some way, shape, or form. Perhaps you feel defeated, and that when it comes to the Christian life, you're a loser.

Why, you ask yourself, *did God even call me to begin with? If He has foreknowledge of everything that will happen, why would He pick a loser like me?*

Here is what we need to realize. God doesn't just see you in your weakness. *He sees you for what you can become.*

My little granddaughter Stella and I were hanging out recently, and she was looking at my face, peering into my eyes. Then she got up really close to me, pressed her nose against my nose, and said, "Papa, I can see myself in your eyes."

She could see her own reflection in my eyes. Well, I looked into those pretty blue-green eyes of hers and said, "Stella you are always in my eyes, and in my heart, too."

What would we see if we got really close to the Lord and looked into His eyes? Would we see ourselves? Would we say, "Lord, I can see myself in Your eyes. I can see that You love me and care about me"?

Over in Hawaii they have an expression they use if you look at someone askance or with a mean expression. They call it "stink eye." They will say, "Hey, bra. You no be giving me stink eye!" Sometimes we may feel that God is collectively giving stink eye to all of us.

But that isn't true.

If you look closely — and you have to be very close — you will see yourself in His eyes. God sees you for what you can become. When the psalmist realized this truth, it filled him with wonder. David wrote, "How precious it is, Lord, to realize that you are thinking about me constantly! I can't even count how many times a day your thoughts turn towards me. And when I waken in the morning, you are still thinking of me!" (Psalm 139:17-18, TLB).

Jesus looks at you and sees you for what you could be.

Remember when the Lord gave a new name to Simon? He was plain old "Simon, son of Jonas." But Jesus said to him, "You are Peter," a word that means "a rock."

I wonder whether the other disciples laughed up their sleeves a little when Jesus said that. "*Simon? A rock?* He's joking, isn't He? If there is anything Simon is *not*, it's a rock. He's impetuous. Impulsive. Hotheaded. Shooting off his mouth when he should keep quiet. He's not a rock!"

But that was the reflection of Simon in Jesus' eyes. The Lord saw a rock. The Lord saw Simon for what he would become. And that is the way He sees you, too.

We see problems, God sees solutions. We see failure, God sees potential. We see a dead end, God sees a new beginning.

You might say, "Greg, you have no idea. I have a horrible failure in my past." Yet I am here to tell you that God can not only forgive you, but He can also recommission you. We will see that played out beautifully in the story before us in Matthew 26.

"THIS NIGHT . . . YOU WILL DENY ME"

We pick up the story in a moment of great intensity. We're in the Upper Room with Jesus and the disciples, and Jesus has just revealed that one of them is about to betray Him.

Have you ever heard the old cliché "You could have cut the tension with a knife"? That expression fits this moment to a T. The disciples were staggered by this revelation and couldn't seem to comprehend it. *One of them? Betray Jesus? How could it be?*

That's when Jesus turned to Judas Iscariot and said, "What you are about to do, do quickly" (John 13:27, NIV). And Judas left the room and went out into the night. Even then, the disciples didn't make the connection. They simply couldn't conceive of their fellow disciple ever doing such a thing. When Judas had gone, Jesus celebrated the Last Supper with the remaining eleven. They broke the bread, and they drank the cup together.

That was when Jesus hit them with another bombshell:

"All of you will be made to stumble because of Me this night, for it is written: 'I will strike the Shepherd, and the sheep of the flock will be scattered.' But after I have been raised, I will go before you to Galilee."

Peter answered and said to Him, "Even if all are made to stumble because of You, I will never be made to stumble."

Jesus said to him, "Assuredly, I say to you that this night, before the rooster crows, you will deny Me three times."

Peter said to Him, "Even if I have to die with You, I will not deny You!"

And so said all the disciples. (Matthew 26:31-35)

Luke's version of this same story adds a detail we don't find here in Matthew. According to Luke 22:31-32, Jesus went on to say, "Simon, Simon! Indeed, Satan has asked for you, that he may sift you as wheat. But I have prayed for you, that your faith should not fail; and when you have returned to Me, strengthen your brethren."

So let's put it all together, this series of shocking pronouncements the Lord made to that little body of men that night in the Upper Room. Not only was one of their number about to betray Jesus to the authorities, but they would all desert Him in the moment of crisis, leaving Him alone.

Peter, however, just wasn't buying it. He basically said, "Not me, Lord. These other guys, maybe. But not me. I wouldn't desert You if my life depended on it!"

That's when the Lord had to give Peter a jolt of reality therapy. He looked him right in the eyes and said, "Simon, let Me say this plainly. Before the rooster crows twice, you will deny three times that you ever knew Me. And you need to know this, too. Satan has been asking, over and over again, that you would be taken out of the care and protection of God."

Now, that is a terrifying thought.

Can you imagine Jesus saying that to you? "Oh, by the way, Satan himself has been asking for you by name, so he can destroy you."

The devil is a created being and is not the equal of God. While God is all-powerful and present everywhere, Satan's knowledge is limited, and though he has many demons serving him, he can't be in more than one place at one time.

According to this Luke 22 passage, the devil has to actually request to harass someone. And why would he request Peter? Perhaps because he saw Peter as a potential leader and a future threat.

God isn't the only one who recognizes leadership; Satan does too. And the evil one often sets his sights on those whom he supposes to be the greatest threat to his kingdom. He isn't going to waste his energy flogging a dead horse, but he (or his demons) will harass and attack those whom God might use.

So if you have been tempted or spiritually beaten up lately, that could be very good news and an indication that God is using you. The reason the devil is after you is because he sees you as a potential threat.

But Jesus went on and told Peter, "I have prayed for you, that your faith should not fail; and when you have returned to Me, strengthen your brethren."

In other words, "Yes, Peter, you are going to have a lapse, wander away from Me, and even deny that you know Me. But you will learn from this. And when you return to Me, you will be a better man for it, and you will be able to bring words of encouragement to others."

Crushed as he may have been to get that news, Peter should have been encouraged by one thing. Jesus specifically told him, "I am praying for you."

You know what an encouragement it is when someone you know and love says to you, "I have been praying for you night and day." How much more if that someone is Jesus Himself?

And He is praying for you, too.

Listen to these incredible words from Romans 8:

Who dares accuse us whom God has chosen for his own? No one — for God himself has given us right standing with himself. Who then will condemn us? No one — for Christ Jesus died for us and was raised to life for us, and he is sitting in the place of honor at God's right hand, pleading for us.

Can anything ever separate us from Christ's love? Does it mean he no longer loves us if we have trouble or calamity, or are persecuted, or hungry, or destitute, or in danger, or threatened with death? (verses 33-35, NLT)

In other words, Christ is in your corner. Jesus Himself is praying for you. And because of that, you never will be separated from God. Were it not for the prayers of Jesus, I wouldn't stand a chance. Neither would you.

Scottish preacher Robert Murray McCheyne once made this statement: "If I could hear Christ praying for me in the next room I would not fear a million of enemies. Yet the distance makes no difference. He is praying for me."[1]

And Jesus was praying for Peter in those dangerous, critical moments of Peter's life.

I don't believe that anyone "suddenly" falls. I think

there were distinct steps that led to this worst stumble in Peter's life.

THE ANATOMY OF A BACKSLIDE
First Step Down: Too Much Self-Confidence

Again, looking at Matthew 26:33, Peter declared, "Even if all are made to stumble because of You, I will never be made to stumble."

Peter was saying, in effect, "I don't know about James and John, and I'm not sure about Matthew or Philip or all the rest of them. But I will tell You this, Lord. I will never stumble. It will never happen to me. You can take that to the bank."

Be careful of making statements like that.

Be careful of saying, "Oh, I would never do that. I'm really strong in that area. I would never commit that sin in a million years."

Yet that may be the very area where you will fall.

Don't ever put confidence in yourself, in your own strength of character, in your own value system, in your own sense of dignity, in your own common sense.

That's what Peter did.

The Lord told Jeremiah, "The heart is hopelessly dark and deceitful, a puzzle that no one can figure out" (Jeremiah 17:9, MSG).

When you and I point an accusing finger at someone, we have three more pointing right back at us. We all have the propensity for doing great wrongs, and the moment we think we don't, we're in great peril. It's like the hymn says, "Prone to wander, Lord, I feel it, prone to leave the God I love . . ."

So don't put confidence in yourself. Cling to the Lord and walk in His protection. The simple fact is, an unguarded strength is a double weakness.

Second Step Down: Neglecting to Pray

A little bit later in Matthew 26, when Jesus and His men were in the Garden of Gethsemane, we read of the following incident:

> [Jesus] went a little farther and fell on His face, and prayed, saying, "O My Father, if it is possible, let this cup pass from Me; nevertheless, not as I will, but as You will."
>
> Then He came to the disciples and found them sleeping, and said to Peter, "What! Could you not watch with Me one hour? Watch and pray, lest you enter into temptation. The spirit indeed is willing, but the flesh is weak." (verses 39-41)

It was surely the lowest moment of Jesus' life at that point. He was in utter anguish as He contemplated the horrors of the cross. All He wanted from His disciples in that moment was to be present and praying.

Instead, they were slumbering and sleeping.

This was a direct result of the first sin of self-confidence. Why? Because pride and prayerlessness go hand in hand. We must never forget that prayer is not only for petition, but also for protection and for preparation. Prayer not only gives us what we want; it prepares us and protects us from what we don't want.

Most of us pray when we are faced with a specific need. A crisis hits. We get bad news from the doctor. We're having trouble with our marriage. We just got let go from our job. The rebellious child is acting up. "Oh man," we say, "we'd better start praying. We need to bring these things to the Lord."

And that is exactly what we should do.

But what about when things are going well? We're feeling healthy, the bills are paid, the job is looking good, and there seems to be good news all around. Do we pray as much then?

Jesus said, "Watch and pray, lest you enter into temptation."

We need to pray for daily protection from the attacks of the evil one and all his minions.

Jesus knew very well what He was about to face: not only the physical torture of dying on a cross, but also the righteous wrath of His Father as Jesus took upon Himself all of your sin, all of my sin, and all of the world's sin, past, present, and future.

He recoiled from that. Of course He did! He prayed, "Father, if it is possible, let this cup pass from Me." All He asked for was some companionship in those darkest of all moments. He didn't need a sermon; He needed some friends. But His friends had totally checked out and were fast asleep.

Their defense, according to one of the Gospels, was that they slept from sorrow. Have you ever cried yourself to sleep, where you literally fell asleep because you were so exhausted from weeping? I've been there. I know what that is like. And these disciples just didn't know what to think, how to react, or what to do. Their whole world was unraveling. There was Jesus, their Lord, sweating blood in the garden and crying out to His Father in the darkness, over and over again. They stayed awake for a little while, but they finally just fell asleep in their sorrow.

Jesus had told them to watch and pray, but instead, they slept.

In Ephesians 5:14, the apostle Paul used sleep as a metaphor for spiritual lethargy and apathy. He wrote, "Wake up,

O sleeper, rise from the dead, and Christ will shine on you" (NIV).

When we're really sleepy, we can act just a little bit delirious. Have you ever noticed that when someone wakes you up with a phone call, you always deny it?

It may be 3:00 a.m., and they say, "Did I wake you?"

Well of course they did! But you will answer, "Umm, no, I was awake. I'm up." Yes, you may be "up," but you're still half asleep.

Years ago I went to speak in Australia to a group of Christian broadcasters. I had decided that I wanted to make it a real fast trip, just jetting in and jetting out. So I told them, "I'll tell you what. I will speak on the same night that I arrive."

Normally, when I go to Australia or New Zealand, I'll get there a few days ahead of time to acclimate myself to the huge time change. But this time, I decided to dispense with all that. Big mistake!

While we were driving to the venue where we were going to have the event, I was doing radio interviews in the car on the cell phone. We finally got to the venue with an hour to spare before my message . . . and my brain was scrambled like an omelet. I was so tired and so jetlagged that I couldn't even put a sentence together, let alone a one-hour message.

I grabbed one of my friends and said, "Okay, here is what you need to do. Go get me a triple espresso, and I'll drink it five minutes before I go out." So he brought it to me just as they told me, "You're on in five minutes."

Gulping down the coffee, I walked out in front of the audience and began to speak. It was almost like having an out-of-body experience. It was a strange sort of detachment, where I was listening to myself speak at the same time I was speaking. *But what was I saying?* Between the surge of caffeine and the extreme jetlag, I couldn't be sure. It didn't seem to be making much sense.

I finally told myself, *Just read your notes, Greg. When you wrote those, you were in your right mind. Because right now, you're delirious.*

But that's what being half asleep is like. You don't think clearly. Your thoughts are foggy. You don't make good decisions. And spiritual sleep is something we can all slip into, as the disciples did in Gethsemane. If ever those followers of Jesus needed to focus and pray with all their hearts, it was right then.

Did you know that failure to pray can actually be a sin? Sin isn't just breaking a commandment, though it includes that. There is also the sin of *omission.* In James 4:17 we read, "To him that knows to do good and does not do it, to him it is sin." And what does the Bible say about prayer?

> Men always ought to pray and not lose heart.
> (Luke 18:1)

> Pray continually; give thanks in all circumstances, for this is God's will for you in Christ Jesus.
> (1 Thessalonians 5:17-18, NIV)

So Peter was self-confident and neglected to pray.

Third Step Down: Trusting Human Effort Instead of God's Power

Matthew 26:51 says, "Suddenly, one of those who were with Jesus stretched out his hand and drew his sword, struck the servant of the high priest, and cut off his ear." That was Peter, of course. Matthew goes on to record this:

> But Jesus said to him, "Put your sword in its place,
> for all who take the sword will perish by the sword.
> Or do you think that I cannot now pray to My Father,
> and He will provide Me with more than twelve legions
> of angels?" (verses 52-53)

Poor Peter got everything turned around. He was boasting when he should have been listening and sleeping when he should have been praying. And then he was fighting when he should have been surrendering.

Fourth Step Down: Following at a Distance

Verse 58 tells us, "Peter followed Him at a distance to the high priest's courtyard. And he went in and sat with the servants to see the end."

Distance from fellowship and a closeness with the Lord is at the heart of every person's fall.

We could illustrate this with a marriage that is falling apart. People will cite all the usual reasons: money, parenting, communication, sexual intimacy, and on and on.

Yes, those are important elements in a happy marriage. But those aren't the places where the marriage broke down. It broke down in *communication*. Something happened to the friendship and companionship on which the marriage was built. The closeness and warmth turned cool, and as a result, all of those other issues found their way into an already fractured marriage.

The same is true of our relationship with God. When our communication with Him breaks down, it is not because He ceases communicating with us; it is because we stop listening to Him. We get too busy to open the day with Bible study and prayer. We allow unconfessed sins to linger. We actually begin closing our ears to the voice of the Holy Spirit. Then, before we know it, we find ourselves following at a distance.

That is what happened to Peter.

I heard the story of a little boy who fell out of bed in the middle of the night. When his mom asked him what happened, he replied, "I think I stayed too close to the place where I got in."

That is why we fall away. We try to walk the edge between our new life and our old life; we stay too close to the place where we got in. In Peter's case, look where he ended up: at the enemy's fire.

Fifth Step Down: Standing at the Enemy's Fire

> Now Peter sat outside in the courtyard. And a servant girl came to him, saying, "You also were with Jesus of Galilee."
>
> But he denied it before them all, saying, "I do not know what you are saying."
>
> And when he had gone out to the gateway, another girl saw him and said to those who were there, "This fellow also was with Jesus of Nazareth."
>
> But again he denied with an oath, "I do not know the Man!"
>
> And a little later those who stood by came up and said to Peter, "Surely you also are one of them, for your speech betrays you."
>
> Then he began to curse and swear, saying, "I do not know the Man!"

Immediately a rooster crowed. And Peter remembered the word of Jesus who had said to him, "Before the rooster crows, you will deny Me three times." So he went out and wept bitterly. (verses 69-75)

Peter was trying to go undercover, keeping tabs on events without really committing himself one way or another. He thought he could just blend into the woodwork. Have you ever tried to be an undercover Christian? I heard a story about a man who only went to church on Christmas and Easter. So after the service one Christmas, the pastor stopped him at the door and said, "My friend, I only see you about twice a year. You need to join the Lord's army."

At that, the man whispered into the pastor's ear, "I'm in the Secret Service."

Is that you? Are you a Secret Service Christian?

At this point, Peter was worn down, defeated, weak, and vulnerable. Yes, he was following Jesus, but at a distance. And following at a distance, Peter had become cold and was attracted to the warmth of a fire in the high priest's courtyard—*the enemy's fire.*

Why was he even there? Matthew gives the answer in verse 58: "He went in and sat with the servants to see the end."

How sad. Peter had evidently forgotten all that Jesus had said about rising from the dead. Now he was just waiting for the end: the end of Jesus' life, the end of his hopes and dreams, the end of everything he held dear.

But it wasn't the end at all. In fact, it was very, very near to a new beginning.

Here was Peter's problem: He was in the wrong place with the wrong people about to do the wrong thing. That's what happens when we fall into sin. We're in the wrong places, hanging out with the wrong crowd. Before we know it, we're swept along and begin doing the wrong thing.

Some girl says, "Oh man, I really made a big mistake. My boyfriend and I had sex. How did this happen to us?"

"Where did this happen?"

"In a hotel room."

"How did you happen to be in a hotel room with your boyfriend?"

"Well, we just went and booked it. And then . . . we were tempted."

"No, you had already given in to temptation by being in the wrong place with the wrong person at the wrong time for the wrong reasons. What happened after that was just an expected outcome."

Or maybe a man with a drinking problem is crestfallen because he has gone back to the bottle. "I fell off the wagon," he says so mournfully. "I have been clean and sober for almost a year, and then I went out and got totally drunk. How could this happen?"

"So where were you?"

"In a bar."

"Why in the world were you in a bar?"

"They've got those nice flat-screen TVs, and I wanted to watch the game."

Seriously?

It really isn't rocket science. When you hang out with the wrong people at the wrong place at the wrong time, it's only a matter of time until you do the wrong thing.

Psalm 1 says it so well:

> Blessed is the man
> Who walks not in the counsel of the ungodly,
> Nor stands in the path of sinners,

Nor sits in the seat of the scornful;
But his delight is in the law of the Lord,
And in His law he meditates day and night.
     (verses 1-2)

What a picture of backsliding! Have you ever noticed the regression in these verses? First the man *walks* in the counsel of the ungodly. Then he *stands* in the path of sinners. Finally, he *sits* in the seat of the scornful.

The fact is, if he had refused to walk anywhere near the counsel of the ungodly, he would never have found himself standing in the path of sinners or, finally, sitting around with those who were utterly scornful of God and His people.

It's like telling yourself one night that you have to lose weight. The next morning, it seems like a good idea to take a different route to work, avoiding the Krispy Kreme doughnut shop.

But then you say to yourself, *That's ridiculous. What could it hurt to walk by the place? I don't have to go in.*

So you walk by, and the scent of freshly baked doughnuts (is there any sweeter fragrance than that?) wafts under your nose. You glance at the store and see the "open" sign on. Then you look through the window and happen to see those beautiful glazed doughnuts coming down the little conveyor belt, glistening in the light. You were walking, then you were standing—with your face pressed up against the glass, looking and salivating. And the next thing you know, you're sitting inside with a doughnut in each hand. That's how it always happens.

The fire wasn't Peter's problem; it was the people around that fire and the subsequent conversation that got him into trouble. So it is with us. When the passion and fire we had for Jesus begin to tail off and grow cold, we look elsewhere for warmth.

That brings us to Peter's final step down.

Sixth Step Down: The Denial

Luke's gospel reveals that there was plenty of time between each of Peter's three denials. First, some girl says, "Hey, wait a second. I know you. You're one of those followers of Jesus!"

Peter, still in his undercover mode, tries to brush her off. "No. You've got the wrong guy. Not me."

Another one says, "I know you. You were with Jesus of Nazareth, right? Come on! You were one of them."

Peter gets more gruff. "No. It's not me. *I don't even know this Jesus.*"

Why didn't he just leave? Why didn't he walk away from that fire at the very first challenge? He wouldn't have had to say a word!

We could ask ourselves the same question, couldn't we?

The last time you were tempted, why didn't you just get up and leave? Why didn't you walk out of the theater when that compromising scene came on the screen? You knew you shouldn't have gone to that movie in the first place. And then there it is, right in your face. Why didn't you walk out the door?

Or maybe it was a time when you were in a group of people and somebody started making fun of the Christian faith and even mocking God. Why didn't you speak up?

Sometimes it's not so easy to "just walk away." You get worn down, and you stop fighting. That's where Peter was. He was worn down, emotionally exhausted, and spiritually numb. He allowed himself to become weak and vulnerable to the attack from Satan that he knew was coming. As a result, he got caught in a miserable web of cowardice and compromise.

Even after he had denied the Lord twice, there was still time for Peter to get out of there. So why did he stay at the fire? It might have been cold, but it wasn't *that* cold.

Nevertheless, in Matthew 26:73, we read, "And a little later those who stood by came up and said to Peter, 'Surely you also are one of them, for your speech betrays you.'"

What does that mean? For one thing, it meant that Peter had been talking with people around the fire. And at least one person had picked up on the fact that he had a Galilean accent.

Busted! At that moment, he could have come clean and said, "Okay, you're right. I am a Galilean, and I am a disciple of that innocent Man being unfairly tried in that house right there."

Instead, he dug himself in deeper. Verse 74 says, "Then he began to curse and swear, saying, 'I do not know the Man!' Immediately a rooster crowed."

This doesn't mean that Peter swore like a sailor, even though he was one. The word *cursed* here is a strong term that means you pronounce death on yourself at the hand of God if you are lying. It's the worst case of taking the Lord's name in vain imaginable. Peter was, in essence, saying, "May God kill and damn me if I'm not speaking the truth." Or to state it another way, "I swear to God. I take an oath that I don't know Jesus."

And then the rooster crowed. Luke added this heartbreaking detail: "The Lord turned and looked straight at Peter. Then Peter remembered the word the Lord had spoken to him: 'Before the rooster crows today, you will disown me three times.' And he went outside and wept bitterly" (Luke 22:61-62, NIV).

What was in that look? Hurt? Reproach? Was the Lord giving Peter the stink eye?

We don't know, of course. But I think that if Peter could have managed to get very, very close to Jesus in that moment, he would have seen himself in Jesus' eyes, just like little Stella could see herself in my eyes.

He would have seen that Jesus loved him. He would have remembered that Jesus had predicted this very specifically, but He had also predicted Peter's strong return and restoration: *"When you have returned to Me, strengthen your brethren."*

As Peter thought about it, he would have remembered Jesus' warnings. He would have recalled how the Lord had said to him, "Peter, you're going to fail badly. But then you're going to repent and turn back to Me. And when you do, you'll be a better man for it. You will learn from your mistakes, and you will help many people turn to Me for salvation."

The repentance began as Peter finally left the fire of his enemies and went out and wept bitterly for his sin.

Three days later, Jesus rose from the dead, and the angels gave Mary a very specific message to deliver to the apostles. And what was that message?

"Go, tell his disciples and Peter, 'He is going ahead of you into Galilee. There you will see him, just as he told you.'" (Mark 16:7, NIV)

You have to love that! The angels didn't say, "Go tell His disciples and James and John."

Nor did they say, "Go tell His disciples and Mary, Jesus' mother."

No, it was, "Go tell His disciples *and Peter.*"

Why Peter? Because Peter desperately needed some encouragement.

As far as he was concerned, life was pretty much over for him. He had failed his Lord at the most crucial moment, after bragging in front of everyone about how brave and loyal and fearless he would be. He had denied his Lord in his Lord's own hearing, swearing that he didn't even know anyone named Jesus. So how could he go on pretending he was a follower? There was no hope or future for him.

And yet, through that message, Jesus was saying, "I remember you, Peter, and I want you to know I am risen."

Peter had done things and said things he was ashamed of. But Jesus was calling him back. Jesus wanted to forgive him, restore him, and fill his life with hope and purpose once again.

It's like that commercial on TV for a little device that senior citizens can wear around their necks. If you fall, you can push a button on the electronic pendant, and it will call emergency medical help. In the commercial, the elderly person who has fallen is shouting into the pendant, "I have fallen, and I can't get up!"

That's the way Peter probably felt. And perhaps that's the way you feel, too. You know that you're far away from the Lord, but the road back seems difficult or even impossible to you.

But that isn't true.

Just change your mind about the direction in which you've been heading and turn toward Jesus, calling on Him to rescue you, forgive you, and restore you.

You don't even have to push a button. Just speak His name.

19

MAKE UP YOUR MIND

In a rare moment of personal reflection, songwriter Jimmy Buffet once stated, "Indecision may or may not be my problem."

Make up your mind, Jimmy!

For the most part, I think of myself as a decisive person. I generally know what I want to do, where I want to go, and what I want to say. It is not that hard for me to make up my mind and just go with it.

When Cathe and I go out to eat at one of our favorite restaurants, I don't even need a menu. I already know what I want when I walk in the door. I'm usually hungry, so I just want to sit down, order the food, and get things moving along.

But then Cathe says to the server, "I'd like to see a menu, please."

A menu?

"Why do you want to look at the menu?" I ask her. "You order the same thing every time."

"Yes," she says, "but I'd still like to look at the menu."

When the server comes back, she asks a dozen questions—all the details about this dish or that dish. And then . . . she orders what she always orders.

I don't really understand it. It's evidently a ritual she feels she needs to go through. I just want to order the food, because I've known what I wanted to order since we left the house.

Even so, ordering off a menu isn't what you'd call a life-altering decision. There are many other decisions and choices in life that are truly weighty, and you want to be very sure about your direction before you make them.

Deciding whom you will marry, for instance, is a decision that could shape your destiny and literally impact generations to come. It's never something you want to treat casually or rush into. Someone has wisely said, "Keep your eyes wide open before marriage and half-shut afterward." Too many couples, however, do the opposite. They go into marriage with their eyes half-shut, and then somewhere down the road find themselves in an eye-opening moment when they say, "Oh no! What have I done?"

The most important decision we ever will make is what we do with Jesus Christ. That's a question that not only will touch every part of your life, but it will also determine your eternal destiny.

In this chapter, we will consider an indecisive man who ended up letting others do his thinking for him. He was a man who tried to appease a fickle, bloodthirsty mob and then somehow reconcile that decision with his own troubled conscience.

His name was Pontius Pilate, the Roman governor of Judea.

DECISION TIME

Back in those days, they didn't elect their governors as we do. They were appointed by Rome, and it was a very important position.

In the account we'll be considering in this chapter, Pilate found himself in Jerusalem at a critical time. Normally, he would have been relaxing in his beautiful palace in Caesarea, on the Mediterranean coast. But on this occasion his duties required him to be in Jerusalem, at a time when thousands of Jewish pilgrims filled the city for Passover. During his time there, the well-ordered life of the Roman governor collided with Jesus Christ.

Once that happened, there was no escaping the situation in which Pilate found himself. He tried everything he could to get out of or get around the circumstances, but nothing worked.

Pilate had to make up his mind about Jesus of Nazareth.

The last thing the Roman governor wanted at that moment was some kind of conflict with the Jews. He'd already had a number of run-ins with the people, and he certainly didn't need to have negative reports getting back to Caesar in Rome.

History tells us that Pilate was a brutal man and an anti-Semite; he hated the Jewish people under his supervision. Nevertheless, he had been appointed governor of Judea and had to somehow make the best of it.

In one historical record from that era, a letter from Herod Agrippa to Caligula, the Roman emperor, has surfaced. Agrippa described the governor in unflattering terms: "Pilate is unbending and recklessly hard. He is a man of notorious reputation, severe brutality, prejudice, savage violence, and murder."

If even hard cases like Agrippa and Caligula thought Pilate was over-the-top ruthless, he must have been a cruel man indeed. That's one reason the otherwise unbending, prejudiced Pilate appeared so indecisive in this account. Normally he was a guy who could dish out death penalties with ease. *"Okay, you're going to get executed. Now, get out of my court. Next?"*

But when Pilate was confronted with Jesus, he found himself strangely torn. For political reasons, he didn't want to offend the religious leaders who had hauled Jesus into his court. But on the other hand, he *knew*—way down in his heart of hearts—that Jesus was an innocent Man and didn't deserve to die.

There were, of course, other forces at play in this story. God Himself was involved in these events, as was Satan and the powers of darkness. And while the objectives of God and the devil were not the same, their desired outcome was the same: the death of Jesus Christ on a Roman cross. Satan wanted to bring this about to stop and silence Jesus. God the Father wanted to bring it about so that Jesus could die in our place, absorb the wrath of God for us, and allow us to be forgiven of our sins. So both heaven and hell were bending events toward Calvary, and Pilate was caught at the crossroads.

Even so, Pilate had a choice in the matter, and we can't let him off the hook for what he did. As with Judas Iscariot, he became a willing accomplice in the devil's plan. He was about to find out that everyone has to make a decision about Jesus Christ.

Some people have a difficult time deciding what they want to do. I remember hearing about a man back in the days of the Civil War who couldn't make up his mind whether to fight for the North or the South. He finally chose to wear the coat of the North and the trousers of the South. When he stepped out onto the battlefield, he ended up getting shot at from both sides.

That's pretty much what happened to Pilate. What was he going to do with Jesus Christ? He had to decide, even though he didn't want to decide. Nevertheless, it's a question every one of us must face in life. It isn't so much the *sin* question as much as it is the *Son* question. We will have to give an account of what we decide about Jesus Christ.

Sometimes we call this event in Scripture "Jesus before Pilate." But we could just as easily call it "Pilate before Jesus." Which man was really in the place of judgment? Pilate may have thought he was giving a ruling that determined Jesus' fate, but in another sense, he was about to decide his own eternal destiny, based on what he would do with Jesus.

THE HORNS OF A DILEMMA

Pilate found himself on the proverbial horns of a dilemma—never a very comfortable place to be.

The Jewish leadership had cross-examined Jesus, deciding He had to die because He had claimed to be the Messiah. They had managed to win over many in the large, teeming crowd of Jewish pilgrims, persuading them to also cry out for Jesus' blood.

They sent Him to Pontius Pilate, placing the governor in a quandary. If he didn't go along with the Jewish leaders, they could enflame the crowds into a major riot—and Rome wouldn't like that at all. But on the other hand, he immediately recognized that Jesus was completely innocent of the charges they had made.

Pilate might have wished he was back in Caesarea on a terrace in a hammock with a lemonade. But wishing wouldn't do any good.

He had to make a decision.

> Now Jesus stood before the governor. And the governor asked Him, saying, "Are You the King of the Jews?"
>
> Jesus said to him, "It is as you say." And while He was being accused by the chief priests and elders, He answered nothing.
>
> Then Pilate said to Him, "Do You not hear how many things they testify against You?" But He answered him not one word, so that the governor marveled greatly. (Matthew 27:11-14)

The gospel of John fills in some key gaps in Matthew's account. The Jewish leaders didn't want to execute Jesus themselves, and Pilate didn't want to have to deal with the situation at all. "Judge Him according to your law," he told them (John 18:31). In other words, he was effectively saying, "You want to execute Jesus? So execute Him. Don't bother me with this. I don't want to deal with this. Take this out of my courtroom."

"Oh no," they essentially reminded him. "We're not allowed to put people to death."

But that really wasn't true; they stoned Stephen to death in the book of Acts. This time, however, they wanted Pilate to do their dirty work for them, and they demanded a Roman execution.

What they didn't realize, of course, was that their actions would bring about the fulfillment of Bible prophecy. The Scriptures not only said the Messiah would die, but also specified how He would die, painting a very clear picture of crucifixion hundreds of years before that horrific means of execution had even been dreamed up by evil minds.

Passages in the Old Testament give graphic details of what would happen to the Messiah, including these verses in Psalm 22:

> They pierced My hands and My feet;
> I can count all My bones.
> They look and stare at Me.
> They divide My garments among them,
> And for My clothing they cast lots. (verses 16-18)

Fulfilling prophecy, however, was the furthest thing from the Jewish leaders' minds. They just wanted Jesus dead and out of the way, and they wanted Pilate to do it.

Pilate didn't want any part of it. But there was Jesus, beaten and bloodied, standing before him, so what could he do?

In Matthew 27:11, Pilate asked Him, "Are You the King of the Jews?"

Did he ask it sarcastically or with sincerity? We don't really know.

Jesus answered, "It is as you say."

In his years as governor, Pilate thought he had seen everything. All criminal penalties in Judea were subject to his ultimate approval or veto, either directly or indirectly through courts that operated under his oversight. He had presided over hundreds, perhaps even thousands, of criminal proceedings. And usually at this point when someone was brought before him, they were either protesting their innocence or groveling on the tiles, pleading for mercy.

Jesus was doing neither.

He had never seen anyone like Jesus.

It reminds me of a story I read about Frederick the Great, King of Prussia, who was visiting one of his country's prisons. As the king spoke with each of the inmates, he heard endless tales of innocence, misunderstood motives, and exploitation. Finally, the king stopped at the cell of a convict who remained silent.

"Well," said the king, "I suppose you are innocent, too."

"Oh no, sir," the man replied. "I am guilty of the crime that I committed, and I deserve the punishment they're going to give me."

Hearing that, the king said to the warden, "Quick, release this rascal before he corrupts all of these fine, innocent people in here!"

It's pretty rare for someone to simply admit to wrongdoing. Most people insist on their own innocence or describe all the extenuating circumstances. Police officers hear this all the time: "I didn't do it, officer, I swear. I'm innocent."

That was what Pilate had been expecting. But that is not what he heard from this quiet Man standing before him. Jesus didn't say He was innocent, and He didn't admit to being guilty. He just stood there serenely, regally, and calmly and faced it head-on. That really bothered Pilate, because he had never seen anything like it. The more he saw of Jesus, the less he wanted to condemn Him.

"I DON'T WANT TO TALK ABOUT IT"

Again, this wasn't Jesus before Pilate; it was Pilate before Jesus. In that moment, Pilate didn't know what the outcome would be. But Jesus knew the outcome very well.

According to John's gospel, at this point the Lord said to Pilate, "You say rightly that I am a king. For this cause I was born, and for this cause I have come into the world, that I should bear witness to the truth. Everyone who is of the truth hears My voice" (John 18:37).

The governor replied, "What is truth?"

Pilate was your classic pagan, with no core beliefs beyond that of self-preservation. His descendants today would be moral relativists or postmodernists, those who believe that all truth is relative and up to the individual. You've no doubt heard people express that view, saying things like, "Your truth may not be my truth." It's a shocking statistic, but a recent poll in our country revealed that 67 percent of Americans do not believe in absolute truth.

Pilate, however, wasn't just facing an opinion or a philosophy about truth; he was in the presence of Truth incarnate. In John 14:6, Jesus said, "I am the way, the truth, and the life."

To Pilate He said, "Everyone who is of the truth hears My voice."

In other words, "You want to know truth, Pilate? Well, you're looking at it. *I am Truth.*"

If only this tired, cynical man could have opened his eyes and opened his heart for a moment. Pilate could have asked Jesus any question and received an answer. Pilate could have brought any need, any burden before Jesus, and the Lord could have resolved it. If Pilate had repented of his sin, Jesus could have forgiven him then and there. He could have made Pontius Pilate brand-new.

What an opportunity! What a *lost* opportunity.

Pilate could have found everlasting life in that moment. And a million years from that tense day in Jerusalem, if he had given his heart to Christ, he might have been looking back on that encounter with overwhelming joy.

But he couldn't be bothered. He just wanted out of the situation.

Pilate did what many do when confronted with the gospel. They change the subject. They say, "I don't want to hear about it." It's as though they put their fingers in their ears and start yelling, "La-la-la-la! I can't hear you!"

Writing these words, I can't help but think of my mom. Though she was raised in a Christian home, she rebelled against the Lord for most of her life. Whenever I would try to bring up the topic of my faith in Christ, her default response would be, "I don't want to talk about it." Whenever we edged closer to any kind of a serious discussion about the meaning of life, the afterlife, or God, she would say it again: "I don't want to talk about it."

One day when she was very ill, just a month before she died, I felt strongly impressed to go to my mother and have a conversation with her.

I remember telling Cathe, "I have to go see my mom today."

"I'll be praying for you," she said.

So I went over, walked into her room, and sat down. I looked at her and said, "Mom, I want to talk to you about your soul. I want to talk to you about the meaning of life and what happens after we die."

Mom said, "I don't want to talk about it."

But this time I said to her, "Today, we *are* going to talk about it."

And we talked. As a result of our conversation that day, my mom made a recommitment of her life to the Lord and went into His presence just a month later. I'm so glad we had that conversation, even though it wasn't an easy one to have.

Mom at that time had been married to a man named Bill. Bill had told me he had a belief in Christ, but I never saw any real evidence of it in his life. One day I was getting ready to leave on a ministry trip and got word that Bill was very ill and wanted to see me.

I remember thinking to myself, *I really don't have time for this. I have to pack. I've got a plane to catch. I just can't do it today. I'll go see him tomorrow.*

But then I felt impressed by the Lord, *You go see him right now.* So I went over to where he was staying and sat down at his bedside. He was very, very ill. We had a very candid discussion, and once again I presented the gospel to him. Bill responded that he wanted to put his faith in Christ. We prayed together, and he committed his life to Jesus.

Driving back home I thought, *Thank God I did that. Thank God that I went ahead and had that meeting with him.* I still managed to catch my plane, and when I landed at my destination, I had a text that Bill had just died.

Just like the conversation with my mom, it hadn't been easy or convenient for me to talk to Bill that day. But I am so glad I responded to the Lord and went to his bedside with the gospel.

I know that it's often hard, awkward, and uncomfortable to have these sorts of conversations with people who need the Lord. It's especially difficult to broach these subjects with family members. But difficult or not, we have to step into the gap when the Lord prompts us to speak. It isn't our job to convert anyone; that's God's job. Our job is to simply present the gospel. Someday, we may end up being very happy we swallowed our discomfort and took the plunge.

PILATE'S BRIEF REPRIEVE

Pilate wanted off the hot seat but didn't know what to do. He didn't want to condemn an innocent man, but he also had his career to think about. He had a taste of power and didn't want to let go of it. Even so, he probably kept on telling himself, *There just has to be a way out of this.*

Luke's gospel tells us that at this point Pilate said, "I find no fault in this Man" (23:4). The Jewish leaders, however, kept insisting, "He stirs up the people all over Judea by his teaching. He started in Galilee and has come all the way here" (verse 5, NIV).

Galilee?

When Pilate heard that word, his eyes must have lit up. He must have thought to himself, *Maybe there is a way out. The gods are smiling on me today. Galilee isn't my jurisdiction. That's the jurisdiction of Herod. I'll just send them to Herod, get them out of my court, and pack my bags for Caesarea.*

Pilate no doubt congratulated himself as they left the hall. *That was a brilliant move, Pontius. Now Jesus is Herod's problem. And anyway, I hate Herod, so it serves him right.*

Luke tells us that Herod was excited at the opportunity to see Jesus. He had heard about Him and had been hoping for a long time to see Him perform a miracle.

When Jesus was brought into Herod's presence, however, He didn't say one word to him. Though Herod peppered Jesus with questions, the Lord wouldn't speak to this evil puppet king at all.

In all the New Testament narrative, Herod is the one man to whom Jesus had nothing to say. Throughout His years of ministry, Jesus had a great deal to say to all manner of people, young and old, rich and poor, male and female, devout and sinners. He had spoken to the woman caught in adultery, to the rich young ruler, and to Nicodemus, who came by night. He even stopped under a sycamore tree to talk to Zacchaeus, the tax collector, who was sitting up in the branches to get a better view of the Lord.

Jesus even had words for Pontius Pilate. But with Herod, He didn't speak a single word. Why? Because Herod's heart was irreparably hardened. Herod was responsible for the death of John the Baptist, and his father was the Herod who tried to have the child Jesus executed, murdering all those baby boys in Bethlehem in the process. This was a wicked dynasty.

Besides that, Herod just wanted Jesus to do a trick, like some kind of parlor game. He wanted Him to give a little entertainment. But Jesus was unwilling to do any such thing. So Herod mocked and ridiculed Him, clothing Him in a royal robe and sending Him back—back to Pilate!

And there He was, standing before the governor again. Pilate wasn't off the hook after all, reminding us there is no escaping Jesus or making a decision about Him.

The governor, however, had one more trick up his sleeve.

ONE LAST TRY

Now at the feast the governor was accustomed to releasing to the multitude one prisoner whom they wished. And at that time they had a notorious prisoner called Barabbas. Therefore, when they had gathered together, Pilate said to them, "Whom do you want me to release to you? Barabbas, or Jesus who is called Christ?" For he knew that they had handed Him over because of envy. (Matthew 27:15-18)

Pilate may have reasoned to himself something like this: *Maybe there's a way out of this yet! The Jews have this custom of having a prisoner released during Passover. We've got this guy Barabbas, who's a notorious criminal—an insurrectionist, a terrorist—and doesn't have a friend in the world. I'll put this lowlife alongside Jesus, the miracle worker, the one who raises the dead and feeds multitudes. Surely they will choose Jesus over Barabbas!*

But they didn't.

The crowds picked Barabbas for rescue rather than Jesus, and Pilate was still facing the greatest dilemma of his life. Then, to make matters worse, he got a note from his wife. We read in verse 19: "While he was sitting on the judgment seat, his wife sent to him, saying, 'Have nothing to do with that just Man, for I have suffered many things today in a dream because of Him.'"

Can't you just see the governor rolling his eyes when he reads that message from Mrs. Pilate? I can hear him saying under his breath, "Oh good night! What now?"

The fact is, we don't know what happened in her dream or how she happened to suffer many things because of Christ. Had she come face-to-face with her own sin? Had the Lord revealed to her the enormity of what her governor husband was about to do? We don't know. But we do know this: Instead of having nothing to do with Jesus, they should have had everything to do with Jesus because He would have forgiven them, changed their bored, empty lives, and given them something to live for.

But sadly, once again, the opportunity was lost as Pilate continued to dither. He knew Jesus was innocent. He knew He was a "just Man," as his wife had just told him. He knew he should let Jesus go. But he was afraid of the repercussions and afraid of losing his political base.

As a result, he was about to make a decision based on his fear rather than on his convictions. And that sort of decision is wrong from the get-go.

Many times men are defined by what they do in their career. Pilate had worked hard, worming his way through all the layers of Roman politics to get where he was, and he didn't want to lose it.

The people said they wanted Barabbas, and Pilate didn't know what to do.

> Pilate said to them, "What then shall I do with Jesus who is called Christ?"
>
> They all said to him, "Let Him be crucified!"
>
> Then the governor said, "Why, what evil has He done?"
>
> But they cried out all the more, saying, "Let Him be crucified!" (verses 22-23)

Even to a man who had seen all the cruelties and injustices that Pilate had seen, this event must have been shocking to him — bloodchilling. They wanted Jesus put to death, a Man who had lived a good life and helped so many people.

Wasn't it just hours ago when Jesus had ridden into town on a donkey and everyone had cut down palm branches to spread in the street before Him? Hadn't they cried out, "Hosanna! Hosanna to the Son of David" (see Matthew 21:1-11)?

But that was then and this was now. Jesus was good to have around if you were hungry or bored or needed a miracle. But after He had served their purposes, they couldn't have cared less about Him.

So now what was Pilate going to do? The answer is in Matthew 27:24-25:

> When Pilate saw that he could not prevail at all, but rather that a tumult was rising, he took water and washed his hands before the multitude, saying, "I am innocent of the blood of this just Person. You see to it."
>
> And all the people answered and said, "His blood be on us and on our children."

This is typical of so many people today. They want to put off what they don't want to deal with. But you cannot put off Jesus Christ.

Someone might protest, "Wasn't Pilate, in effect, being used by God? Didn't Pilate bring about God's purposes by sending Jesus to the cross?"

Yes, he did. But that doesn't excuse his actions any more than it excused the actions of Judas Iscariot. Pilate heartlessly had Jesus scourged, beaten, and tortured. He listened to the wrong voices, made the wrong decision, and hardened his heart against God.

Sometime later, in the book of Acts, the young church of Jesus Christ raised their voices to God and prayed:

> In fact, this has happened here in this very city [Jerusalem]! For Herod Antipas, Pontius Pilate the governor, the Gentiles, and the people of Israel were all united against Jesus, your holy servant, whom you anointed. (Acts 4:27, NLT)

This verse clearly points out that Pilate was responsible for what he did.

So what happened to Pontius Pilate? History tells us that seven years after this cruel, self-serving decision, Pilate was banished to Gaul by the emperor Caligula. Gaul was a distant region to the northwest of Italy, beyond the Alps. In that place, the historical records say, he suffered what appears to a mental breakdown. And one night Pilate went out into the darkness and hung himself, just as Judas Iscariot had done.

What a tragic waste of life. He threw his life away because he was more concerned about what others thought about him than what God thought about him. His craving for popularity and power ended up costing him everything.

The saddest fact of all is that for those minutes or hours, however long it was, Pilate had Jesus right in front of him! He was so close to the Truth, the very embodiment of Truth, that he could have reached out and touched Him! He could have believed in Jesus and been instantly forgiven of his sin, just as the thief next to Jesus on an adjacent cross had done.

Pilate, however, did what people do each and every day. They reject Christ. And why do they do it? There are no good reasons. There are only excuses. For some it may be a concern over their career or the cares of this life. In an earlier chapter we considered Jesus' parable of spiritual growth, where He spoke about the good seed being sown on four different soils. In one of the examples, Jesus talked about seed sown on ground imbedded with weeds and how those weeds choke the growth out of the young plants. He said, "Still others, like seed sown among thorns, hear the word; but the worries of this life, the deceitfulness of wealth and the desires for other things come in and choke the word, making it unfruitful" (Mark 4:18-19, NIV).

If you have ever planted a flower and watched weeds grow around it, you know the weeds don't lunge suddenly out of the ground and start violently strangling the flower. It's a gradual process—so gradual you wouldn't even be able to see it if you were watching. But if you set up a camera and did time-lapse photography, you would see the weed slowly wrapping its tentacles around the flower and strangling it in slow motion.

That's how it works in our lives as well. We might say, "I'm not really rejecting the Lord. It's just that I have a full plate right now. I have a mortgage payment, responsibilities, and a living to earn. I'm just too busy to think about it right now."

The more we prioritize money, position, fame, and career, however, the less we will be able to make truly wise decisions. Anything that becomes more important to us than God can end up choking the life out of us. For the sake of a lucrative career, some men and women will cast aside their integrity and even their friends and family. They will give up everything to obtain and hold on to a certain position or status in life.

And in the end, what do they have? A handful of ashes.

That was Pilate. It was more important for him to be in power than anything else—even more important than God.

Others will choose people or certain relationships over Jesus. Peer pressure doesn't end with high school. We still care about what people think and want people to like us and approve of us. I have seen people make the worst compromises imaginable simply out of fear of what other people might think about them.

That was in Pilate's mind, too. He cared about what

the crowd thought, what the religious rulers thought, and what Rome thought.

He should have been more concerned about what Jesus thought.

The fact is, if you give up a position or some friends or certain pleasures for the sake of Jesus Christ, God will more than make it up to you, in this life and in the life to come.

Peter once said to Jesus, "We've given up everything to follow You. What will we get?"

> Jesus replied, "I assure you that when the world is made new and the Son of Man sits upon his glorious throne, you who have been my followers will also sit on twelve thrones, judging the twelve tribes of Israel. And everyone who has given up houses or brothers or sisters or father or mother or children or property, for my sake, will receive a hundred times as much in return and will inherit eternal life. But many who are the greatest now will be least important then, and those who seem least important now will be the greatest then." (Matthew 19:27-30, NLT)

You might say, "Okay, Greg, I've given up some things to follow Jesus. Where are the hundreds of houses He promised?"

I would answer with something like this: "Whatever you may have given up to follow the Lord, hasn't God made it up to you? Yes, you may have had to let go of a few friends. But hasn't He given you better Christian friends in their place? You've had to let go of a handful of so-called pleasures. But now, looking back, you can see they weren't really pleasures at all but instead destructive addictions."

Reflecting on my own life, I'd rather have one day of walking with Jesus than a thousand days doing what I used to do to try to find fun and fulfillment. As the psalmist said, "A single day in your courts is better than a thousand anywhere else!" (Psalm 84:10, NLT).

But this life is only a microscopic fraction of the whole story. The best is yet to come! In heaven, those who have faithfully followed the Lord Jesus on earth will receive rewards beyond imagination. Ultimately, we will rule and reign with Him on a new earth.

If Pilate had only known. He thought that being a Roman governor over the troubled province of Judea for a few years was such a big deal that he had to hold on to that job at all costs. But if he had decided to follow Jesus instead of condemning Him, he would have received more than he ever dreamed. In fact, he would be walking with God in heaven at this very moment.

Pilate couldn't make up his mind what to do with Jesus, and as he dithered and procrastinated, heaven slipped through his fingers.

What you and I decide to do with Jesus in this life will determine what He will say to us in the next one.

Either you will hear Him say, "Welcome home, child. Enter into life," or you will hear Him say, "Depart from me, I never knew you."

Pilate missed his chance for eternal joy.

But you don't have to.

NOTES

Chapter 1: "Follow Me"

1. A. W. Tozer, *The Knowledge of the Holy* (New York: HarperCollins, 1961), 84.

Chapter 2: Following Jesus Through the Storms of Life

1. Susan Olasky, "In the Thick of It," *WORLD,* October 8, 2010, http://www.worldmag .com/2010/10/in_the_thick_of_it/page1.

Chapter 8: What Every Last-Days Believer Needs to Know

1. Documented in Aron Ralston, *127 Hours: Between a Rock and a Hard Place* (New York: Simon and Schuster, 2004) and *127 Hours,* directed by Danny Boyle, Beverly Hills, CA: Fox Searchlight Pictures, 2011.

Chapter 13: How to Pray (and How Not to Pray)

1. R. A. Torrey, *How to Pray* (Grand Rapids, MI: Revell, 1900), 9.

Chapter 15: The God of the Living

1. Randy C. Alcorn, *Heaven* (Carol Stream, IL: Tyndale, 2004), 336.
2. C. S. Lewis, *The Weight of Glory* (New York: HarperCollins, 2001), 173.

Chapter 16: Loving God

1. C. S. Lewis, *The Quotable Lewis,* Wayne Martindale and Jerry Root, eds. (Carol Stream, IL: Tyndale, 1989), 412.

Chapter 18: Fallen but Forgiven

1. Robert Murray McCheyne, *The Works of Rev. Robert Murray McCheyne: Complete in One Volume* (New York: Robert Carter and Brothers, 1874), 138.

Other Books by Greg Laurie

Visit www.kerygmapublishing.com